FEDERALISM AND RESOURCE DE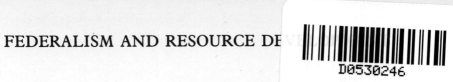

FEDERALISM AND RESOURCE DEVELOPMENT

The Australian Case

Edited by
Peter Drysdale and Hirofumi Shibata

GEORGE ALLEN & UNWIN   Sydney   London   Boston
In association with
The Australia-Japan Research Centre   Australian National University

First published in 1985
George Allen & Unwin Australia Pty Ltd
8 Napier Street, North Sydney NSW 2060 Australia

George Allen & Unwin (Publishers) Ltd
Park Lane, Hemel Hempstead, Herts HP2 4TE England

Allen & Unwin Inc.
Fifty Cross Street, Winchester, Mass 01890 USA

National Library of Australia
Cataloguing-in-Publication entry:

Federalism and Resource Development
　　Bibliography.
　　Includes index.
　　ISBN 0 86861 734 2.
　　ISBN 0 86861 726 1 (pbk.).

　　1. Mines and mineral resources – Government policy –
　　Australia.　2. Federal government – Australia.　3.
　　Investments, Japanese – Australia.　4. Australia –
　　Commerce – Japan.　5. Japan – Commerce – Australia.
　　I. Drysdale, Peter.　II. Shibata, Hirofumi, 1925– 　.
　　III. Australia-Japan Research Centre.

333.8'0994

Library of Congress Catalog Card Number: 84-73432

Set in 10/11.5pt Plantin By Graphicraft Typesetters, Hong Kong
Printed in Singapore by Singapore National Printers (Pte) Ltd

Contents

Tables

Figures

Contributors

Peter Drysdale is Executive Director of the Australia–Japan Research Centre and a specialist in the study of Japan within the Asian–Pacific economy. He has been associated with the major academic and research institutions in Japan (including the Japan Economic Research Center, Hitotsubashi University, Osaka University, and the Institute for Developing Economies). In 1979 he co-authored (with Hugh Patrick, now of Columbia University) a major report to the US Congressional Committee on Foreign Affairs on the future of the Asian–Pacific economy, which led to a number of policy initiatives on the Pacific Community.

Hirofumi Shibata is Professor of Economics in the Economics Faculty at Osaka University, and has made important contributions to the literature, Japanese and English, on international trade, public sector economics and resource economics. He has been Professor of Economics at the universities of Kentucky and Western Ontario.

Cheryl Saunders is a senior lecturer in law at the University of Melbourne. Her main research interests are in the field of public law, especially federalism and Commonwealth–State relations.

Russell Mathews is Director of the Australian National University's Centre for Research on Federal Financial Relations and is a member of the Commonwealth Grants Commission. He has published widely in the fields of taxation and fiscal federalism.

Stuart Harris has recently been appointed Secretary of the Australian Department of Foreign Affairs. He was previously Director of the Centre for Resource and Environmental Studies at the Australian National University, and has written extensively on trade, resource and energy issues.

Michael Crommelin is Zelman Cowen Professor of Law at the University of Melbourne. He is the joint author of several books on the legal regimes governing Australian resource development and has written numerous articles on mineral and petroleum law and constitutional law.

11

Ken Willett is the Deputy Co-ordinator of the Western Australian Department of Resources Development. His work involves a wide range of mining, processing and energy development issues, and he has a special interest in mining taxation.

John D.S. Macleod is a Vice-President (Group Economist) of CRA (a leading Australian mining firm), where he has worked since 1974. He has had worldwide experience of the banking industry, and was voted top business economist in Australia in a poll conducted by the Australian *Financial Review* in 1981.

F.G.H. Pooley is First Assistant Secretary in the Foreign Investment Division of the Australian Department of the Treasury. He is an Executive Member of the Foreign Investment Review Board.

Frances Perkins is a Research Fellow with the Australian National University's Centre for Resource and Environmental Studies. Her present research interest is in policies for the provision and pricing of infrastructure in Australia, particularly in relation to resource development.

Makoto Sakurai is a Research Officer with the Export–Import Bank of Japan in Tokyo. His current research interests include the debt problem for less developed economies and industrial adjustment between Japan and developing countries.

John Warhurst is a lecturer in Australian studies at the Australian Studies Centre of the Institute of Commonwealth Studies at London University. He has published books and articles on numerous aspects of Australian politics and is at present studying intergovernmental relations and interest groups.

Gillian O'Loghlin is a Research Assistant with the Department of Political Science in the Research School of Social Sciences at the Australian National University. She is editor of the Australasian Political Studies Association Newsletter.

Ben Smith teaches in the Australian National University's Faculty of Economics and Commerce, specialising in resource economics and international economics. His published work includes the first analysis of long-term contracts in Australia–Japan minerals trade, and he is one of Australia's leading researchers in the economics of the minerals trade.

Preface

This volume had its origins in a workshop organised by the Australia–Japan Research Centre, in the Research School of Pacific Studies at the Australian National University, as a major element in its work in 1983. The workshop was co-sponsored by the Centre for Resources and Environmental Studies and the Centre for Federal Financial Relations, also at the Australian National University.

The idea for the workshop emerged from a meeting of the Australia–Japan Research Centre's Research Committee with its counterpart research committee in Japan based at the Japan Economic Research Center in Tokyo. The Australia–Japan Research Centre is jointly funded by grants and endowments to the Australian National University by the Australian and Japanese governments, as well as private business organisations in both countries. Its work is directed by a research committee of Australian academics, chaired, at the time this study was undertaken, by Sir John Crawford, and presently by Professor Stuart Harris. The Centre provides research support and co-ordination for Australian and overseas work on various aspects of Australia–Japan economic relations and other policy issues in their international context. This work is undertaken in close cooperation with the counterpart group in Japan.

The Japanese side suggested that work could be usefully done on the workings of the Australian federal system of government and the division of powers and responsibilities within that system. The aim was to pinpoint the areas of difficulty and uncertainty which might be created for overseas purchasers of Australian goods or investors in the Australian resource industry. Given the importance of the resources sector in trade and investment links with Japan, it seemed appropriate to focus the work on the impact of the federal system on resource development and trade. This seemed particularly appropriate because, in much Australian discussion of resource policy issues, conducted largely from a national perspective, the role of the separate States as effective owners of resources had often seemed to emerge as a stumbling block to the pursuit of coherent policy, but there had been little attempt to spell out clearly the extent of conflicts of powers and interests, and the nature of desirable cooperative action, between different levels of government. To those of us interested in resource policy questions, both in Australia and overseas, the

13

Japanese suggestion of work on the implications of federalism was very welcome. The execution of the work exposed other interests and issues of importance, and we hope some fresh insights into the operation of Australia's federal system more generally.

The work of coordinating the research and preparation of papers for the workshop leading to the production of this book was largely the responsibility of Mr Ben Smith, Economics Faculty, Australian National University. He was assisted by Professor Stuart Harris (of CRES) and Professor Russell Mathews (of CFFR) in preparing the program and delivering it over a two-year period. The contributions to the volume, and to discussion at the preceding workshop, are by leading Australian and Japanese scholars engaged in work on the Australian federal system or the resource trade, from various perspectives. A full list of participants in the project is included at the end of the book.

The Centre wishes to thank the authors whose papers and comments appear in the volume and those who participated in the preparatory workshop. Ms Janet Healey undertook the detailed editorial work of refining and drawing the manuscript together. Mrs Beverley Hargreaves was responsible for the huge task of processing the manuscript which was delivered with her usual and exceptional speed and efficiency. The Centre's staff provided the logistic and other support for the organisation of the workshop which yielded the book.

My thanks go to all who helped in these various ways, and especially to my colleagues Ben Smith, and Hirofumi Shibata, of the Economics Department at Osaka University in Japan, who not only co-edited this volume but contributed much to the success of the workshop whence it came.

Peter Drysdale
Canberra, July 1984

1 Perspectives

PETER DRYSDALE
AND HIROFUMI SHIBATA

Australia's federal system has wide-ranging effects on the development of the country's mineral and energy resources and the conduct of resources trade with major trading partners such as Japan. At the same time, Australia's resource-based economy and its development have had a profound influence on the evolution of Australian federalism.

Foreign businessmen and policy makers alike have had considerable interest in how the Australian federal system works in relation to resources trade and development, and how it has evolved over time. Analysis of the workings of Australian federalism and the division of powers within that system identifies the potential difficulties and uncertainties for overseas purchasers of Australian goods and for investors in Australian industry. This volume may provide a source of information for those who need to know how Australia's federal system affects resource development and trade and a reference point for those, inside or outside Australia, who seek to understand its complexities.

Overview

This book has two broad purposes. The first is to provide a clearer understanding of the nature, workings and problems of Australian federalism, especially as it affects the resources sector, for an audience unfamiliar with Australia's federal system but interested in its mechanisms. This should help in avoiding possible uncertainties or misunderstandings in trade or investment; in particular, it should elucidate where impediments in resource developments or resource trade flows are functions of the historically determined system of government in Australia, rather than deliberate constraints aimed at frustrating Australia's trade and investment partners.

The second purpose is to explore more fully the source and nature of policy conflict (within the Australian federal system) over resource development and trade issues, and to consider ways of fostering more cooperative approaches. An important aim is to advance policy discussion to a point where fruitful new directions can be perceived. Inevitably a major outcome is the posing of questions to active participants in policy analysis and debate (several of whom

joined in the discussion of the contributions to this volume at the workshop that
led to its preparation) and in outlining constructive policy approaches and
important research issues.

Overlapping Responsibilities and Conflicting Objectives

To a Japanese observer, who is accustomed to conceiving of the nation as a
unitary state, perhaps the first impression of Australian federalism is the extent
to which the delineation of functions between different levels of government is
not always clear.

In principle, the division of the functions of government between the federal
and State levels is such that matters which are international or national in scope
are assigned to the federal government, and those conceived to be matters whose
effects are confined to a particular State are assigned to the State. Yet the
arguments presented in the book make it clear that there are many fields in
which federal and State governments exercise concurrent powers, and other
fields in which the two levels of government contest the legitimacy of exercising
their respective powers. This is the case in the area of environmental controls,
for example. A consequence is that foreign investors as well as Australian
citizens are often subjected to conflicting demands by the two levels of
government.

In the resource field, a State government obviously tries to regulate resource
developments in the interests of its own residents, but the Commonwealth
viewpoint will reflect the interests of those living in other States that are not
directly involved. If the game played between federal and State governments is a
zero sum game, as in the case of the distribution of the tax base between them,
conflict of interest results. Prospective resource developers may be forced to
perform impossible gymnastics in order to satisfy two conflicting demands at
once, before their proposals are accepted by the officials of the two governments.

A second impression is the predictability of the causes of recent federal–State
conflcts in Australia. To put the case perhaps too simply, State governments
seem to stress the objective of rapid economic development, while the federal
government attempts to modify the single-minded pursuit of basic resource
development objectives through the pursuit of other objectives, such as resource
conservation, environmental externalities, the diversification of industrial structure, the naturalisation of foreign investment, and the maintenance of favourable international trade terms. In short, the objectives of the Commonwealth
tend to represent the views of citizens who are comparatively detached from
the immediate benefits arising from resource developments in a particular
State.

Resource developments inevitably alter the natural environment, and often
involve the large-scale participation of foreign capital. Commonwealth concerns
with environmental issues and foreign ownership may appear to individual

States as obstacles to the pursuit of independent development objectives, and may create conflict between the two levels of government. Commonwealth action can obviously inflict considerable financial damage on the parties involved—both developers and State governments—if it is politically feasible to revoke actions already taken by State governments, and if the States have the capacity to retaliate or claim compensation.

State Policies and Efficient use of Resources

A third issue, which is addressed in three central chapters of the book and is a major theme in the discussion reported in chapter 13, is the method used by the States to allocate mineral rights. The governments of resource-exporting States are generally committed to policies of economic development through the rapid exploitation of mineral resources. They seem to reason that rapid exploitation of resources provides the States with enlarged employment opportunities, increased income and improved public goods through revenue from taxes and levies in various forms on extracted resources.

These State objectives are often pursued in ways that are normally considered to create economic inefficiency and to cause deterioration in the terms of international trade. In particular, the management of the licensing of resource exploration is designed to hasten resources exploitation.

If the maximization of returns from an exhaustible resource is the objective of resource management, there is fairly general agreement that the most appropriate method of allocating private access to resources is to grant resource developers a secure long-term right to use the resource, through lump-sum bidding for the right, so that they can adjust the timing of resource extraction to market conditions. The current practice of allocating exploration leases for a limited period on a first-come-first-served basis clearly hastens exploration and the subsequent extraction of minerals by developers, who wish to pre-empt the mining rights and fear to lose their leases through delay. It encourages competitive acceleration of resource extraction and is likely to cause oversupply of the extracted resource, leading to deterioration in the terms of trade for exports.

The judgment may be that the benefits secured through rapid economic development outweigh the income losses from economic inefficiency and deterioration in the terms of trade. There are also financial and administrative problems associated with the management of auctions of exploration and extraction licences, and these discourage use of the bidding system. Financing up-front payments under a bidding system and the treatment of these payments in the event of exploration failure are two such problems.

Properly administered, a lump-sum bidding system need not cause developers to delay action on project development. If the State's social discount rate is higher than the developer's private discount rate, the State may combine taxation on unused licences with the lump-sum bidding for licences. If licences were negotiable in an open market, their market value would automatically solve the problems of financing and the risk of failure by preventing the State from selling out licences too cheaply, whether intentionally or unintentionally. Indeed, the auctioning method has the added merit of protecting citizens' interests, since developers and government officials often prefer a negotiated sale to an auction in order to maintain secrecy over the distribution of risks and benefits between the two parties.

Charging royalties on mineral output may also create inefficiencies, for it narrows extensive and intensive margins of extraction and leaves some minerals unmined. Profit taxation, which is neutral in its effect on production margins, is more desirable from the point of view of efficiency. More importantly, significant differences exist in royalty and tax rates among the States, and different royalty rates probably result in considerable differentials across States in the marginal costs of mining (net of royalties and taxes). Such differentials encourage the misallocation of labour and capital among States and increase the national average cost of production of any given resource. In this context, it is worth observing, interstate competition for investment from outside sources could have a favourable effect on the Australian economy, through the pressure it generates to reduce taxes and royalties that affect marginal costs and to employ forms of taxation that impinge only upon pure economic rent.

Impact of Resource Development on Federalism

The analysis of federal–State relations in the following chapters gives rise to a speculation. The participants in the political and economic process in Australia tend to think of the Australian federal system as shaping resource developments and trade in a special way. However, the reverse also seems to be true; is it not the case that the Australian resource economy and the nature of resource development and trade have reshaped the Australian federal system over the years, and continue to do so?

Two lines of reasoning can be advanced to support this speculation. The first concerns the special feature of revenues generated from the extraction of exhaustible resources, namely that there is a large economic rent element. Unlike the returns on labour or capital, resource rents are regarded as common wealth, which should not accrue to particular persons, groups or States. While this philosophy is not universal it is quite endemic, and certainly entrenched in Australian law and thinking. But other than an implicit principle of equalisation, no obvious principles emerge that attract automatic agreement on a specific formula for the distribution of resource rents; consequently the distribution of rents will be subject to continual bargaining. The availability of resource rents, alongside the established and highly centralised taxation collection system, encourages the interest in revenue transfer as part of the attempt to equalise income among the States, even between the remotest of towns and the major cities.

One of the purposes of a federal system is to preserve independence in the ways in which different communities maintain their lifestyles and provide public goods. The rent component of tax revenues, however, lays stress upon equal distribution and uniformity in income levels and the provision of public services. Indeed, the services provided may vary progressively less in type and quality, to a point where they are at least as uniform as those observed in a unitary state, such as Japan. There are surely other factors that explain the tendencies towards 'equalisation' across the Australian States through the operation of the federal system. But it seems plausible to argue that the character of the resource economy is one important reason.

The second reason for the influence of Australia's resource-based economy on the nature of Australian federalism is that resources produced in Australia are almost all exported. Control of exports is a federal function under the Constitution. The growth of mineral resource output over the years, and the concomitant growth in mineral exports, has extended the role of the federal government and increased its bargaining strength in dealing with the States. Refusing to grant an export licence may be a relatively minor administrative matter for the federal government, but it is usually a major issue for the State or area in which potential resource production is located. There is a certain irony in the fact that the power of the federal government grows inevitably as the resource-exporting States develop and increase their weight in the economic life of the nation.

These two factors, which are related specifically to the development of Australia's resource economy, have probably influenced the tendency towards the expansion of central government power in Australia's federal system. Furthermore, the Australian federal system took root in an era of rapid improvement in communications technology and extension of scale economies in the provision of public as well as private goods.

However attractive the idea that federalism should preserve variety within a nation, there are inexorable forces, closely related to the bounties of nature and their use, that seem to have strengthened the role of central government in Australia. Other factors have been working in the same direction, as discussed in the argument of this book, especially chapter 13. Obviously it is better to have a problem created by the opportunities to exploit the wealth of nature than no problem at all. It is at least theoretically possible to find solutions to this problem which will benefit everybody, including those who stress the value of variety in the life of a nation.

Australian Policy Perspectives

There seems little dispute that operation of the Australian federal system presents important problems for the resource industry and its management by both levels of government. Whether these problems are unique to Australia and whether, on balance, they damage Australia's competitiveness in the resource trade are not the issues of most importance. The key point is that there are considerable inefficiencies in the various taxation and other arrangements under which the industry operates, and that these inefficiencies, and more particularly any prospect of their amelioration, are inextricably linked to the operation of the federal system.

A central policy question in Australia, therefore, is whether the inefficient taxation regime under which the industry operates can be improved, given the structure of the Australian federal system, the established fiscal arrangements between the States and the federal government, and the political milieu in which these arrangements have evolved. An important contribution of this book, and of the discussion that accompanied its preparation, is that it addresses these questions.

The already heavily centralised character of Australian federal–State arrangements represents a significant barrier to any national attempt to replace the present system for taxing the resource industry with a standardised and more efficient system that would involve some sacrifice of fiscal autonomy by the States, since the States would tend to resist any further concentration of fiscal powers at the federal level. States are unwilling to relinquish one of the few vestiges of revenue-raising autonomy, even though they are extremely shy of autonomy in revenue raising in general. Taxation is unpopular, and the States are quite happy for the federal government to incur that unpopularity, and to blame it if they cannot provide adequate services for their electorates. Resource taxes, however, are not electorally unpopular, since they do not impinge directly upon the electorate, so that in this area of revenue raising States are least willing to yield. In these circumstances, and with markets in recession, it is understandable that the Australian mining industry, conscious as it is of the impost of the present complex regime upon efficiency in mining development, has been anxious that new and potentially more efficient forms of taxation should completely eliminate the inefficiencies of etablished State taxes and levies.

The Constraints of Federal–State Fiscal Arrangements

In trying to judge whether the management of resource industry taxation can be improved, it is important to understand the general arms-length framework within which federal–State fiscal relations presently operate. The system is described in detail in chapter 3, but the focus here is on the structure of incentives in federal–State fiscal arrangements for State governments to treat the resource sector efficiently.

An important feature of federal–State tax-sharing arrangements is the principle of 'fiscal equalisation'. Fiscal equalisation means that States with a relatively low per capita tax base may be compensated by additional grants from the Commonwealth to permit the provision of a standardised level of services. In principle, a State does not receive additional funding if it has merely failed to make an appropriate effort to raise revenue. In practice, however, the capacity to gauge 'revenue effort' is rather limited. In relation to resource developments, it is difficult to know how much revenue could have been raised by an efficient tax mechanism. Thus it may be that States have little incentive to introduce such tax mechanisms. Rather, as already observed, they have an incentive to maximise the rate of resource development (thereby delivering a political good for State residents) and to sacrifice the objective of maximising revenue flows from resource extraction. The same argument suggests that there have been advantages in 'hiding' revenues raised; for example, by overcharging for rail freight services and using the surplus profits to subsidise passenger services elsewhere in the State. The efficient alternative— to raise the maximum possible non-distortionary tax revenue directly from resource developments—might simply reduce revenue grants from the Commonwealth, in so far as the State in question was then perceived as less needy.

The combination of lack of State fiscal responsibility and the fear that explicit revenue raising would be offset by reduced Commonwealth funding tends to reinforce the concern of States with the rate of resource development (and with the creation of direct and indirect employment) and to lessen their concern for managing resources in a way which maximises their value to the community.

A Way out of the Morass

Any significant improvement upon the management and taxation by governments of resource developments in Australia is seen as requiring three elements. The first is the adoption of a taxation regime (such as the proposed resource rent tax combined with an efficient system of tenement allocation for exploration and development leases) that is superior to the royalties and levies currently in place. Second, the States must cede their autonomy of taxing power in the resource area and be prepared to operate under a standardised arrangement. A third and essential element is that any new federal–State system of taxation must be organised so as to provide the States with the incentive to operate resource taxation efficiently, through automatic reimbursement of the lion's share of resource taxation receipts.

Whether, on the grounds of administrative efficiency, the Commonwealth administers such a resource rent taxation arrangement is not the crucial issue. What is crucial is that a comprehensive arrangement, covering States and federal territories, has little chance of being legislated unless the federal and the State governments see the value of entering into a set of cooperative arrangements that embodies these three elements. This is a tall order and is not likely to be delivered quickly, or at one fell swoop, except in quite exceptional circumstances. However, there is no reason why the States should not gradually perceive the value of such cooperation, and eventually join a soundly based initiative from the federal government.

The federal government is now seeking to introduce a more efficient resource taxation system, along the lines discussed in the contributions to this volume. It has chosen to confine its reforms to Commonwealth-administered tenements and to a key sector, new offshore oil developments. Once in place and operational, the Commonwealth resource rent tax and leasing arrangements on new oil developments could serve as an attractive model for the States. In time, inducements could be provided under Commonwealth–State tax-sharing arrangements for the States to join in the extension of resource rent taxation arrangements beyond Commonwealth territories in cooperation with the Commonwealth. This would seem the only sensible way to proceed; unilateral action by the Commonwealth is not practicable and could well make resource taxation less rather than more efficient, fulfilling the worst fears of an industry that already feels burdened by the present competitive taxation arrangements. Whether a more efficient federal–State resource taxation regime evolves will depend on how well the three elements identified above can be provided.

The Politics of Federalism

A federal system of government is one way of organising the resolution of conflicts of objectives and interests, given the presence of overlapping common interests among, in this context, geographically defined political constituencies. Australian federalism is very much a live political process, and the politics sometimes seems to dominate the conduct of federal–State affairs. Whether political issues overrride legal, constitutional or economic issues, and when, are questions upon which the contributions in this volume encourage reflection. The interest in the politics of Australian federalism lurks in the background but is not subject to much analysis in this book (except in chapter 13, where political issues receive some attention in the summary and comment) or for that matter elsewhere.[1]

A central theme that is developed in chapter 2 (which deals with the workings of the Constitution) and pervades the whole volume is that Australian federalism has seen the steady accretion of Commonwealth powers, and operates in some ways (such as the methods of raising and disbursing taxes) in a style that is more centralist than that of many unitary states. This observation is important to an understanding of authority in the management not only of resource trade and foreign investment issues but also of a wider range of issues that have been related to the external affairs power (including environmental matters) or derive from authority under other sections of the Constitution (such as Aboriginal affairs). But how important are the checks of the political process upon the exercise of Commonwealth authority over resource development and resource trade issues?

Political Limits to Central Power

The political process certainly colours the way power is exercised at different levels of government. It could also be argued that political constraints limit the extent to which a Commonwealth government can override or ignore State interests.

The rights of States to exercise their own powers and influence the exercise of Commonwealth powers are jealously guarded, and any serious or effective undermining of these rights has the potential for rebounding to the electoral disadvantage of a federal government. This restraint is made more real by the relative sizes of the States in the Australian federation—each of the six States has a significant share of the political representation at the national level. Restraint on the extension of Commonwealth power may be only really effective, however, in respect of major issues (where State electors can be made single-issue voters); in the more frequent case of less important or emotive matters there is little political restraint on the effective implementation of the Commonwealth's increased legal powers.

A more fundamental point is that the politics of federal–State relations are susceptible to more serious analysis than they are commonly given. To say that outcomes are determined by politics, as is frequently said in discussion of federal–State dealings, does not constitute an adequate explanation. Often there may be good economic reasons for political outcomes and bargains. They may be a consequence of logrolling, where the representatives of one region agree to support another region on one issue in exchange for the latter's support on other issues. The underlying explanations may be economic; they may also, if course, be ideological or party political. Analysis of how and when politics matter in the conduct of Australian federal–State relations deserves more extensive treatment than could be undertaken in this book.

The evolution of Australian federalism, and the accretion of powers to the central government, have been the product of several forces. Some of them are, as suggested, endogenous to the political economy of resource development in Australia. Others have been common influences upon the structure of governments in other industrial democracies; for example, the postwar tendency towards centralised economic management that developed in response to the need to exploit economies of scale. Another factor has been the growth of international interdependence and the extension of international agreements and treaties governing international economic and political transactions. Australia's unique political and economic position in the international community has undoubtedly strengthened the federal government's role because of a strong external affairs interest.

The operation of the Australian and Canadian federal systems provides an interesting contrast. Canada, of course, has its geographically defined cultural divisions. But, perhaps more importantly, it nestles alongside the United States and has most of its international dealings with one giant neighbour. In the conduct of its international economic and political affairs, on the other hand, Australia's circumstances have inevitably demanded more national cohesion: in the process of decolonisation; in the years of war; in international economic relations; and in the development of its role in Asia and the Pacific.

That said, it is salutary to return to the reason for compiling this volume. Much Australian discussion of resource policy issues is conducted from a primarily national perspective, while the role of the separate States as effective owners of resources has often seemed to emerge as a stumbling block to the pursuit of coherent policy. Little attempt has been made to spell out clearly the extent of conflicts of power and interest (and the nature of desirable cooperative actions) between the different levels of government. This book seeks to redress that omission.

The book therefore begins with a chapter by Saunders, which spells out the constitutional division of powers between the Commonwealth (federal) and State governments. The economic context is established in the following chapter, by Mathews, which outlines federal–State fiscal arrangements and contains a comprehensive discussion of the basis on which these arrangements have been founded and the extent to which they meet the various allocative and distributive objectives of the parties involved. In the fourth chapter Harris draws out the conflict in State and federal policy objectives in the area of resource development and use, emphasising the dynamism of the system.

The core study of federalism as it impinges upon resources development and trade is contained in the next five chapters. Crommelin provides a succinct account of the mineral exploration and production regime under the federal system; Willet gives an extensive survey of resource taxation arrangements and policy issues in the federal system; Macleod assesses the impact of the federal system upon developer interests; Pooley reviews State and federal attitudes towards foreign investment and the mode of foreign investment regulation; and Perkins looks at questions surrounding financing and charging for resource-related infrastructure.

In the three penultimate chapters, the effects of the federal system on essential foreign investor interests and resource trade management are addressed. Sakurai examines Australian resource development and trade from the perspectives of Japanese investors and purchasers; Warhurst and O'Loghlin describe the detailed management of these external economic relations by State and federal authorities; and Smith analyses the implications of federal–State rivalry for the effectiveness of policies that influence the climate for investment in resource projects and Australia's international market position.

The final chapter summarises the argument of the book and offers a commentary, from other standpoints, on the contributions in each chapter and on other issues germane to a fuller understanding of Australia's federal system as it affects resource development and trade.

2 Australia's federal system and the division of powers

CHERYL SAUNDERS

The Division of Powers in Federal Theory

The federal principle has been defined as 'the method of dividing powers so that the general and regional governments are each, within a sphere, coordinate and independent'.[1] This definition has three elements. First, there must be two sets of governments, operating directly on the same citizens; both, presumably, will be chosen by those citizens in accordance with constitutional requirements. Second, powers must be divided between these governments. Third, the governments must be able to exercise their allotted powers independently—in other words they must be able to act, within the confines of their limited powers, with the same latitude as individual governments in a unitary system.

In practice, as experience has shown, it is almost impossible to divide powers in such a way that governments can operate completely independently of each other: it is generally conceded that in a modern federation some interdependence is inevitable. Nevertheless, it is also accepted that at least a degree of autonomy of the respective governments in the exercise of their powers is an essential characteristic of federalism and an underlying aim of a federal division of powers.[2] Continued adherence to this principle need not be based on constitutional theory alone. It is also consistent with political propriety for democratically elected governments to exercise and be responsible for the exercise of powers without interference from another source.

There is no single accepted method of dividing federal powers. The United States, Canadian and West German constitutions each provide a different model. The most familiar model is that of the United States, which later was adopted by Australia. This model vests specific legislative powers in the centre, leaves the remainder with the regions and confers paramountcy on an exercise of central power in the event of conflict between the two. Whatever method is used, the division of powers will inevitably be entrenched in a formal, written constitution. In turn, a system of judicial review to ensure compliance with the constitution is likely to be provided.

Dicey described the principle that should guide the allocation of particular powers between the centre and the region as follows:

25

A federal State is a political contrivance intended to reconcile national unity and power with the maintenance of 'state rights'. The end aimed at fixes the essential character of federalism. For the method by which federalism attempts to reconcile the apparently inconsistent claims of national sovereignty and of state sovereignty consists of the formation of a constitution under which the ordinary powers of sovereignty are elaborately divided between the common or national government and the separate States. The details of this division vary under every different federal constitution, but the general principle on which it should rest is obvious. Whatever concerns the nation as a whole should be placed under the control of the national government. All matters which are not primarily of common interest should remain in the hands of the several States.[3]

The principle is obviously correct; its application is less easy. Certain powers, of which the defence power is an example, are universally acknowledged to be national in character. Another natural limitation on powers that are capable of being exercised by the regions is provided by territorial considerations. These factors aside, however, there is room for considerable divergence on which powers 'concern the nation as a whole' or are 'of common interest'. In all but a few matters the allocation of powers in fact is likely to be made subjectively, in the sense of being influenced more by historical and contemporary political considerations than by any generally applicable principle. Objective criteria may be harder to identify and more complex than Dicey's formula suggests.

The Formal Division of Legislative Powers under the Constitution

Method of division

The scheme of the Australian Constitution is to vest specific powers in the Commonwealth Parliament and to leave the remainder with the States, as far as they are constitutionally capable of exercising them. The starting point for the implementation of this scheme is section 107, which provides that

> [e]very power of the Parliament of a Colony which has become or becomes a State shall, unless it is by this Constitution exclusively vested in the parliament of the Commonwealth or withdrawn from the parliament of the State, continue as at the establishment of the Commonwealth ...

Elsewhere, other sections ennumerate the legislative powers of the Common-wealth or withdraw particular powers from the States. Sections vesting powers in the Commonwealth are scattered throughout the Constitution, but most are concentrated in sections 51 and 52. Additional limitations on State power can be found in several sections, of which the most significant and familiar is the guarantee of freedom of interstate trade, commerce and intercourse in section 92.

Only a few of the legislative powers vested in the Commonwealth are expressed to be exclusive and therefore unable to be exercised by the States at all. The most important of these is the power in section 90 to 'impose duties of customs and of excise, and to grant bounties on the production or export of goods'. Other powers are effectively exclusive because the provision vesting power in the Commonwealth is complemented by another withdrawing power from the States. Thus the Commonwealth has exclusive power to raise naval and military forces (sections 51(6), 114) and to coin money (sections 51(12), 115). For the most part, however, powers vested in the Commonwealth are concurrent powers, exercisable also by the States. Many of the powers in section 51 fall into this category. Some of those which do not are inherently incapable of exercise by the States. The power of 'borrowing money on the public credit of the Commonwealth' is an example.

The Commonwealth also is subject to specific prohibitions in the exercise of its powers. Section 92 applies to the Commonwealth as well as to the States.[4] The Commonwealth may not discriminate between States in exercising its power to tax, or give preference to States or parts of States in matters of trade, commerce or revenue (sections 51(2), 99). Commonwealth legislation for the acquisition of property must provide for just terms (section 51(35)). There is a limited guarantee for freedom of religion in section 116.

Resolving conflict between Commonwealth and State laws

A division of power under which the Parliaments of the Commonwealth and the States can legislate on the same matters necessitates a procedure to resolve the conflicts between laws that inevitably will arise. The relevant provision under the Commonwealth Constitution is section 109, which provides that

> [w]hen a law of a State is inconsistent with a law of the Commonwealth, the latter shall prevail, and the former shall, to the extent of the inconsistency, be invalid.

Most of the uncertainties about the operation of this section in fact concern the ambit of the legislative power on which paramountcy is conferred. A current controversy, for example, is the question of whether the Commonwealth's power to legislate for taxation under section 51(2) extends to State taxation, so as to enable the Commonwealth to override State taxation laws. However, two questions about the meaning of section 109 itself should be mentioned. First, it has been held that the section operates not only in the case of direct inconsistency between Commonwealth and State laws but also in cases where the Commonwealth law evinces an intention 'to cover the subject matter and provide what the law upon it shall be'.[5] This type of inconsistency can give rise to problems where it is not clear what are the precise limits of the subject matter covered. Second, although section 109 does not accord paramountcy to an exercise of delegated legislative power by the Commonwealth, a similar result can be achieved with an appropriate expression of intention in the enabling statute.[6] Thus State legislation that is inconsistent with an award of the Commonwealth Conciliation and Arbitration Commission is invalid as a result of section 65 of the *Conciliation and Arbitration Act* 1904, which is designed to attract section 109.

Commonwealth legislative powers

The National Australasian Convention which met in Sydney in 1891 to 'consider and report upon an adequate scheme for a Federal Constitution'[7] began its deliberations with debate on a series of general resolutions moved by Sir Henry Parkes. The first resolution proposed

> [t]hat the powers and privileges and territorial rights of the several existing colonies shall remain intact, except in respect to such surrenders as may be agreed upon as necessary and incidental to the power and authority of the National Federal Government.

The three subsequent resolutions dealt with particular aspects of the division of powers that were accepted as fundamental. They were the guarantee of freedom of interstate trade and intercourse, the conferral on the central government of exclusive power to impose customs duties, and the centralisation of military and naval defence under federal control. These two themes, of a free trade unit within Australia and a common defence system, permeated the eventual division of powers. Their achievement constituted major aims of the federal movement.

There appears to have been little general debate, either in this convention or in the later one of 1897–98, on the criteria that should be used to identify the powers that are 'necessary and incidental' to a federal government. Most powers were assigned to the Commonwealth Parliament either because they were considered necessary for intercolonial free trade or defence, or because they represented problems which individual colonies historically had been unable to solve. Many of the powers were virtually transcribed from the existing federal constitutions of the United States and Canada. Many also had appeared in proposals for Australian federation since 1849, and therefore were obvious candidates for inclusion in the list of federal powers in 1891.

The relatively uncontroversial nature of the proposed division of powers is shown by the fact that few changes of major substance were made in subsequent drafts to the powers proposed to be vested in the Commonwealth Parliament by the draft Constitution Bill of 1891. Quick and Garran summarised them as follows:

> The legislative powers of the Federal parliament were substantially the same (in 1891) as at present (1901), with the following exceptions: Astronomical and meteorological observations, insurance, invalid and old age pensions, conciliation and arbitration, and the acquisition of property for public purposes were not included. In the 'banking' sub-clause there was no exception of State banking. The river question was only represented by a power to legislate as to 'river navigation with respect to the common purposes

of two or more States, or of the Commonwealth'. There was no clause providing for the acquisition of State railways, or railway construction and extension; but the power to make laws for the control of railways 'with respect to transport for the purposes of the Commonwealth' was not limited, as it is now, to 'naval and military purposes.'[8]

To this it should be added that the ambit of the exclusive power of the Commonwealth Parliament to impose excise duties was widened in 1897 and the power in section 96 to make conditional grants to the States was included during negotiations between colonial Premiers in 1899. Neither of these changes would have been seen as particularly relevant to the division of legislative powers at the time, although both have had a profound impact on the practical operation of that division since.

Since 1901 there have been three constitutional amendments that have directly altered the division of powers. In 1946, paragraph (23A) was inserted in section 51 to enable the Commonwealth to provide a wide range of specified welfare benefits. In 1967, the exclusion of the Aboriginal race from the power to make laws for the people of any race was removed from section 51(26). In 1929, section 105A invested the Commonwealth with power to make agreements with the States with respect to their debts, providing constitutional authority for the financial agreement by which the Loan Council is established. This last amendment led to a most significant increase in effective Commonwealth economic power.

The substantive powers presently vested in the Commonwealth Parliament under section 51 can be divided into three categories. The first comprises powers that are inherently national in character, in the sense that they are generally accepted as necessary central powers in any federal system. The most obvious example of this category is the defence power. Another is the external affairs power, and other powers ancillary to it, which enable Australia to act with unity in international matters (sections 51(1), (7), (8), (9), (10), (19), (27), (28), (30)).

The second category can be described as comprising commercial powers: powers designed to create and facilitate the internal free trading and national commercial system sought by the framers of the Constitution. This is the largest category of powers, including interstate trade and commerce; taxation; bounties; borrowing; postal, telegraphic, telephonic and other like services; census and statistics; currency, coinage and legal tender; banking; insurance; weights and measures; bills of exchange; bankruptcy; copyright; foreign, trading and financial corporations; acquisition and construction of railways with State consent; and conciliation and arbitration.

In the third category are powers that relate to various aspects of social welfare or organisation. It comprises the marriage and divorce powers; power to make various welfare payments; and power to legislate for the people of any race for whom it is deemed necessary to make special laws.

Parkes' resolution suggested that only 'necessary' powers should be conferred on the federal Parliament; that otherwise the powers of the existing colonies should 'remain intact'. If this approach were adopted, however, it was foreseeable that in due course the powers vested in the Commonwealth would prove inadequate. The Constitution therefore provided for the extension of Commonwealth power, without resort to formal constitutional amendment, through a power to legislate on matters referred to the Commonwealth by the States. It is a commentary on the Australian approach to the federal division of legislative powers that, while a reference power is unique to the Australian federal system, a comparable provision appeared in most major proposals for federation in Australia from the mid-1850s onwards. The advantage of a reciprocal power, to enable the States to legislate on matters constitutionally within the exclusive competence of the Commonwealth, was not recognised at this stage, largely because the significance of the few Commonwealth exclusive powers was not foreseen.

One other power should be mentioned: section 51(38), which enables the Commonwealth to legislate with respect to

the exercise within the Commonwealth, at the request or with the concurrence of the Parliaments of all the States directly concerned, of any power which can at the establishment of this Constitution be exercised only by the Parliament of the United Kingdom or by the Federal Council of Australasia.

Until comparatively recently this somewhat obscure provision was widely assumed to be meaningless. With hindsight, however, it is possible to speculate that it was inserted in the Constitution as a precaution; in case some of the advantages potentially secured for the colonies by the *Federal Council of Australasia Act* 1885 had inadvertently been lost under the new federal Constitution. The possible use of the power in relation to the remaining links between Australia and the Parliament of the United Kingdom has been the subject of much discussion in recent years. The project currently being conducted under the auspices of the Premiers' Conference to sever the remaining imperial links with the United Kingdom is expected to be based partly on section 51(38).

To complete the description of the division of powers, it is relevant to note the possibility of an implied Commonwealth power to legislate for 'national' purposes other than those expressly identified in the Constitution. To the extent that such a power exists, it is justified by reference to the position of the Commonwealth as the only single jurisdiction capable of representing Australia as a nation. The implied national power of the Commonwealth Parliament has been relied upon to support both the appropriation and the spending of public moneys for purposes outside express Commonwealth power and substantive legislation on particular matters. In either context there is uncertainty about its extent, although there is little doubt about its existence.

Judicial Review

Judicial review of the constitutional validity of legislation is an almost inevitable concomitant of a division of legislative power in a federal system. The

Constitution does not provide expressly for judicial review, although it can be argued that is is recognised indirectly in several sections.[9] In any event, the function has been assumed and performed by the High Court since its establishment in 1903.

The function of determining whether laws fall within constitutional heads of power is necessarily a creative one. The heads of power themselves are briefly described and inherently ambiguous, and their meaning is subject to greater uncertainty and strain as circumstances change in ways that were not contemplated when the division of powers was settled. Very different results can be produced by different approaches to interpretation adopted by the Court, or by the same approach applied by different members of the Court.

For the first two decades after federation the High Court adopted an approach to constitutional interpretation which tended to restrict the scope of Commonwealth legislative power. By this approach any ambiguity in the operation of a power was resolved in favour of the narrower interpretation, on the ground that section 107 of the Constitution reserved to the States all powers not withdrawn from them by the Constitution. For obvious reasons this approach became known as the doctrine of reserved powers. It was one of two doctrines espoused by a majority of the High Court during this time that depended on implications drawn from the federal nature of the Constitution rather than on any express constitutional requirement.

The doctrine of reserved powers and the philosophy on which it was based were repudiated by the High Court in 1920 in the *Engineers* case.[10] The Constitution was an Act of Parliament and therefore, according to the majority, should be interpreted in accordance with the ordinary rules of statutory construction. The new doctrine was best described by Higgins J, a member of the majority, who delivered a separate judgment:

> The fundamental rule of interpretation, to which all others are subordinate, is that a statute is to be expounded according to the intent of the Parliament that made it; and that intention has to be found by an examination of the language used in the statute as a whole. The question is, what does the language mean; and when we find what the language means, in its ordinary and natural sense, it is our duty to obey that meaning, even if we think the result to be inconvenient or impolitic or improbable. Words limiting the power are not to be read into the statue if it can be construed without a limitation.[11]

The joint majority judgment of Knox CJ and Isaacs, Rich and Starke JJ concluded with the following rather pompous analysis of the aims of the majority, which suggests that the Court may have underestimated the problems of constitutional interpretation that would arise in the future:

> We have anxiously endeavoured to remove the inconsistencies fast accumulating and obscuring the comparatively clear terms of the national compact of the Australian people; we have striven to fulfil the duty the Constitution places upon this Court of loyally permitting that great instrument of government to speak with its own voice, clear of any qualifications which the

people of the Commonwealth or, at their request, the Imperial Parliament have not thought fit to express, and clear of any questions of expediency or political exigency which this Court is neither intended to consider nor equipped with the means of determining.[12]

Discovering the meaning of the 'comparatively clear terms' of the Constitution is not always as straightforward as the majority in the *Engineers* case seemed to expect. There are inherent uncertainties in some of the terms used; what, for example, are trading corporations, excise duties, aliens or industrial disputes? Even greater difficulties are posed by the process of characterising a law as one with respect to a particular head or heads of legislative power: a law which imposes an income tax is obviously a law with respect to taxation; a law which imposes an income tax on the investment income of superannuation funds, subject to an exemption where the assets of the fund are invested in certain kinds of public securities in specified proportions, has been held to be a law with respect to taxation,[13] but the proposition is less obvious.

Nor has it proved possible to eliminate implications entirely from the process of constitutional interpretation. The implied national power has been described earlier, but even implications based on federalism are hard to eradicate entirely. It is ironic that the broader the sweep of Commonwealth power as a result of the *Engineers* doctrine, the greater is the need for a degree of protection for the States to some implied minimum level. This need appears to have been recognised by the High Court, at least in the abstract, in several recent cases.[14]

The principles of constitutional interpretation expounded in the *Engineers* case are still theoretically accepted as correct and followed by the High Court. Whatever modifications those principles have undergone since the case was decided, the old doctrines of implications remain discredited. In the words of Mason J in *Commonwealth* v. *Tasmania* (*Dams* case), they are 'grave constitutional heresies'.[15] The practical result has been a steady expansion of Commonwealth legislative power. The recent decision in the *Dams* case on the extent of the external affairs power in many ways represents the high-water mark of this process. Although the division of powers undoubtedly imposes a constraint on the Commonwealth which is felt at earlier stages in the legislative process, Commonwealth laws seldom are invalidated now by the Court on grounds of *ultra vires*.[16]

The Division of Executive and Judicial Power

The discussion so far has been concerned solely with the division of legislative power. The federal principle also requires the powers exercisable by the other arms of government, traditionally the executive and the judiciary, to be divided between the Commonwealth and the States. It would be logical for the division of these powers to mirror the division of legislative power, subject to minor necessary adjustments. This was achieved in the constitutional division of judicial power,[17] although recent decisions by the High Court have considerably expanded the area of jurisdiction that is ancillary to federal jurisdiction and hence exercisable by federal courts. The basis for the division of executive power is not made explicit in the Constitution, however, and the result is uncertainty about the scope of the executive power and a lack of symmetry in the powers exercisable by the different arms of Commonwealth government.

Section 61 constitutes the only attempt to delineate the general executive power of the Commonwealth. It provides that

> [t]he executive power of the Commonwealth is vested in the Queen and is exercisable by the Governor-General as the Queen's representative, and extends to the execution and maintenance of this Constitution and of the laws of the Commonwealth.

It would have been possible to interpret this section as confining federal executive power to two sources: the Constitution itself, and laws passed by the Parliament. If this view had been adopted, the executive power would have been tied by definition to the ambit of the legislative power of the Commonwealth, and the problem of the federal division of executive power would not have arisen. Although it was espoused for a time by some members of the High Court,[18] this limited interpretation of section 61 did not ultimately prevail. With hindsight, this was inevitable in view of the constraint it would have placed on the power of the Commonwealth executive to contract without parliamentary authority. Its acceptance became even less likely when the High Court decided that parliamentary authority was not necessary to support the validity of ordinary contracts made by governments of the States.[19]

Rejection of the more literal interpretation of section 61 did not necessarily mean that the executive power of the Commonwealth was significantly wider than its legislative power. In the *Wool Tops* case,[20] for example, Isaacs J rejected the need for parliamentary authority for executive contracts but nevertheless held the contracts invalid on the ground, among others, that they exceeded 'the limits of the constitutional domain of the Commonwealth executive power'. He appeared to identify these with the limits of Commonwealth legislative power, together with whatever other power was necessary for the 'maintenance of the Constitution'.[21]

The limits have been hard to preserve. In one respect erosion was facilitated by the words of section 61 itself. The concept of power to 'maintain the Constitution' inevitably suggests the existence of inherent power flowing from the very existence of the Commonwealth and undefined in scope. This tendency was supplemented by acceptance of the proposition that the sources of executive power were not confined to those mentioned in section 61, which in turn introduced the possibility of common law or the prerogative as additional sources. In the absence of any express constitutional limit on the ambit of federal executive authority, it fell to the High Court to develop such limits, if any. The task of the Court was further complicated in due course by the development of Australian independence from the United Kingdom, with the consequence that certain executive powers previously exercised by the United Kingdom on behalf of Australia passed, by some uncharted process, to Australia itself. Section 61 provided the vehicle for the argument that these powers became vested in and exercisable by the Commonwealth government.

The result is not entirely clear. The scope of the Commonwealth power to contract has not been settled by judicial decision. Although most authorities suggest, without finally deciding, that the validity of federal contracts should be measured against the possibility of valid federal legislation on the subject, some commentators have argued persuasively that the federal power to contract is in fact unlimited.[22] Further, while it is settled that the Commonwealth executive derives some prerogative power from section 61 and that the power is limited, it is far from clear what the precise limits are.[23] In *Victoria* v. *Commonwealth* (*AAP* case), Mason J described the executive power as confined to the 'area of responsibilities of the Commonwealth', which he equated with 'the distribution of legislative powers, effected by the Constitution itself and the character and status of the Commonwealth as a national government'.[24] The terms in which he proceeded to amplify that description, however, by reference to 'enterprises and activities peculiarly adapted to the government of a nation and which cannot otherwise be carried on for the benefit of the nation', suggest a potential for federal executive power that far exceeds the substantive legislative powers vested in the Commonwealth Parliament.

Some additional points should be made. The first is that the view that all relevant prerogative powers are exercisable by the Commonwealth executive under section 61 is difficult to reconcile with the existence of section 2, under which the Governor-General is authorised to exercise 'such powers and functions of the Queen as Her Majesty may be pleased to assign to him'. The inconsistency is made more puzzling by the fact that an assignment was advised and made under section 2 as recently as 1973.[25] The relationship between these two sections in the light of currently accepted views about section 61 is impossible to explain satisfactorily other than by reference to historical factors.

Second, it should be noted that section 51 itself provides a mechanism whereby Commonwealth legislative power can be extended to the limits of the executive power. Section 51(39) invests the Parliament with power to legislate with respect to '[m]atters incidental to the execution of any power vested by this Constitution in ... the Government of the Commonwealth'. Commonwealth legislation on a matter incidental to the executive power would appear to be supported by this provision, even though independent action could not have been taken by the Parliament under any head of substantive power.

The final point is one of principle. A constitutional structure under which the executive power, either separately or in combination with the power to appropriate, is broader than the legislative power provides an additional incentive to bypass the parliamentary process. It is unsatisfactory for this reason, as well as for its potential for making inroads on the federal distribution of power. It is particularly inappropriate at a time of increasing emphasis on the virtues of public accountability and open government.

Constitutional Amendment

The formal procedure for amendment of the Commonwealth Constitution is provided by section 128. It first requires an amending bill to be passed by both Houses of the Commonwealth Parliament, or by a single House in accordance with the prescribed deadlock procedure. The bill must then be passed at referendum and receive the royal assent. Passage at referendum usually requires the approval of a majority of electors voting and of a majority of electors in a majority of States.

The conventional wisdom is that the Commonwealth Constitution is hard to amend. Thirty-eight Constitution alteration bills have been put to referendum since federation: only eight of those, varying in substance from trifling to highly significant, have been passed. Many of the rejected bills contained multiple proposals for change, and many other proposals foundered at some earlier stage in the constitutional amendment process. The actual casualty rate is therefore even higher than the bald referendum statistics suggest. Although an obvious inference is that the form of the Constitution is effectively rigid, there is an alternative view that less partisan attempts at constitutional change would produce more positive results. Nor should it be assumed that the attitude of the electorate to constitutional amendment has necessarily remained unchanged over the course of 82 years.

Proposed alterations to the division of powers have constituted a substantial proportion of the proposals put to referendum and a smaller proportion of those that have succeeded. Only two of the successful referendums directly altered the division of powers. One was the social services amendment of 1946, which included section 51(23A) in the Constitution. The other was the Aboriginals amendment of 1967, which removed the provision excluding Aboriginals from the power to make laws for the people of any race in section 51(26). A third amendment, investing the Commonwealth with power to make agreements with the States with respect to State debts (section 105A), in fact has resulted in the most significant accretion to Commonwealth power of all. As noted earlier, it is unlikely that it was viewed in that light at the time of its passage.

Most of the proposals put to referendum in the first 50 years after federation concerned Commonwealth powers. Many of them were repetitive. The referendums of 1911, 1913 and 1919 put to the people substantially the same four proposals for extensions to Commonwealth power over trade and commerce, corporations, industrial matters and monopolies, although in 1911 and 1919 they were included in omnibus 'legislative powers' bills and in 1913 each was put separately. All except the trade and commerce proposal reappeared again in the referendum of 1926. Altogether five proposals to amend the industrial power were put to the people during this period.

Since 1951 the pattern has changed. Proportionately fewer proposals (fourteen) have been put to referendum. The practice of including multiple proposals in the same bill has almost disappeared. A higher proportion of the proposals were passed. A much smaller proportion involved direct alteration of the federal distribution of power.

It is not necessarily the case that there is any causal relationship between the relatively greater success at referendum over the past 30 years and the fact that fewer proposals have involved extensions to Commonwealth power. Three of the four successful proposals are attributable to the work of the Constitutional Convention, which aims to develop consensus on proposals for constitutional change. They also were fairly minor by comparison with many of those that have been unsuccessful in the past.

The decline in the number of referendum proposals dealing with federal powers in recent decades should be attributed to the pessimism of successive governments over the referendum process as a means of increasing Commonwealth power, rather than to a state of satisfaction with the extent of federal powers as they stand. This attitude is much assisted by the expansive approach of the High Court to the interpretation of Commonwealth powers. Many of the proposals which were put to referendum and rejected in the first 50 years of federation have been substantially effected since through judicial decision. The history of the Constitutional Convention provides further evidence either of an assumption that referendums directed to the federal division of power are doomed to failure, or of a belief that an adequate consensus on changes to the division of power is impossible to achieve. In the ten years of its existence, the Convention and its committees have made no serious attempt to examine and recommend changes to the extent of federal powers. However, the work at present being done by three Convention subcommittees in the areas of external affairs, industrial relations and fiscal powers may require this proposition to be qualified.

It is at least worth arguing that a reappraisal of the division of powers, followed by whatever constitutional change is necessary, would be appropriate at this stage in the development of Australian federalism. Judicial review and intergovernmental arrangements can be used effectively to alter the existing distribution, but the results are often incomplete, uncertain or tenuous. De facto alteration of the division of powers in these ways also removes the text of the Constitution further from reality, a result which presumably should be avoided if possible.

A reappraisal of the division of powers should be preceded by an attempt to formulate criteria to identify powers that are properly national. A comprehensive and universally applicable set of criteria may be impossible to find, but the result should provide some guidance. In any event the process will stimulate debate on an aspect of the federal system which hitherto has received too little attention. The debate should canvass the relevance of such factors as the nature of the subjectmatter of the power (that is, whether particular powers are so important that national control is necessary or desirable), the need for uniformity, and the practicability of individual action by States in view of the territorial limitations on their powers.

Modifying the Division of Powers other than by Formal Constitutional Change

It is clear that the division of powers can effectively be modified through the process of judicial review. Indeed, the significant extensions to Commonwealth power that have occurred since federation are almost entirely due to judicial review and only in relatively minor instances to the referendum process. Attempts to change the division of powers at referendum have generally proved unsuccessful.

The division of powers can be modified by other means as well. All involve some interaction between the Commonwealth and the States, although the States have not always been willing participants. The courts have also played an important role in relation to some of these practices.

Reference of powers

Section 51(37) invests the Commonwealth Parliament with power to legislate with respect to

[m]atters referred to the Parliament of the Commonwealth by the Parliament or Parliaments of any State or States, but so that the law shall extend only to States by whose Parliaments the matter is referred, or which afterwards adopt the law.

This represents a unique Australian contribution to the methodology of dividing powers for federal purposes. Nevertheless, it has been used surprisingly little. This is usually attributed to some unresolved questions about the legal operation of the power, but it is undoubtedly due in part to political and practical factors as well. Suspicion of the use the Commonwealth might make of a referred power has inhibited references from the States. This problem is aggravated by the legal uncertainties referred to earlier over whether, for example, a reference, once made, can be recalled by a State. The Commonwealth for its part has been reluctant to encourage or accept references made by only a few States, on the ground that it cannot make adequate use of the power in those circumstances.

As a result, comparatively few references have been made under section 51(37), dealing with relatively minor matters. A majority of references made have conferred on the Commonwealth transitional postwar powers; most of the rest relate to aspects of aviation. On one uncharacteristic occasion Tasmania referred to the Commonwealth power to legislate for trade practices, but that reference has since expired.

Negotiations for references of power are more frequent. The decline of faith in the referendum as a means of altering the division of power has been matched by a revival of interest in the potential of the reference power. Thus debate over the inadequacies of Commonwealth power in such fields as family law, defamation, company law and industrial relations has almost always taken place in the context of references of power—without, however, any tangible results.

The legal deficiencies of the existing reference power are recognised now as twofold. First, there are doubts about the extent of the power of the States over references they have made. Second, there is no reciprocal arrangement under which matters presently within the exclusive legislative competence of the Commonwealth can become the subjects of State power. Such matters include the imposition of excise duties, legislation for Commonwealth places, and the investiture of federal courts with jurisdiction.

The Constitution Alteration (Interchange of Powers) Bill 1984, which was put to referendum in December 1984, would have remedied both these defects. A new section 108A would have invested the Commonwealth Parliament with a power to 'designate' a matter within its exclusive power as one with respect to which the States can legislate. A new section 108B would have removed the existing legal doubts over the operation of section 51(37) and ensured that they cannot arise in relation to section 108A. Despite broad all-party support in the Constitutional Convention the proposal nevertheless was defeated at referendum, providing support for the pessimistic view of the feasibility of constitutional change.

Intergovernmental fiscal arrangements

The ability of the Commonwealth to influence policies on matters outside the range of federal legislative powers under the Constitution has been considerably enhanced by the way in which intergovernmental financial relations have developed since federation. Chapter 3 contains a detailed discussion of these arrangements; only certain aspects are briefly mentioned here.

Even at the time of federation it was recognised that there would be an imbalance in the revenue resources available to the States under the Constitution, creating a situation that would necessitate the redistribution of revenue from the Commonwealth to the States. The principal cause of the imbalance in 1901 was section 90, which invested the Commonwealth with exclusive power to impose customs and excise duties.

The need for a system of revenue redistribution not only has continued since federation, but has become more acute as a result of the expanded definition of excise duties and the effective exclusion of the States from income taxation. The revenue redistribution scheme prescribed by the Constitution itself was mandatory only for the first ten years after federation, and was duly terminated as soon as possible. Subsequent arrangements were left to the discretion of the Commonwealth government and Parliament, in consultation, to the extent they considered necessary, with the governments of the States.

Payments of a revenue nature from the Commonwealth to the States can be categorised as revenue redistribution payments, special grants and specific purpose grants. The first two categories comprise general revenue grants. Payments in the third category are restricted in varying degrees in the purposes for which they may be used and the manner in which they may be spent. The vehicle for payment of all three categories of grant is section 96, which provides that ' ... the Parliament may grant financial assistance to any State on such terms and conditions as the Parliament thinks fit'.

The High Court has been more than usually generous in its interpretation of section 96 in the context of both general revenue and specific purpose payments. For present purposes it is relevant to focus on the nature of the terms and conditions which the Parliament can attach to a grant of financial assistance. On the authorities as they presently stand, there appears to be no limit to the power of the Commonwealth in this respect as long as the conditions do not infringe express prohibitions or guarantees elsewhere in the Constitution.

The most extreme formulation of the extent of Commonwealth power under this section can be found in the judgment of Latham CJ in the *First Uniform Tax* case:[26]

> If the Commonwealth Parliament, in a grants Act, simply provided for the payment of moneys to States, without attaching any conditions whatever, none of the legislation could be challenged by any of the arguments submitted to the Court in these cases. The amount of the grants could be determined by the satisfaction of the Commonwealth with the policies, legislative or other, of the respective States, no reference being made to such matters in any Commonwealth statute. Thus, if the Commonwealth Parliament were prepared to pass such legislation, all State powers would be controlled by the Commonwealth—a result which would mean the end of the political independence of the States. The determination of the propriety of any such policy must rest with the Commonwealth Parliament and ultimately with the people. The remedy for alleged abuse of power or for the use of power to promote what are thought to be improper objects is to be found in the political arena and not in the Courts.

On one point at least, Latham CJ must surely have been wrong. The power to attach conditions to the grants is clearly vested in the Parliament by section 96; as a matter of law, therefore, the executive could not attach conditions of its own without parliamentary authority. Even if such a power resides in the Parliament, however, its implications, if used in the way foreshadowed by Latham, are startling. Its existence is entirely inconsistent with the federal principle discussed at the beginning of this chapter. So far, the Commonwealth has not in fact attempted to use the power in this way. To the extent that it has been used, however, it has enabled the Commonwealth to participate actively in such fields as education, health, transport, environmental control and aspects of social welfare which would not otherwise fall within its sphere of competence.

Government borrowing in Australia is now formally regulated through the Loan Council, established under the Financial Agreement of 1927. Constraints on borrowings by local and semi-government authorities also are imposed by the Loan Council, under the Gentlemen's Agreement of 1936. For a variety of reasons (which will be described elsewhere) the Commonwealth has obtained extensive de facto control of decisionmaking by the Loan Council. This has facilitated the extension of Commonwealth economic power in several respects.

To the extent that governments rely on Loan Council funding, it enables the Commonwealth to determine the level of public expenditure on capital works; it also provides a means by which the Commonwealth can influence interest rates. For the most part, however, intergovernmental borrowing arrangements have not yet developed to a point where the Commonwealth can directly affect substantive areas of State activity requiring capital funding.

Other intergovernmental arrangements

The Commonwealth and the States participate in a variety of cooperative arrangements designed to overcome the effect of constitutional constraints, including the federal division of powers. Arrangements designed to achieve uniform law or centralised administration in particular matters have an effect comparable to an exercise of power by the Commonwealth. In many of these arrangements the Commonwealth is dominant, either because substantial Commonwealth funds are involved or because the principal enabling legislation is enacted by the Commonwealth as the only participant capable of providing a legislative framework that transcends State boundaries. Arrangements of this kind provide another means of effectively altering the division of powers.

A common technique of cooperative federalism is the enactment of uniform legislation by the participating jurisdictions. This is unlikely to achieve perfect legislative uniformity. Discrepancies between the initial Acts are almost inevitable, and experience has shown that they are likely to become more severe in the course of subsequent amendments. A more sophisticated device to ensure effective uniformity was developed in Australia recently, in the area of company law. Pursuant to an intergovernmental agreement, the Commonwealth enacted plenary companies and securities industry legislation for the Australian Capital Territory, based on the territories power in section 122 of the Constitution. Each State passed legislation to apply the Commonwealth legislation, as amended from time, within the State concerned. Amendments to the Commonwealth legislation are made in accordance with majority resolutions passed by a ministerial council, on which the Commonwealth and all States are represented. The effect of this arrangement falls short of the investment of a plenary power to legislate for companies in the Commonwealth Parliament, but only to the extent that State ministers participate actively in policymaking.

Legislative uniformity may be inadequate without administrative uniformity. The latter is commonly achieved through the 'bucket' technique: the creation of a single authority invested with power by all participating jurisdictions. The enabling legislation is usually Commonwealth legislation, which may create some difficulty in finding a head of constitutional power to support the initial enactment.

This technique was also used in the companies scheme: the National Companies and Securities Commission was constituted by Commonwealth legislation, and the head of power, again, was the territories power. If the Commonwealth legislation were taken in isolation, the National Commission was an authority established for the Australian Capital Territory. It derived its capacity to administer the companies legislation nationally from legislation passed by each State pursuant to the agreement, investing the Commission with the necessary State powers.

The problem of Commonwealth power was dealt with differently under the Albury–Wodonga development agreement. Under that agreement, the bucket corporation was created by Commonwealth legislation, relying on an assortment of powers that might conceivably be thought to have some relevance to a scheme of this type: interstate and overseas trade and commerce, corporations, immigration, and defence. Almost all the powers actually exercised by the corporation for the purposes of planning and developing the Albury–Wodonga area, for which it was created, derive from laws passed by New South Wales and Victoria. In the case of both the companies and the Albury–Wodonga scheme, ancillary State authorities perform supporting roles. This is neither a necessary nor a usual feature of such schemes.

Current variations on the bucket technique include the creation of separate positions by the Commonwealth and a State to which the same person is appointed, and the cross-vesting of jurisdiction exercisable by Commonwealth and State authorities. Further variations can be expected as the potential of these devices as a means of circumventing constitutional difficulties is more generally realised. It is to be hoped that this realisation will be matched by an understanding of the capacity of these arrangements to impinge upon fundamental constitutional principles and an enthusiasm to structure them as far as possible to avoid unwarranted effects.

The High Court has recently conferred its imprimatur upon cooperative arrangements between the Commonwealth and New South Wales in the context of the coal industry scheme. The scheme is based upon the premise that neither the Commonwealth nor the State possesses adequate power to provide a comprehensive arbitral system for the New South Wales coal industry. Both jurisdictions therefore have enacted legislation to provide for the establishment of a coal industry tribunal and to invest it with power. The same person in fact is appointed to constitute the tribunal under both Acts. In *Re Duncan; ex Parte Australian Iron and Steel Pty Ltd*[27] questions were raised about the validity and effect of this arrangement, but it was held to be valid in a unanimous decision. Some justices went further, conferring a more general blessing on cooperative arrangements. Thus Deane J discovered cooperation to be 'a positive objective of the Constitution'. For Mason J,

> [a] federal constitution which divides legislative powers between the central legislature and the constituent legislatures necessarily contemplates that there will be joint legislative action to deal with matters that lie beyond the powers of any single legislature.

The Commonwealth Constitution divides legislative, executive and judicial power between the Commonwealth and the States. The original basis of the division was that it should confer upon the Commonwealth powers that were necessarily national in character, although it is not clear that any general principles were developed to enable those powers to be identified. Certainly the question has received almost no systematic thought since.

There has been little formal amendment of the division of powers since federation. Nevertheless, the effective operation of the Constitution has been significantly altered by other means. The most important of these have been judicial review and various forms of intergovernmental arrangements. The time has now arrived when it would be appropriate to decide whether we are content to allow the federal system to continue to be adapted and moulded in the ad hoc way that has prevailed for the past 80 years, or whether a more systematic and comprehensive review is required.

The effect of the modifications that have occurred has been, without exception, to expand Commonwealth power. The division of powers still operates as an important constraint on Commonwealth action, but the barriers are crumbling. Ironically, the increasing professionalism of State governments and administrations in recent years has accentuated the significance of the role of the States at a time when sweeping extensions to Commonwealth power are taking place through the courts. In the short term, the result may be an increase in cooperative actions of increasingly ingenious kinds. If present trends continue, Australian federalism will rest almost entirely on political rather than on legal sanctions.

3 Federal–State fiscal arrangements in Australia

RUSSELL MATHEWS

This chapter examines the structure of fiscal arrangements in Australia, with special reference to taxation and federal–State financial relationships. References to the Australian States should be taken to include the Northern Territory, which has been self-governing since 1978. The Australian Capital Territory continues to be administered by the Commonwealth (federal) government.

Taxing and Borrowing Powers and Expenditure Responsibilities

The Constitution gives the Commonwealth and the States concurrent powers over all forms of taxation other than customs and excise duties, which are exclusive to the Commonwealth. However, the Commonwealth has effectively established a monopoly over income tax collections, and the High Court has excluded the States from collecting sales taxes on commodities (but not on services) on the ground that they are excise duties.

Except for rents or royalties from offshore minerals, which the Commonwealth has agreed to share with adjoining States, the States control natural resource revenues arising from the reservation of mineral rights for the Crown. States are also able to derive revenues from resource development indirectly, for example through charges for rail or electricity services. Although the States are generally precluded from granting any bounties on the production or export of goods, this restriction does not apply to metals, and they are able to subsidise mineral production indirectly through the prices they charge for services. For its part, the Commonwealth has been able to control some mining operations indirectly by refusing to grant export licences; it also has the power to impose export taxes.

Commonwealth and State governments originally had concurrent powers with respect to borrowing and the public debt. Following a Financial Agreement between the Commonwealth and the States in 1927, the Constitution was amended to establish the Australian Loan Council, consisting of the Prime Minister and the State Premiers or Treasurers, with the power to control the

amounts, terms and conditions of virtually all long-term public sector borrowing in Australia. For reasons discussed below, the Commonwealth has now
assumed effective de facto control over the Loan Council, and hence over public
sector borrowing.

Under the Commonwealth Constitution, the Commonwealth government has
the responsibility for those functions of government which are international in
character (such as defence and foreign affairs), involve national matters (such as
citizenship and currency) or have interstate ramifications (such as activities
extending beyond the limits of individual States). The States have the formal
responsibility for most aspects of law and order, social services, local government, community and economic services, and resource development. In many
of these areas responsibility is shared between the Commonwealth and the
States, depending on whether the activities have international or interstate
dimensions or are confined within individual States. Thus international and
interstate trade and commerce, conciliation and arbitration in relation to
industrial disputes extending beyond the limits of any one State, and banking
other than State banking within a State are the subject of Commonwealth
powers, while similar activities within States are controlled by State laws. In
addition, the Commonwealth has used its financial powers, especially a general
grants power where by it can provide financial assistance to States on such terms
and conditions as it sees fit, to involve itself in various ways in functions, such as
education, health and transport, that are formally State responsibilities. Both in
this way and as a result of the interdependence of the two levels of government
in relation to many areas of decisionmaking, there is a significant degree of
sharing of responsibility for social and economic policies.

Although the Australian Constitution does not distinguish between the
economic stabilisation, income distribution and resource allocation functions of
government, the Commonwealth has assumed primary responsibility for the
first two while the States retain a large measure of control over resource
allocation decisions within the public sector. While the Commonwealth and the
States both exercise important regulatory functions (again depending on
whether activities are international, interstate or intrastate), the States and their
local governments undertake most final expenditures by the public sector on
goods and services. The Commonwealth's budget is essentially a redistributive
mechanism for making financial transfers between and within the private and
public sectors. Not only does the Commonwealth raise more than 80 per cent of
all taxes and effectively control all government borrowing, but some 80 per cent
of total Commonwealth outlays consist of transfer payments to persons or
families and payments to the States or to other government agencies.

The Commonwealth has explicit constitutional responsibility for the provision of cash social service benefits. This, combined with its involvement
through grants to the States, means that the Commonwealth shares responsibility for social welfare with the States, which have the task of organizing the direct
provision of education, health, housing and other social services.

The Commonwealth and the States both operate business undertakings in
fields such as banking, transport, electricity and gas, and water supply. The

Commonwealth has constitutional responsibility for postal and telecommunication services.

The responsibilities of local government have traditionally been largely restricted to the provision of roads and services to property. Activities such as fire protection, police services, education, health and housing, which in other federations are often carried out by local governments, have been almost exclusively the concern of the States in Australia. Likewise, business undertakings in fields such as electricity, gas, water supply and sewerage tend to be operated by so-called semi-government or statutory authorities established by the States to provide services throughout the State or the metropolis. Nevertheless, local government activities have recently been expanding quite rapidly in both range and scale as councils have assumed greater responsibility for social welfare, community and recreation services. In rural areas local authorities usually have the additional task of providing water and sewerage services, as well as engaging in many other forms of business undertakings.

The Structure of Australian Taxation

The principal Commonwealth taxes are individual and company income taxes, customs and excise duties, and a selective wholesale sales tax.

The individual income tax is applied according to a progressive scale above a tax-free threshold. Wage and salary earners are taxed on a pay-as-you-earn basis, while some other forms of income are taxed at source or are liable to provisional tax. Numerous concessional allowances and tax-exempt expenditures are available in the form of tax rebates or deductions from income.

Company taxes are payable on total company incomes without regard to dividends paid, which are taxable in the hands of shareholders. Public companies are differentiated from private companies, which are liable for additional tax on undistributed profits. Tax concessions available to businesses include: accelerated depreciation on plant; investment allowances on the cost of new plant; full deduction in the year of expenditure for capital expenditures by primary producers for such purposes as soil and water conservation; income equalisation and averaging schemes for primary producers, and a different form of averaging for authors and inventors; generous film industry concessions; rapid write-off provisions for capital expenditure by the mining industry and for expenditure on certain facilities for the transport of minerals.

Customs duties are mainly import duties imposed to protect Australian industry, but they also include an export duty on high-grade coking coal, an excise component in respect of excisable commodities and a revenue duty of 2 per cent on most imports not bearing protective duties. Very high excise duties are imposed on liquor, tobacco and petroleum products, but the most important excise duty is the crude oil and liquefied petroleum gas levy.

The oil levy is designed to bring the prices to refiners for oil produced from Australian fields discovered before 1975 up to import parity prices, with producers receiving those prices less the excise levy payable to the Commonwealth; the levy is payable at progressively higher rates as production from each field increases. Oil produced from newer fields is not subject to the levy. Similar arrangements operate for the liquefied petroleum gas levy, except that the domestic price is set at the lower of the export parity price and an indexed price based on movements in the import parity price of Australian crude oil; the excise duty is related to the weighted average of domestic and export prices; and fields brought into production after 1977 are free of excise. Excise rates and the excise component of customs duties are now subject to half-yearly indexation in accordance with changes in the consumer price index.

The Commonwealth has indicated its intention to introduce a resource rent tax, which will replace the crude oil and liquefied petroleum gas levies and its own royalties on offshore oil and gas production, and which it would also like to replace State royalties on minerals produced within State boundaries (presumably on the basis of some kind of revenue-sharing arrangement). However, State agreement to such an arrangement is unlikely to be forthcoming. What the Commonwealth has in mind is a cash flow tax which will allow development and other capital expenditure to be recouped before tax becomes payable. It has been indicated that the tax is likely to involve a progressive rate structure above an exemption threshold, with the rate of tax depending on the rate of return on either shareholders' funds or total investment.

The wholesale sales tax is a partial tax payable on designated commodities at the point of sale to retailers. It applies to only about 25–30 per cent of final consumption expenditure; services are not subject to the tax. In 1983 the Commonwealth introduced a tax on bank account debits at very low rates, while a 1 per cent levy on taxable incomes will operate from February 1984 to help finance the new health insurance program, Medicare.

There are virtually no Commonwealth taxes on capital, death duties having been abolished. There is no capital gains tax as such, but some capital gains are taxed as income.

The principal State taxes are payroll tax, stamp duties, financial institutions duty, motor taxes, business franchise tax, liquor taxes, gambling taxes, levies on public corporations and land tax.

Local government rates, which constitute virtually the whole of local taxation revenues, are based on unimproved or site values in some States, while in others councils have the option of using, as alternatives to unimproved or site values, improved capital values or annual rental values.

Table 3.1 sets out the structure of Australian taxation by type of tax and level of government imposing the tax for the year 1981/82. The principal features are worth noting here.

First, the Commonwealth, which received 81 per cent of the total collections compared with 15 per cent for the States and 4 per cent for local government, dominates tax raising in Australia. Second, there is an almost complete separation of taxes among the three levels of government, the only shared revenue base being that for State and local property taxes (land taxes and rates). (State-type taxes collected by the Commonwealth relate to the Australian

Table 3.1 The structure of Australian taxation, 1981/82 ($m)

	Commonwealth[a]	State[b]	Local	Total
Income tax				
Individual				
—wages and salaries	17 417	—	—	17 417
—other	3 087	—	—	3 087
Company	5 215	—	—	5 215
Customs duties				
Imports	2 060	—	—	2 060
Coal exports	97	—	—	97
Excise duties				
Crude oil and liquefied petroleum				
gas	3 163	—	—	3 163
Other	2 830	—	—	2 830
Sales tax	2 854	—	—	2 854
Payroll tax	16	2 398	—	2 414
Stamp duties	11	1 350	—	1 360
Motor taxes	10	1 009	—	1 020
Business franchise taxes	—	267	—	267
Liquor taxes	4	231	—	235
Gambling taxes	—	729	—	729
Levies on public corporations	—	121	—	121
Property taxes	21	370	1 718	2 109
Other	487	629	88	1 204
Total	37 992	7 103	1 806	46 901

Notes: a Includes the Australian Capital Territory
    b Includes the Northern Territory
Sources: ABS *Taxation Revenue Australia 1981–82* Cat. No. 5506.0, Tables 1, 5, 16, 17;
    Commonwealth of Australia *Budget Statements 1982–83* 1982–83 Budget Paper
    No. 1, p. 245

Capital Territory.) The table does not throw any light on Commonwealth–State revenue competition with respect to mining revenues. In 1979/80, the most recent year for which figures are available, the Commonwealth, in addition to the oil and liquefied petroleum gas levies, collected $905 million in company tax from companies whose main source of assessable income was mining, while mining royalties collected by the six States amounted to $239 million (excluding Commonwealth payments in respect of offshore fields). But the company tax statistics are too crude to enable worthwhile comparisons to be made. A third feature of the Australian tax system is the heavy reliance on income taxation, with personal income taxes accounting for 45 per cent of all taxation and company taxes for another 11 per cent. Moreover, a very high proportion of personal income taxes (82 per cent) is paid by wage and salary earners. Fourth, there is widespread use of selective taxes on goods and services, many of which can be characterised as low-yielding nuisance taxes, combined with the absence of a broad-based consumption tax. Fifth, there is no general tax on capital or capital accretion in the form of death duties, an annual tax on wealth or a capital gains tax. The property taxes levied by State and local governments are not only partial, being mainly restricted to land, but are indirect taxes to a significant extent because they fall on business enterprises as well as individuals.

By international standards the overall level of Australian taxation, as measured by the proportion of tax collections to gross domestic product, is not high. Although the tax system in Australia has some virtues associated with the uniform tax arrangements and the absence of overlapping jurisdictions, when judged by criteria of simplicity, efficiency, equity and effectiveness it must be considered most unsatisfactory. Many low-yielding taxes involve very high administrative and compliance costs, while futile attempts to plug avoidance loopholes in the income tax legislation, combined with the use of taxation concessions to promote social and economic objectives which have nothing to do with the basic goals of taxation policy, have resulted in an income tax system of unbelievable complexity. This and the widespread use of discriminatory taxes have also had the effect of distorting both production decisions and consumer choices.

The prospects for significant tax reform seem virtually non-existent. Three principal measures would enhance the simplicity, efficiency, equity and effectiveness of the Australian tax system. The first would involve reduced reliance on income taxation and changes in its revenue base and rate structure. Among other things, net cash flow should be substituted for the unmeasurable and easily manipulated concept of income as the revenue base. This would of course have important consequences for the mining industry, because it would permit the immediate writing off of all capital expenditure for taxation purposes and the consequential sharing by the Commonwealth of the risks as well as the gains from mining operations. The second requirement would involve the restoration of capital taxes, including both death duties and an annual tax on capital. The third would require the introduction of a broad-based consumption tax in the form of a value-added tax or retail sales tax. This would be designed not only to compensate for the reduced revenue from income taxation but also to replace the miscellany of partial outlay taxes such as the Commonwealth sales tax, the State payroll tax and the large number of Commonwealth and State taxes on particular forms of transactions.

Such reforms would require cooperative action by the Commonwealth and the States. A reduction in the level of income tax would open the way for the States to impose income tax surcharges, as permitted by existing legislation, in substitution for many of their existing low-yielding and inefficient taxes. Capital taxes would no doubt need to be reserved to the Commonwealth to prevent a repetition of the precipitate action which recently led to the abolition of State death duties. Because both the Commonwealth and the States would need to give up existing taxes to facilitate the introduction of a value-added or retail sales tax, some kind of revenue-sharing agreement would be necessary, under which each level of government would be able to nominate the tax rate to apply to a common base.

While tax-sharing arrangements of this kind have operated successfully in Canada (in respect of income taxation) and West Germany (in respect of the value-added tax), it is difficult to see agreement being reached by Australian governments. Even at the Commonwealth level, ideological differences among political parties and the short time span between elections make it extremely unlikely that root-and-branch tax reform could ever the achieved, even if it were to be attempted. While the non-Labor parties support the increased use of indirect taxes but oppose capital taxation in any form, the Labor Party takes the opposite view on both. About the only taxation policy which can be characterised as bipartisan is the continued heavy reliance on income taxation, an approach which assumes that people pay the taxes that they are supposed to pay, that tax avoidance and evasion can be eliminated by closing loopholes without having to make structural changes to the tax system, and that income taxes, with all their faults, are more efficient and equitable and less destabilising in their effects than any alternative.

Existing Tax-Sharing Arrangements

Not the least unsatisfactory feature of the Australian taxation system has been its effect on intergovernmental financial relations, resulting especially in a loss of fiscal responsibility at both the Commonwealth and State levels and a breaking of the nexus between taxing and spending decisions throughout the public sector. The financial dominance of the Commonwealth, which has resulted primarily from the income tax monopoly achieved under the uniform taxation arrangements introduced during the second world war, manifests itself in three principal ways, each of which reflects a state of vertical fiscal imbalance between the Commonwealth and the States.

The first is the tax-sharing arrangement whereby the Commonwealth makes general revenue grants to the States (and to local governments) in substitution for the income taxes the States used to collect for themselves. The second is the extensive use of specific purpose payments, whereby the Commonwealth uses its financial powers under the Constitution and its superior resources to influence the manner in which services are provided in functions which are the constitutional responsibility of the States. The third is the Commonwealth's de facto control over the Australian Loan Council, whereby it effectively determines the level, terms and conditions of virtually all public sector borrowing.

In addition, the Commonwealth's fiscal dominance has enabled it to influence the distribution of tax-sharing grants, specific purpose payments and loan funds among the States and among local government authorities, and thereby to play a decisive role in determining the extent to which there is horizontal fiscal balance within each level of government.

In their present form, the tax-sharing arrangements have the following characteristics.

1   The States in the aggregate receive a fixed proportion (20.72 per cent) of total Commonwealth tax collections in the previous year. The distribution of this amount among the six States reflects the past distribution of general revenue grants, but is purportedly being shifted towards relativities assessed by the Commonwealth Grants Commission on the basis of fiscal equalisation principles.

2   Without departing from the system of uniform personal income tax assessment and collection, any State may impose a percentage surcharge on or grant a percentage rebate to its residents to its own benefit or cost. (So far, no State has taken advantage of this provision.) Any income tax surcharge so imposed by one of the four less populous States will be subject to equalisation through the Commonwealth Grants Commission to bring its yield up to the average per capita revenue that such a surcharge would yield to New South Wales and Victoria.

3   The Commonwealth may declare a change in any Commonwealth tax made for economic management purposes to be a special surcharge or rebate which will be excluded from the tax-sharing base.

4   In addition to a continuing guarantee that no State will receive a lower grant in absolute money terms in any year than it received in the previous year, the Commonwealth has guaranteed that in 1983/84 and 1984/85 each State will receive an increase of at least 1 per cent per annum in its grant in real terms. (The real terms guarantee is partly financed from moneys set aside from the States' 20.72 per cent aggregate share of the tax base, but in 1983/84 an additional Commonwealth allocation (bringing the total to 21.16 per cent) was necessary to fund the guarantee.)

5   No State may apply for a special grant through the Commonwealth Grants Commission before 30 June 1985.

6   The Commonwealth is supposed to consult the States on changes in Commonwealth taxation which affect the tax-sharing base. (This requirement does not appear to have been observed.)

7   Local governments receive, in aggregate, 2 per cent of Commonwealth personal income tax collections in the previous year, the distribution among the States reflecting the advice of the Commonwealth Grants Commission and the distribution within States being determined by State grants commissions in accordance with broad criteria specified by the Commonwealth, whereby funds are distributed partly on the basis of population and partly on a fiscal equalisation basis.

Although the Northern Territory does not participate in the tax-sharing arrangements as such, it receives a direct tax-sharing grant from the Commonwealth, which is increased from year to year in proportion to both the increase in total Commonwealth tax collections in the previous year and the increase in the Territory's population in the current year. The Territory is not eligible for the real terms guarantee, but it can apply for special grants through the Grants Commission (and in fact received a special grant in 1983/84), and is subject to other special financial arrangements with the Commonwealth. It may impose personal income tax surcharges or grant rebates on the same basis as the States (although, like them, it has not chosen to do so), and its local governments receive direct tax-sharing grants from the Commonwealth in a manner analogous to the State arrangements.

In addition to the tax-sharing grants, the States and the Northern Territory also receive general revenue funds in the form of so-called identified health grants, which have replaced the specific purpose grants that used to be paid for the sharing of hospital, community health and school dental service costs. These will eventually be absorbed into the tax-sharing grants; meanwhile they are increased each year in proportion to the increase in the tax-sharing grants.

In 1983/84 only, the States received special temporary revenue assistance grants to alleviate their severe budgetary difficulties; these were distributed on the same basis as the tax-sharing grants.

When the tax-sharing arrangements were introduced in 1976, it was claimed that they would improve the basis of intergovernmental fiscal relations by giving the States an effective voice in revenue-raising decisions and restoring their access to the personal income tax base for the first time since 1942. However, the new arrangements did not result in any significant change in the position of the States; if anything, Commonwealth control over State finances has been strengthened.

Not only has there been no real State participation in decisions relating to the tax-sharing arrangements, but the right to impose income tax surcharges was effectively precluded by the Commonwealth's failure to make tax room by reducing its own rates, which it could easily have done by simultaneously reducing the tax-sharing grants by an equivalent amount. Nor has the Commonwealth taken decisive action to improve the distribution of the grants among the States in accordance with two reviews of tax-sharing relativities by the Grants Commission. Unilateral Commonwealth decisions have had the effect of reducing the aggregate amount of State entitlements on several occasions; it is not too much of an exaggeration to say that, through the tax-sharing arrangements, the specific purpose programs and the Loan Council, the Commonwealth now exercises the same degree of overall fiscal control over the States as over its own departments and agencies.

At the June–July 1983 Premiers' Conference, however, a working group of Commonwealth, State and Northern Territory Treasury officers was appointed to examine longer term issues affecting the distribution of taxation powers between the Commonwealth and State (and Northern Territory) governments. The working group was also to advise on the terms of reference for a further review of State tax-sharing relativities.

Horizontal Fiscal Equalisation: the Commonwealth Grants Commission

Since 1933 an independent statutory authority—the Commonwealth Grants Commission—has had the responsibility for advising on applications for special financial assistance by individual States. This it has done by applying what it calls the principle of fiscal equalisation, where by the special grant recommended for a State will make it possible for that State to provide a standard level of services to its citizens if it also makes a standard revenue-raising effort.

The Commission arrives at the level of its recommended grant by assessing revenue and expenditure needs for each category of recurrent revenue (taxes, land and mineral revenues) and recurrent expenditure (social services expenditures, other expenditures and the results of those business undertakings which have an impact on State budgets because they cannot be operated profitably). The revenue need for a particular category is calculated by applying a standard revenue-raising effort to the difference between a standard per capita revenue base and the per capita revenue base of the State seeking assistance, and multiplying the result by the latter's population. The expenditure need for a category is calculated as the differential per capita cost of providing standard services multiplied by the claimant State's population. The differential cost may be attributable to demographic, scale, dispersion or environmental factors beyond the control of the State seeking assistance, but not to policy differences between that State and the States used as the standard. These are the two States with the highest fiscal capacity, New South Wales and Victoria.

The revenue and expenditure needs in individual categories (which may be positive or negative) are then summed to arrive at the claimant State's total assessed needs. To the extent that the claimant State's tax-sharing and some other revenue-augmenting grants (such as those for education and health) exceed what it would receive under an equal per capita distribution of grants, the assessed needs are being partially met by those other grants, and the special grant recommended is calculated as the difference between the assessed needs and the differential amount of the other grants.

The Grants Commission's recommendations on special grants have always been accepted by the Commonwealth. The procedures developed by the Commission have played a major role in reconciling fiscal equality and diversity in the Australian federation. The special grants are general purpose grants and leave claimant States with the freedom to determine their own levels and patterns of revenue raising and spending (subject to the overall fiscal constraints within which they have to operate). Their own policies do not affect the levels of financial assistance they receive.

The Commission's procedures for assessing a State's needs in respect of mineral revenues may be used to illustrate its concern to ensure that, as far as possible, its assessments reflect differences in revenue-raising capacity and not differences in revenue-raising effort (that is, in State policies). The Commission applies the average revenue effort of the standard States, as reflected in their royalty rates, to the difference between the average per capita revenue base of the standard States and the per capita revenue base of the State being assessed, the measure of the revenue base for this purpose being one that reflects the relative profitability of the mining operations in the standard States and the claimant States (and not actual royalty collections). The resulting per capita difference in revenue-raising capacity is then multiplied by the claimant State's population to derive its assessed needs for mining revenues, which will be positive or negative depending on whether its per capita revenue base falls short of or exceeds the average of the standard States.

The claimant State's revenue needs are thus independent of its revenue-raising effort, and it is free to fix its royalty rates at whatever level it considers appropriate having regard to its own budget priorities and its attitudes towards resource development. In practice, data problems may complicate the tasks of determining standard royalty rates (for example, when a particular mineral is mined in the claimant State but not in the standard States) or of measuring revenue bases (for example, when it is suspected that the revenue base of the claimant State has itself been influenced by its resource policies). The Commission's response to such problems has been described in some detail elsewhere;[1] in brief, the general thrust of its procedures is designed to ensure that the claimant State's needs reflect its potential revenue-raising capacity relative to that of the standard States and not merely its revenue collections.

It will be clear that whether a special grant is recommended for a State will depend not only on its assessed needs but also on how it fares in the distribution of the tax-sharing grants and certain other grants.

During the past 25 years, the distribution of general revenue grants has shifted from a system predominantly based on population to one which, at the time of the introduction of the tax-sharing arrangements in 1976, applied population adjustment factors (so-called State factors) to State populations in order to determine the distribution of the tax-sharing grants. Relative to a Victorian base of 1.00, these factors ranged from about 1.03 for New South Wales to about 2.00 for Tasmania, with the factors of the other three States at varying positions between those limits. The factors reflected ad hoc political decisions taken at various times and had not been systematically determined by reference to the relative fiscal capacities of the States. The decisions frequently represented political deals between the Commonwealth and individual claimant States, whereby a State's share of general revenue (tax-sharing) grants had been increased to such an extent that it no longer needed to seek special assistance through the Commonwealth Grants Commission.

By 1976 the three less populous States, which, as the States with the lowest fiscal capacity, had been the original claimant States, had all withdrawn from claimancy and, through the tax-sharing grants, were in fact being overequalised at the expense of the other three States. Only Queensland, which was not the State with the lowest fiscal capacity but which was receiving a relatively unfavourable share of the tax-sharing and other relevant grants, remained a claimant State until special grants arrangements for the States were replaced by new arrangements in 1982. However, the Northern Territory continues to be assessed for special grants on the foregoing basis.

Under the tax-sharing arrangements introduced in 1976, provision was made for a review of the tax-sharing relativities in accordance with fiscal equalisation principles. An expanded Grants Commission carried out two such reviews, being required to report on whether it considered that the existing relativities (as represented by the State factors) needed to be changed. In its two reports, presented in 1981 and 1982, the Commission advised that in its view the factors should be changed, and provided assessments of the relativities which it said would be consistent with the application of fiscal equalisation principles. In reaching these conclusions, the Commission adapted the procedures for assessing needs which it had developed for the purposes of its claimancy reviews.

In oversimplified terms, the distribution model adopted by the Commission involved the calculation of each State's per capita share as an equal per capita share of the total amount of tax-sharing funds available, plus or minus its per capita revenue and expenditure needs and its differential per capita specific purpose grants. With needs and grant differentials assessed by reference to a population-weighted six-State standard, the total per capita variation to the equal per capita amount for a State could be positive or negative. The adjusted per capita amounts then represented the tax-sharing relativities, which were converted to population adjustment factors by expressing them as ratios of the Victorian amount. The relativities calculated by the Commission implied that the three most populous States—New South Wales, Victoria and Queensland—should receive larger shares of the tax-sharing funds and that the other three States should receive smaller shares.

At the June 1982 Premiers' Conference, it was announced that, subject to the modification of the Commission's relativities for South Australia and Tasmania to take account of the fact that their hospital cost-sharing agreements with the Commonwealth were still in force, the assessed relativities would be phased in over the three years from 1982/83 to 1984/85. However, the Commonwealth also decided that each State would be guaranteed an increase of at least 2 per cent in real terms in 1982/83 and 1 per cent in real terms in each of the following two years.

The Commonwealth made virtually no new funds available to finance the guarantee, so that in the first instance it had to be funded from the tax-sharing pool itself. In 1982/83 the three States whose factors were to be reduced (South Australia, Western Australia and Tasmania) were subject to the guarantee, which in effect was therefore financed by the three States whose relative shares were supposed to be increased. All states except Queensland were subject to the guarantee in 1983/84, so that, with the exception of a shift towards Queensland, little progress was made during the first two years towards phasing in the Commission's assessments.

A further review of tax-sharing relativities was commenced in 1984 as part of a general review of the present tax-sharing arrangements which expire on 30 June 1985. Unless the Commonwealth makes additional funds available to facilitate the phasing in of whatever new relativities may be assessed, it is difficult to see that the third review will be any more successful than its predecessors in shifting the distribution of the tax-sharing grants to one based on fiscal equalisation principles.

Nevertheless, the fiscal equalisation arrangements in Australia, with all their faults and limitations, go much further in the direction of systematically equalising the fiscal capacities of the States than any comparable arrangements in other countries. This is because the Grants Commission's assessments now embrace all States, so that States with above-average fiscal capacity are equalised down to the six-State average at the same time as below-standard States are equalised up to the average. Expenditure needs as well as revenue needs are subject to assessment—among other things, resource revenues are fully equalised—and differential specific purpose grants likely to affect fiscal capacity are taken into account. Although there is disagreement among the States and with the Grants Commission on many issues with an important bearing on its assessed relativities, the Commission's essential methodology is not in dispute and the Commission itself seems to be generally accepted as an impartial arbiter. All that is needed to complete the process of fiscal equalisation in Australia is a continuing review process and the injection of additional funds by the Commonwealth to facilitate the phasing in of new relativities.

Specific Purpose Payments

Another manifestation of the Commonwealth's fiscal superiority is the importance of specific purpose payments in Australian federal fiscal arrangements. There has been some retreat from the position reached in the mid-1970s, when specific purpose payments in aggregate approached the level of Commonwealth general purpose payments and financed about a third of all State expenditure (recurrent and capital). But they are still very influential in State budgets and finance nearly one-fifth of the States' total expenditure.

Specific purpose payments take the form of either grants (both recurrent and capital) or loans, the latter often being used where the payments finance revenue-producing activities such as housing, railway projects and programs directed to economic development. To a much greater extent than in most other countries, specific purpose grants are usually free of matching requirements, although they may incorporate other revenue conditions as well as the expenditure conditions which govern the ways in which the funds are used. As a result, the grants are often similar in their effects to general revenue grants; the States can readily substitute them and the expenditures they finance for their own revenues and expenditures. Nevertheless, the Commonwealth is able to impose its own policy decisions on the States in relation to the assisted programs, even though the States are better placed to interpret and respond to the preferences of their citizens with respect to these programs. The result is a weakening of State responsibility and administration.

During the early 1970s, most of the large specific purpose programs were developed and administered by statutory commissions appointed by the Commonwealth to advise on the financial needs of the States in relation to the specific purpose programs. The Commonwealth Grants Commission still has the seldom-exercised responsibility for advising on the interstate distribution of local government tax-sharing grants, while the Australian Heritage Commission advises on grants to the States for the restoration, preservation and improvement of the national estate.

Apart from these relatively minor tasks, the only surviving programs administered by statutory Commonwealth bodies are those for tertiary education (universities and colleges of advanced education and technical and further education) and schools (government and non-government), which are the respective responsibilities of the Commonwealth Tertiary Education Commission and the Commonwealth Schools Commission. In both cases these Commissions still have a statutory responsibility to advise on the financial needs of the education sectors for which they are responsible. In the light of that advice the Commonwealth government determines the levels of grants that will be provided and issues guidelines to the Commissions to govern their allocations to States or educational institutions.

Although most universities and colleges of advanced education remain State institutions, the Commonwealth now provides all their funds. It also provides about 15 per cent of the recurrent costs and about two-thirds of the capital costs of technical and further education colleges, about 10 per cent of the average costs of government schools, and up to about 50 per cent of the average costs of non-government schools.

The principal specific purpose programs, payments for which in 1982/83 are recorded in Table 3.2, are those for debt charges assistance, tertiary education, schools, welfare services, housing, roads, natural disaster relief, employment and local government. In 1983/84 grants were also made under the new Medicare program to compensate the States for revenue losses and medical costs directly related to the program. Hospital cost-sharing grants and two smaller health grants were recently replaced by general purpose health grants.

There are several small programs (other than those recorded separately in Table 3.2) directed towards resource development and trade, including assistance for depressed primary industries, a national soil conservation program, water projects, and infrastructure support for the three main steel-producing regions in Australia.

The distribution of specific purpose payments among the States has usually reflected political decisions or arbitrary criteria rather than any systematic evaluation of relative needs. Of course, many grants for particular projects are necessarily restricted to the States in which those projects are undertaken, and individual projects are particularly susceptible to pork-barrelling. But even broad national programs do not necessarily take relative needs or effort into account for the purpose of determining the distribution of payments among the States. For example, at the same time as the new schools program in the mid-1970s was providing relatively large grants to States which had been spending comparatively small amounts on their schools, the distribution of the new hospital cost-sharing grants favoured those States which had been spending relatively large amounts on their hospitals.

Table 3.2 Major Commonwealth specific purpose payments to States, 1982/83 ($m)

	States			Northern Territory
	recurrent	capital[a]	total	total
Debt charges assistance	59.0	—	59.0	31.1
Universities	918.2	52.1	970.3	—
Colleges of advanced education	597.9	39.6	637.6	—
Technical and further education	99.0	124.5	223.5	8.9
Government schools[b]	432.0	132.3	564.3	11.2
Non-government schools	552.1	48.2	600.4	
School-to-work transition	40.5	—	40.5	0.5
Pre-schools	32.8	—	32.8	0.3
Hospital running costs[c]	207.4	—	207.4	—
Home care services	17.7	—	17.7	0.1
Children's services	16.0	1.1	17.1	0.3
Aboriginal advancement	29.0	4.8	33.8	2.1
Housing	5.5	312.7	318.2	20.2
Roads—general[d]	—	736.0	736.0	24.7
Bicentennial roads program	—	110.7	110.7	6.2
Railway upgrading	—	21.8	21.8	—
Transport upgrading	—	65.0	65.0	—
Rural adjustment	3.0	14.3	17.3	0.5
Brucellosis and TB eradication	24.4	—	24.4	3.7
National water resources program[e]	—	34.3	34.3	2.0
Special employment programs	97.6	53.1	150.7	1.2
Drought—fodder subsidy	103.7	—	103.7	—
Natural disaster relief	48.1	98.0	146.1	0.2
Northern Territory Electricity Commission	—	—	—	60.0
Local government tax-sharing assistance	424.5	—	424.5	2.0
Other	64.5	161.3	225.8	5.0
Total	3 772.9	2 009.8	5 782.7	180.2

Notes: a Grants and loans
 b Includes joint government and non-government school programs
 c South Australia and Tasmania
 d Includes $26.7m for special Tasmanian projects
 e Includes some recurrent payments

Source: Commonwealth Government *Payments to or for the States, the Northern Territory and Local Government Authorities 1983–84* 1983–84 Budget Paper No. 7, Tables 49, 105

In addition to grants for local government that are passed through the States, of which the most important are the tax-sharing grants recorded in Table 3.2 and grants for roads (of the $736.0 million roads grants to the States shown in Table 3.2, an amount of $178.0 million was passed on to local governments), the Commonwealth made direct payments of $59.1 million to local governments in 1982/83. Of these, the most important were for aerodromes ($29.6 million), children's services ($15.5 million) and nursing homes and aged or disabled persons' homes and hostels ($11.0 million). Northern Territory local governments received roads grants of $0.9 million and direct grants for children's services of $0.4 million.

Public Sector Borrowing: the Australian Loan Council

Partly as a result of constitutional amendment in 1928 following the Financial Agreement between the Commonwealth and the States (which covered Commonwealth and State government borrowing) and partly as a result of a so-called Gentlemen's Agreement in 1936 (which covered borrowing by semi-government and local authorities), virtually all public sector borrowing in Australia is formally subject to the control of the Australian Loan Council as to amounts, forms, terms and conditions. The Council consists of the Prime Minister and the State Premiers or Treasurers, and under the voting rules the States can outvote the Commonwealth. Since the second world war, however, the Commonwealth has used its income tax monopoly and its influence over the Reserve Bank to impose its will on the Loan Council. In most years since the early 1950s, it has not been possible for the States to raise loans from the public to the extent necessary to cover State borrowing programs formally approved by the Loan Council (but in practice determined by the Commonwealth). The Commonwealth has been prepared to make up any shortfall in State programs from its own budget (through so-called special loans made on the same terms as treasury bonds issued to the public), provided it is able to decide on the amounts, terms and conditions of those programs. As a result of these developments, during recent years the Council has become one of the main instruments for the exercise of the Commonwealth's policies of fiscal restraint.

Apart from borrowing by the Commonwealth itself, there are at present five categories of public sector borrowing in Australia: State Loan Council programs; borrowing by electricity authorities; infrastructure borrowing; other borrowing by larger semi-government and local authorities (those borrowing more than $1.8 million in a year); and borrowing by the smaller semi-government and local authorities.

Although all are subject to Loan Council decisions, in practice the Council (and hence the Commonwealth) has imposed varying degrees of detailed control over the level, terms and conditions of borrowing. During recent years, borrowing by State semi-government and local authorities has been progressively freed from Loan Council regulation and permitted to operate under market-oriented conditions.

State Loan Council programs provide the States' general purpose capital funds and, with the Commonwealth's own borrowing, are the only programs constitutionally subject to Loan Council control. The Commonwealth finances one-third of the total State programs approved by the Council through general purpose capital grants, leaving the remaining two-thirds to be financed by borrowing. No doubt partly because of the cost of the capital grants and partly because State programs form part of the Commonwealth's own budget (whether or not they involve special Commonwealth loans as well as borrowing from the public), State programs represent the form of public sector borrowing that is most subject to severe Commonwealth fiscal restraint. Since 1976/77 the money amount of State programs has remained roughly constant, but the real value has been nearly halved. It is difficult to find any economic rationale for this reduction in resources made available for State programs at a time when there has been both heavy and growing unemployment as well as a running down of the public sector capital stock to dangerously inadequate levels. The conclusion must be that, of all the items in the Commonwealth's budget, this is the one which can most easily be cut back in order to accommodate the Commonwealth's obsessive concern with the size of its budget deficit.

From the viewpoint of the States, the Loan Council programs nevertheless have the advantages that they provide general purpose funds, some in the form of grants, and that the States are assured of receiving the funds allocated. States may also allocate part of their loan programs to public housing, and they receive the same favourable terms for that allocation as for other Commonwealth advances under the Commonwealth–State Housing Agreement. Although the Northern Territory is not a member of the Loan Council, the Commonwealth makes allocations to the Territory (capital grants and loans) on the same basis as to the States.

Until recently semi-government and local borrowing programs have also been subject to Loan Council decisions with respect to amounts, terms and conditions, although since the early 1960s smaller authorities (at present those borrowing no more than $1.8 million in a year) have been exempted from the need to obtain Loan Council approval for their loans, while still needing to conform to the Council's guidelines with respect to interest rates, terms and conditions. Most States have recently established central borrowing authorities to coordinate loan raising and to enable smaller authorities to borrow on competitive terms.

In 1978/79 the Loan Council adopted guidelines for so-called infrastructure financing whereby it was possible for some larger authorities to obtain special additions outside their borrowing programs. These additions were approved case by case for projects related to economic development; specific Commonwealth approval was needed. While the general effect of the additions was to increase the flexibility of public sector borrowing in the direction of projects and States with development potential, the increased funds available were generally offset by reductions in other Loan Council programs, so that there was little improvement in the States' aggregate level of capital funds. Because no new projects have been approved since 1980/81, infrastructure financing is diminishing in importance after reaching a peak of one-third of all larger authority borrowing in 1981/82.

About half of the infrastructure financing was for electricity projects, and in 1982 the Loan Council decided that for a trial period of three years the amounts and terms of domestic borrowing by Commonwealth and State electricity authorities could be determined by their own governments without Loan Council approval.

So far as the remaining larger authorities are concerned, the Council decided in 1983 to limit its control over domestic borrowing to the aggregate level of the program and to leave interest rates, timing and terms and conditions to individual governments to determine. However, there was to be consultation between governments, and overseas borrowing by all authorities (including electricity authorities) was to be subject to an upper limit and to Loan Council and Commonwealth approval for each case; the distribution of loans raised overseas was to be mutually agreed by the States.

In 1984 the Council adopted for a trial period a system of global limits on authority borrowing from all sources, including leasing arrangements, commercial credits and other devices which States had been using to circumvent Loan Council controls. Other controls over amounts and conditions of authority borrowing were removed to give the States greater flexibility in their borrowing both in Australia and overseas.

Despite these changes—indeed, partly because of them—the Loan Council arrangements remain a most unsatisfactory feature of Australian fiscal federalism. This is so for several reasons, of which the most important are the Commonwealth's domination of the Loan Council and its use of the Council as an instrument of fiscal restraint. The aggregate level of public sector borrowing in Australia has been kept much too low relative to the need for public investment. By any standards, the public sector capital stock is in a deplorable condition, and there can be no excuse for the severe curbs that the Council has placed on general purpose State Loan Council programs.

A second major defect of the Loan Council arrangements, which has been accentuated by recent developments, has resulted from arbitrary decisions that have favoured some categories of borrowing relative to others, discriminated against States general purpose funds, distorted the allocation of public sector resources, unnecessarily inhibited the States from determining their own capital works priorities, and made them resort to all kinds of devices in order to finance capital spending. Through its influence on the Loan Council and the distribution of its specific purpose capital payments, the Commonwealth has effectively determined the pattern as well as the level of public sector investment, even though it has no way of obtaining detailed knowledge of expenditure needs across different capital works categories. The result is inefficiency, a lack of accountability and the absence of financial responsibility for decisions on the part of both the Commonwealth and the States.

The third major weakness of the Loan Council is the absence of any systematic basis for determining the interstate distribution of capital funds. This is mainly due to the provisions of the Financial Agreement itself, which make it very difficult to effect any change in distribution from year to year to reflect relative needs. While they may be criticised on other grounds, the recent decisions to favour development projects and the Commonwealth's allocations of specific purpose capital payments have probably improved the overall interstate distribution of capital funds, albeit arbitrarily and without reference to any systematic criteria.

Commonwealth Payments to or for the States

Table 3.3 summarises the main forms of Commonwealth financial assistance and other payments to the States and local authorities for 1982/83, distinguishing between recurrent and capital funds, general purpose and specific purpose funds, and categories of borrowing. As well as total amounts for the six States, per capita figures for the States and the Northern Territory are presented to facilitate comparisons.

The Structure of the Australian Public Sector

Table 3.4 provides an outline of the outlays and receipts of the three levels of government in 1981/82, the most recent year for which figures are available. Outlays are classified by economic categories.

The table illustrates the relative importance of State and local governments with respect to final expenditure on goods and services, and the predominance of the Commonwealth in transfer payments—intergovernmental, benefits to persons, interest and other transfers—and taxation. Interest and dividend payments include transfers to other governments; the amount shown in column (4) consists almost wholly of State payments to the Commonwealth. The last column represents a consolidation of public sector transactions, so that transfers between governments are netted out. The deficits recorded in the last row are partly financed for individual levels of government by advances from other governments, but these also need to be netted out in determining the consolidated financing transactions for all public authorities, which are therefore restricted to borrowing from the overseas sector, public loan raising and Reserve Bank and other residual financing.

To evaluate the size of public sector deficits in 1981/82 (the consolidated deficit of $4614 million represented about 3.3 per cent of gross domestic product), it should be noted that about $1800 million of Commonwealth capital expenditure on goods and services represented investment by authorities outside the budget, mainly business undertakings. The comparable figure for capital expenditure by State non-budget authorities was $4100 million.

It will be clear from this analysis of intergovernmental fiscal arrangements that Australia has a public sector financial system in which taxing, spending and borrowing decisions are all highly centralised. Indeed, it has a fiscal system which is highly centralised not only relative to other federations, such as the United States, Canada, West Germany and India, but also by comparison with many countries with unitary systems of government, such as the United Kingdom and, in some respects at least, Japan.

While it might have been expected that some benefits would flow from these arrangements in terms of the potential provided for greater equity and control

Table 3.3 Commonwealth payments and Loan Council funds available for the States and the Northern Territory and their authorities, 1982/83

	Total ($m)	Six States ($ per capita)						Total	Northern Territory ($ per capita)
		NSW	Vic.	Qld.	SA	WA	Tas.		
Tax-sharing grants and other special assistance	7 783	443	439	615	656	676	842	522	3 029
Health grants	1 017	88	75	38	7[a]	104	12[a]	68	180
General purpose capital funds (State loan council programs)[b]	1 373	83	86	74	134	94	223	92	918
Total general purpose funds	10 173	614	600	728	797	873	1 078	682	4 127
Specific purpose payments									
—recurrent	3 773	234	259	220	362	239	331	253	853
—capital	2 010	114	115	168	162	161	225	135	518
Total specific purpose payments	5 783	348	373	388	524	400	556	388	1 371
Direct payments to local authorities	59	3	2	6	4	4	16	4	4
Total payments	16 015	965	976	1 122	1 325	1 277	1 650	1 074	5 502

Table 3.3 Continued

		Six States							Northern Territory
	Total ($m)	NSW	Vic.	Qld.	SA ($ per capita)	WA	Tas.	Total	($ per capita)
Borrowing by larger semi-government and local authorities[c]	877	61	71	76	25	35	5	59	53
Infrastructure borrowing[c]	166	12	6	24	—	4	24	11	—
Borrowing by electricity authorities	2 612	101	205	238	133	264	305	175	178
Borrowing by smaller authorities	533	26	35	58	30	40	44	36	14
Total borrowing by semi-government and local authorities	4 187	200	317	396	187	342	377	280	245
Total payments and funds available	20 202	1 165	1 293	1 518	1 512	1 619	2 027	1 354	5 747

Notes: a Hospital cost-sharing grants are included in specific purpose payments
b Capital grants and borrowing programs
c Excludes electricity authorities

Sources: Commonwealth Government Payments to or for the States. the Northern Territory and Local Government Authorities 1983–84 1983–84 Budget Paper No. 7, Tables 13, 50, 71, 72, 82, 84, 105; calculations by author

Table 3.4 Australian public sector receipts and outlays, 1981/82 ($m)

	Commonwealth authorities (1)	State authorities[a] (2)	Local authorities (3)	Transfers between governments (4)	All public authorities (1) + (2) + (3) − (4)
Outlays					
Net expenditure and goods on services					
—current	8 708	15 520	1 257	—	25 485
—capital[b]	2 077	6 771	1 733	—	10 580
Total goods and services	10 785	22 291	2 990	—	36 065
Transfer payments					
—to States and local authorities	13 181	757	54	13 992	—
—cash benefits to persons	13 091	327	—	—	13 418
—interest and dividends paid	3 140	3 193	384	1 750	4 967
—transfers overseas	667	—	—	—	667
—other	1 434	269	—	—	1 703
Total transfers	31 513	4 547	438	15 742	20 755
New advances					
—to State and local authorities	862	21	—	883	—
—other	60	105	4	—	169
Total net advances	922	126	4	883	169
Total outlays	**43 220**	**26 964**	**3 431**	**16 625**	**56 990**

Receipts					
Taxation	37 996	7 098	1 811	—	46 905
Grants					
—from Commonwealth	—	13 154	28	13 182	—
—from other government authorities	—	54	756	810	—
Other receipts	4 130	2 616	467	1 750	5 471
Total receipts	**42 126**	**22 922**	**3 070**	**15 742**	**52 376**
Deficit	**1 094**	**4 042**	**361**	**884**	**4 614**

Notes: a Includes the Northern Territory
b Includes increase in stocks and purchases of existing assets

Source: ABS *Government Financial Estimates Australia 1982–83* Cat. No. 5501.0, Table 8

over the stability of the Australian economy, if not with respect to its efficiency, such benefits are far from being realised.

By the criteria of effectiveness, simplicity, equity, efficiency, and its effects on economic stability, the Australian taxation system is badly defective. With the income support and social services system generally, it is capable of being exploited and manipulated by various groups—often the rich and the power-ful—so that there is little relationship between the benefits that flow to individuals or groups from the fiscal arrangements and the relative capacities of those individuals or groups to pay taxes or their relative needs for cash benefits or social services. The taxation system discriminates especially against wage and salary earners and business enterprises, with damaging consequences not only for equity but also for the performance of the economy and its stability in terms of prices, employment, profitability and the balance of payments.

The tax-sharing and grants arrangements have achieved considerable success in contributing to fiscal equalisation between States; indeed, they must be judged as being much more effective than arrangements in other federations. Even here, however, the full potential for fiscal equalisation has not been realised. More generally, the conclusion must be that Australia's tax-sharing, grants and borrowing arrangements have inhibited the effectiveness of govern-ment by blurring lines of responsibility for taxing and spending decisions, weakening political and administrative accountability and, by making govern-ments less responsive to the needs and preferences of their citizens, failing to take advantage of the opportunities for decentralised decisionmaking and diversity which provide the principal rationale of a federal form of government.

4 State and federal objectives and policies for the use and development of resources

STUART HARRIS

Resources have a special position in the consideration by governments of their aims and objectives and the policies they should follow to achieve them. The reasons are varied. Resources are basic to the life of any community, and even in market enterprise economies governments are expected to accept responsibility for the security of supply and to some extent the level and stability of prices of basic foods and raw materials—energy and strategic minerals in particular.

An economy with a significant natural resource endowment has different concerns. Development of natural resources is seen as a means of economic, social and political growth, and questions related to it become important public policy issues. Such questions are in some ways no different from those touching any other form of economic development, but in other ways they differ substantially. Differences include the location-specific nature of the resources themselves and the existence of economic rents, which arises from the fixed supply of resources or the higher costs of the next available supply source. They may also involve questions of the rate of depletion where exhaustible resources are concerned.

In Australia, further factors of practical importance are the high foreign investment levels in resource development, raising questions about who gains most from resource development; and the high dependence on the international market, again influencing the benefits from resource development and their distribution, this time between domestic and foreign consumers. Within Australia, conflicts of interest exist between the States that consume and import resources as well as between those that produce and export them. For the most part, however, issues affecting the latter are considered here.

Historical concern at the vulnerability of an agriculturally based export economy has led to continuing attempts to diversify the Australian economy. This has stimulated efforts to develop a manufacturing sector, normally through tariff or other protection. Limited success has been achieved overall, but it has probably contributed substantially to concentrating populations in the urban centres of south-east Australia, imposing, at the same time, a burden on the less developed regions. For regions endowed with mineral resources, development of these resources can be seen as a means of reversing this situation and achieving the social, economic and perhaps political development that would improve their relative positions while countering the various other influences towards greater power for the population and financial centres.

These factors obviously affect, and are affected by, the fact that Australia is a federation. Before considering the implications of Australia's federal system, however, it is useful to examine the nature of the benefits from resource development and their distribution, in order to relate resource objectives and policies to them.

The Benefits from Development

As well as the immediate benefits from resource development, a variety of external or indirect benefits are normally assumed to arise, consisting of the economic growth that comes from what have been called backward and forward linkages.[1] Backward production linkages stem from the purchase of inputs leading to investment in input production, and forward production linkages involve investment in handling and processing. Forward consumption linkages arise because income growth leads to investment in consumer goods supply to meet increased demand.

The extent to which such linkages occur autonomously depends upon many factors. The experience in other countries, however, is that in regions not already well developed economically, resource development often takes place in an economic enclave. In such cases linkages are few, most of the spending generated by the development going outside the region, often overseas. In Australia, the evidence on regional linkages seems to support this view. Because mining commonly occurs in areas of extensive agriculture with low population concentrations, the output, income and employment multipliers associated with mining at the regional level are frequently small.[2] Thus the flow-on effects of the more important mining projects in Australia occur mainly in the State capitals, and to a lesser extent overseas. Moreover, the evidence suggests that the consumption-induced effect arising from household expenditure is frequently the largest regional multiplier component, and that mining contributes relatively less to household income where large-scale mining operations are involved.

In these circumstances, to gain significant benefits from resource development the government may have to raise, and use, revenue from the development, and the substantial taxable capacity is likely to be that of the economic rents. The government can seek to appropriate these rents through direct taxes and royalties or through charges on governmentally provided services. The benefits from development can also be appropriated through conditions imposed on resource exploitation. These often include producing at a different rate or with a different pattern of resource exploitation from that which would be best for the developer, requiring the use of local (higher cost) inputs, or specifying local (higher cost) processing. These are unlikely to be economically efficient paths to development in terms of net revenues, but presumably other benefits—resource conservation, or employment and population growth—are expected, and are given higher weights. Employment and population growth in particular are commonly critical objectives for the low-income States, who see resource development and the expected population growth associated with it as a way of catching up with the more developed States. In any case, the imposition of such conditions will normally appropriate some of the benefits to subsidise these linkage activities.

The Question of Rent

Any autonomous increase in economic activity gives some economic gain by employing otherwise unemployed factors of production or because, if factors of production are already employed, higher prices will have to be paid to attract them away from their existing use, implying that the new use for these factors has some competitive advantage. Normally such advantage will be lost by competition to where the new activities earn only a normal profit—the returns, including a return to risk, needed to make it worthwhile to engage in that activity—in which case any rents from the innovative activity will disappear.

In most economic activities, the existence of rent is likely to arise from the presence of artificial barriers and can be eliminated by policies aimed at removing those barriers, such as policies against restrictive practices, with consequent gains in economic efficiency. For natural resources rents arise from natural barriers such as a fixed supply or from rising costs of additions to the resource supply.

The importance of this is that rent is a surplus, or unearned income, and has no influence on production decisions—nor does who gets the rent make any difference to productive efficiency. Since rents are surpluses, however, there are no rules for allocating the rents to which one can appeal on the grounds of economic efficiency. Much of the benefit from resource development is in the generation of such rents, and it is of interest, therefore, who gains such rents. I have discussed this elsewhere in a bargaining framework,[3] looking at the bargaining that takes place at various levels to gain the rents, including bargaining between governments and developers as well as between State and federal governments (though bargaining within the State and between labour and capital is also relevant).

The need for bargaining arises not just from the existence of rents but also because in practice it is difficult to define the rents. There is no clear measure of the normal profit (including the risk premium) required by a developer. If rents were clearly definable, governments could argue that as owners of the property rights in the resources they should receive the rents. As a practical matter, they need not give the developer the rents—they need only allow the developer the normal profit necessary to make it worthwhile to exploit the resource. In practice, certainty on the part of the government about whether a normal profit in this sense (and no more) has been realised or not can only be achieved (at best) with a false judgement—if the developer decides that he would not receive enough to proceed and the tax is the deciding factor. The rent is what the developer can potentially offer for the right to develop the resource; he hopes, however, that he does not have to offer it. Consequently resource policies are influenced substantially by government objectives with respect to rent and the bargaining strategies which are pursued.

Private and Social Rent

Resource policies are also influenced substantially by differences between rents to a private developer and 'rents' to the community—the surpluses over all social costs. This requires that allowance be made not only for all social benefits but also for social costs. The most obvious of these are environmental costs, but they include such things as the impact on Aboriginal interests and community concerns about loss of sovereignty from foreign investment. Because of the normally non-market characteristics of these social costs they are difficult to measure, and judgments of their importance depend heavily upon subjective assessments.

In effect, since to internalise these costs to exploitation requires government action, governments have to judge how far such social costs must be accepted to attract development and the associated social benefits. These social costs can increase because of real factors, such as measurable effects of a diminishing absorptive capacity of environmental resources, or because community perceptions of these costs rise—as, of course, they have done in recent decades. Moreover, as discussed elsewhere in the context of uranium mining, there are difficulties in assessing social costs before the event on questions depending substantially upon community perceptions.[4] Such problems emerge directly in assessing the social costs involved in the use of environmental resources and the impacts on the Aboriginal cultural heritage, as well as in the conflicts with a nationalistic approach to resource development.

The Federal System

Before considering these various questions in detail, it is necessary to consider the federal system itself. The objectives of the States reflect, or are constrained by, the legal responsibilities specified in the Constitution for each level of government and the legislative and regulatory mechanisms established under them. The States own the subsurface or mineral rights of most mineral deposits, with constitutional powers over many aspects of resource development. The federal government also influences resource development in many ways, including its constitutional responsibility for management of the economy and its trade and external affairs powers.

Within the constraints offered by these constitutional provisions, the objectives of different governments are determined by different political, economic or geographic circumstances. Objectives often differ between governments of differing political complexions. They have also been influenced more generally by attitudes, only partly linked to partisan policies, about the appropriate role of

governments. Views held widely in the early postwar decades required governments not simply to provide a minimum framework within which economic
activities were pursued but to participate more actively in economic as well as
social aspects—some reversal of which seemed to occur in the mid- to late 1970s,
at least at the federal level. Yet differences in methods and in objectives,
including the trade-offs between economic efficiency and objectives such as
stability, equity and political or economic autonomy, commonly arise from
other factors, such as local or regional interests and the differential impact of the
international system. For example, their high export dependence makes
Queensland, Western Australia and the Northern Territory vulnerable to
international market conditions. Yet it also gives them a substantial outward
orientantion and independence from domestic constraints; ties with the other
State or federal governments often seem to be barriers to further development
based on foreign capital and foreign markets.[5]

Government objectives have to reflect, at least in part, prevailing community
beliefs and values; they are influenced by community attitudes to the environment, to Aboriginal values and to the role of foreign enterprises, as well as to
how well the market handles high-risk activities such as oil and other minerals
exploration. Public attitudes to resource development generally and to which
particular level of government—State or federal—should manage such development are also important.

Since different governments have different interests, conflicts between policy
objectives are common, and to some extent the federal system institutionalises
these conflicts, particularly in the resources field. Some States are net importing
States (for some resources at least) and have different interests (lower prices)
from net exporting States, who want higher prices—as with natural gas piped
from South Australia to New South Wales. There are also differences of interest
between federal and State governments over a variety of matters: foreign
investment controls, export policies, State borrowing programs, policies affecting the environment and Aborigines, exchange rates, and particularly the direct
sharing of rents. Substantial differences also exist between the resource
development States and territories (Western Australia, Queensland, the Northern Territory and to some extent New South Wales) and the States with a
relatively smaller interest in such development (Victoria, South Australia and
Tasmania), who are concerned not to lose secure access to resource supplies nor
to be disadvantaged financially. These latter differences arise particularly over
the provision of loan funds and over the redistribution of revenue at Premiers'
Conferences.

Many such differences relate to the distribution of the rents from resource
development and, as with the division between developer and government,
there are no rules for determining the extent to which rents collected by
governments should go to the region or State in which the resources occur rather
than to the nation as a whole. While the resource policies that each level of
government can implement are constrained to some degree by the delineation of
constitutional powers and their legal interpretation, many of these powers,
including the taxation powers, overlap. Federal and State powers overlap in

many other economic areas, and have done so since federation. For minerals and energy, however, these overlaps have grown in importance as government interest, and the rents involved, have increased.

The policies that any particular level of government is able or willing to implement influence significantly the extent to which the rents are gained by developers or governments, by those in the region or State in which the resources occur (through State government tax collections, or low prices to consumers, as with Victorian natural gas), by the national community, or by overseas consumers. Within the given legal and institutional framework, however, they will reflect State and federal political and economic relationships.

The Nature of Federation

Part of the problem in looking at differences between federal and State objectives and policies in the field of resources arises from different understandings of the nature of the Australian federation. As a political nation-building process, the federation implies an equity argument for the redistribution of wealth and income across the nation and an argument for achieving increased economic efficiency through the economies of scale provided by a larger political and economic entity without internal barriers. On that interpretation, State governmental objectives often seem to conflict with the objectives of federation. On the other hand, if federation is seen as an expression of the physical and social separation of populations and a means by which regional interests are represented and institutionalised, these distributive effects and efficiency gains will be given a lower priority; such a position has received increased community acceptance in the past decade or so as tangible external threats encouraging national cohesion have diminished. That the economies of scale of a federal government outweigh the diseconomies is not simply an argument advanced by regional interest groups. Tullock notes that, rather than a highly centralised administration being the most efficient form of government (although it may be the most orderly), 'if we want the voters' wishes to be served by the government, then a system under which the voters are able to communicate those wishes to the government through the voting process in a more detailed and particular way is more efficient'.[6]

One view of what constitutes the Australian federation is not self-evidently more correct than another. The common argument that collecting the benefits of resource development as revenue is more efficient than obtaining the benefits indirectly, and that revenue collection is likely to be more effectively carried out at the federal than at the State level, cannot be considered simply on its own terms. Taxation is inevitably an instrument of economic management as well as of revenue raising; consequently, to argue for a centralised revenue-raising role is to argue for a centralised economic management role. Nevertheless, despite reservations about the costs as well as the benefits of centralised governments, the orthodox economic view remains that national economic efficiency would increase with the management of resource development by federal governments, with the management of consumption rather than more production seen appropriately as the States' area of responsibility.[7] Yet, although the States are net spenders rather than net revenue raisers, the latter view to a degree at least, conflicts with the State-oriented view of mineral resource management that is supported by the Constitution.

Swings between the two views are likely to remain a characteristic of community attitudes. Moreover, although the Constitution emphasises the States' powers in managing resource production, in practice, given the concurrent powers of taxation, the economic management role is divided; the particular roles of governments are determined by a variety of factors, including their political strength and the nature of their objectives. It will be useful to look first at the general objectives of federal and State governments, and then to look at them in specific contexts.

The Development Objective

'Development' has been an overriding objective for Australian governments of all political complexions and at all levels for a long time. In recent years a number of writers have noted that 'development' has accreted values of its own. Loveday, Harman and others have referred to the 'ideology' of development, pointing to the political advantage that, unlike distributional issues, it is an objective difficult to find fault with, and to which almost anything can be justified as contributing.[8] Donald Horne sees the concept of development as having religious overtones, referring to the 'secular faith of national development'.[9] Without discussing in detail why this has occurred and the extensive evidence suggestive of its significance offered by these commentators, it obviously has important implications for the objectives and policies of State and federal governments. If 'development' is believed to provide benefits over and above those measurable in net revenue terms, the government is likely to be 'weak' in its views about sharing net revenue with the developer—concessions will be made of the net revenues in exchange for the assumed external benefits.

An uncritical belief in the merits of development, leading to a failure to perceive the more subtle relationship between material progress and improved well-being and to a weak bargaining stance in relation to developers, is widely argued to have been generally evident in Australia in the early postwar decades and to have persisted in some jurisdictions in later periods. Such approaches tend to be self-reinforcing. Undue electoral emphasis on development—in terms of its pace and volume—encourages public attitudes that make it difficult for governments to adopt stronger bargaining approaches in response to developers.

It is not in itself important whether the added (or external) benefits of development are emotional or psychological or are more tangible benefits arising from the enlarging of State populations or the expansion of associated service industries, as long as those community preferences are maintained. Once the perceived benefits are recognised as lacking substance, or change for other reasons, attitudes towards new developmental proposals are likely to alter.

Attitudes to past contractual development arrangements may also change if these are now seen as substantially weighted in favour of the developer. Community pressures for rectifying the imbalance may then arise—as illustrated by Queensland's 1974 variation of the agreements with bauxite and coal producers in order to increase royalty rates.

Australian Objectives in the 1950s and 1960s

This is what appears to have happened with Australian attitudes towards development over the years since the second world war: a previously strong belief in the intangible benefits of development has been modified—though the degree of modification has varied, with significant differences emerging between some States and the federal government, the other States' positions normally depending upon their immediate interests and the party allegiances of particular administrations.

The postwar relationship between governments and developers in Australia until the early 1970s has been described as a 'rentier' relationship.[10] Such a relationship was seen as reflecting partly the strong desire by several States for development investment and partly a belief that the attractiveness of Australia's resource endowment for foreign investors was not high. On this argument, domestic resource policies consisted substantially of accommodating and meeting the needs of predominantly overseas resource developers. Large capital sums and high technology were seen as essential in minerals and energy development; federal tax concessions and State lease arrangements and, later, provision of infrastructure were designed to encourage and facilitate investment by those able to provide them. For the States, overseas investment had the added advantage of reducing dependence on the 'foreign' capital sources of south-eastern Australia.

This phase has been further divided, with particular reference to Western Australia.[11] In the early stage, the 1950s and early 1960s, a piecemeal approach gave assistance as needed to resource developers but was content to accept that resource development, as well as the gains from it, would emerge autonomously in the normal course of events. In the second stage it was accepted that State governments in particular had to be actively involved as part of an overall strategy for encouraging resource development. Governments did not participate in resource development itself, but extensive provision of incentives, including infrastructure and services, became a conscious, rather than reactive, policy. Gains from resource development continued to be seen, generally, as external benefits arising from linkages stimulated by minerals and energy investment.

Various factors combined, including lack of experience of governments and officials, limited economic knowledge and uncertainties about the respective bargaining strengths of the parties, to give the result that in both periods the idea of acquiring a major part of the benefits of resource development by way of direct taxation was largely (but not wholly) discarded. Taxation, it was argued, needed to be low to avoid discouraging investment, and support from State and federal governments needed to be substantial to provide a welcoming environment, particuarly to offset the disadvantages of investing in the less populous States. In practice, while having some general application, this pattern seems to have emerged specifically in Western Australia (and possibly New South Wales). In Queensland, it has been argued, the elements of a bargaining approach appeared in the 1960s for coal,[12] though the low levels of royalties and other rent shares sought suggest that at that time the attractiveness to investors of the resource exploitation opportunities then available was thought to be low.

In the late 1960s and early 1970s there was a reaction to the increased rents available, to concerns at their distribution, domestically and overseas, and to doubts whether the normal process of development of linkages really led to significant growth in employment and real income per head in the development regions. At the same time, growing concerns were emerging at the social costs of development: environmental impacts, loss of national sovereignty and effects on Aboriginal cultures. Thus community beliefs in the external benefits of mineral development were diminishing, just as the costs were being judged to be higher than earlier government policies had acknowledged.

The apparently limited direct linkage effects from mine development in Australia's development regions have been noted. In the past, State governments often sought, with some success, to encourage linkages through the conditions imposed on resource developers in their negotiations with the State for access to resource deposits; the present location of the Australian iron and steel industry reflects the negotiation of such arrangements. Efforts were made after the second world war to encourage such developments, and in Western Australia there were attempts to obtain a commitment to a steel industry. Several States have similarly sought to attract aluminium smelters by offering low-priced energy as well as infrastructure and services. As already observed, these strategies involve either conceding the resource rents to the developer or using them as implicit subsidies.

The federal government's position during this period was substantially similar to that of the development States but for different reasons. Largely for defence and strategic considerations arising from wartime and postwar concerns, federal resource objectives were mostly centred on the achievement of self-sufficiency in resource supplies. This led to interests in the discovery and development of mineral resources, particularly petroleum and iron ore. Early concerns to conserve resources, as with iron ore (which then, as later with natural gas, involved a difference between State and federal objectives), changed as the size of the reserves became evident. The emphasis remained on exploration and development, as it did, for different reasons, in the States.

Further important factors were that, until the mid-1960s at least, the Commonwealth faced continuing balance of payments problems and sought to encourage export- or import-replacing industries. Because of the benefits of capital inflow, considerable attention was given to providing a welcoming attitude to overseas investors. Yet, as the Vernon Committee report suggested, mineral resource development was not then regarded as a likely major contributor to economic growth or to exports.[13] Subsidiary objectives held by federal and State governments included the decentralisation of population and, in particular, settlement in the north of Australia, to which mining development was seen to contribute.

Given these objectives, substantial tax or financial incentives were provided by federal governments for exploration and development, as well as loans to the States for infrastructure related to mineral development. The Vernon Committee was in fact concerned at the extent to which infrastructure costs were being charged to private developers because of the discouragement to remote settlement and to Australian capital participation in resource development.[14] Security of supply objectives, as well as market and industrial stability, had also been part of the motivation for the federal–State Joint Coal Board, which was set up in the late 1940s to manage the coal industry and its development in New South Wales.

Australian Objectives in the 1970s

As Table 4.1 shows, by the early 1970s capital investment in Queensland and Western Australia by the mining industry had grown in relative importance. At the same time market changes had occurred that influenced at least some of the approaches taken by State and federal governments. The extent to which these governments perceived the need for such changes, however, clearly differed.

Table 4.1   Australia: fixed capital expenditure (mining) as a proportion of gross capital expenditure

Percentage of Australia's gross capital expenditure represented by fixed capital expenditure (mining) by State						Percentage of Australia's gross capital expenditure represented by fixed capital expenditure (Australia)
	NSW	Vic.	Qld.	WA	Tas.	SA	Australia
1954/55	0.59	0.16	0.24	0.19	0.06	0.11	1.12
1955/56	0.61	0.20	0.27	0.17	0.05	0.12	1.27
1956/57	0.73	0.24	0.35	0.18	0.05	0.12	1.95
1957/58	0.70	0.21	0.33	0.17	0.05	0.09	1.53
1958/59	0.57	0.25	0.36	0.17	0.04	0.07	1.35
1959/60	0.56	0.22	0.34	0.14	0.03	0.07	1.35
1960/61	0.60	0.21	0.23	0.12	0.04	0.09	1.37
1961/62	0.66	0.25	0.29	0.17	0.05	0.09	1.43
1962/63	0.62	0.22	0.42	0.22	0.03	0.06	1.83
1963/64	0.53	0.21	0.52	0.25	0.02	0.05	1.70
1964/65	0.85	0.28	0.73	0.45	0.10	0.09	2.31
1965/66	0.65	0.15	0.50	0.40	0.27	0.05	4.07
1966/67	0.68	0.28	0.61	0.53	0.39	0.04	4.28

Table 4.1 (Continued)

	NSW	Vic.	Qld.	WA	Tas.	SA	Australia
1967/68	0.59	0.83	0.46	0.57	0.23	0.05	na
1968/69	0.96	2.22	0.83	1.80	0.28	0.17	na
1969/70	0.77	1.18	0.68	1.17	0.26	0.15	4.39
1970/71	0.88	0.91	1.15	2.12	0.29	0.09	5.93
1971/72	0.80	0.33	1.62	1.73	0.17	0.12	5.01
1972/73	0.41	0.25	1.26	0.86	0.12	0.16	3.17
1973/74	0.36	0.37	0.96	0.83	0.11	0.20	2.88
1974/75	0.58	0.59	0.83	1.07	0.14	0.18	3.50
1975/76	0.59	0.54	0.87	0.95	0.10	0.08	3.22
1976/77	0.71	0.48	0.63	0.69	0.07	0.07	2.70
1977/78	0.93	0.46	0.69	1.52	0.10	0.13	3.89
1978/79	0.86	0.44	1.44	1.47	0.09	0.14	4.58
1979/80	0.87	0.50	1.26	0.66	0.12	0.14	4.30
1980/81	1.58	0.67	1.24	1.94	0.12	0.18	6.36
1981/82	2.17	0.60	1.40	2.29	0.07	0.36	7.07

Notes: Gross fixed capital expenditure figures for Australia are from *Australian National Accounts—National Income and Expenditure* (ABS Cat. No. 5204.0). These figures include private expenditure (companies, unincorporated enterprises, dwellings owned by persons) and public expenditure (public enterprises and general government). There are no gross capital expenditure figures for any State.

Mining figures for Australia to 1967/68 are from *Australian National Accounts—National Income and Expenditure* (ABS Cat. No. 5204.0). These figures are for private industry only. Total mining figures for Australia from 1968/69 are from ABS Cat. Nos 10.60 and 8401.0. They include Northern Territory and Australian Capital Territory figures.

State mining figures from 1954/55 to 1968/69 are from the ABS bulletin *Mining and Quarrying*. These figures include all expenditure on new structures and additions (including major alterations, capitalised repairs and improvements) and all plant, machinery and vehicles acquired for use in connection with actual mineral production. Expenditure on mine development is included. The mining figures for the States from 1954 to 1968 were given on a calendar year basis and have been adjusted mechanically to obtain financial year figures. Comparison with the Australia-wide figures shows only a slight difference, which is also due to the inclusion of the Northern Territory and the Australian Capital Territory in the Australian mining figures. State mining figures from 1968/69 to 1972/73 are from ABS Cat. No. 10.60; figures from 1972/73 are from ABS Cat. No. 8402.0. All the State mining figures include public and private enterprise.

Mining figures obtained after 1968/69 include the extraction of minerals occurring naturally as solids such as coal and ores, liquids such as crude petroleum, and gases such as natural gas, by such processes as underground mining, open-cut extraction methods, quarrying, operation of wells or evaporation pans, dredging, or recovering from ore dumps or tailings. Establishments mainly engaged in dressing or beneficiating ores or other minerals by crushing, milling, screening, washing, flotation or other processes, including chemical beneficiation, or mainly engaged in briquetting are included because these processes are generally carried out at or near mine sites as an integral part of mining operations. Natural gas absorption and purifying plants are also included. Excluded are establishments mainly engaged in refining or smelting minerals or ores (other than the preliminary smelting of gold), or in the manufacture of such products of mineral origin as coke, cement, fertilisers, iron ore pellets or metallised iron agglomerates. These figures include disposals.

na Not available

The federal government gradually saw less need to provide specific incentives to encourage resource development, particularly after the commodities boom of the early 1970s. It had sought earlier to limit the control exercised by foreign companies, although, partly because of uncertainty about the federal government's constitutional power to restrict foreign corporations, this had limited effect until 1974. The other social costs associated with development also began to impinge on federal governments through heightened community pressures.

In the resource States, public concern at the indirect and social costs of resource development was less marked than in the major urban areas. State governments often aligned themselves with developers against environmental lobbies, resource nationalists or supporters of Aboriginal rights, or against federal actions thought to reflect such views. In part this was a response to a different assessment of the social costs involved, but it also probably reflected a greater willingness in the development regions to accept those costs in order to achieve the resource development perceived as necessary. Other influential parts of the community, or the governments representing them, weighed these social costs more highly or saw as less compelling the need for rapid resource development. Pressures arose as a result for the federal government to be more active in obtaining some of the resource benefits and redistributing them nationally.

These differences between State and federal governments are resolved in a bargaining process between the two levels of government. This is so both in the short-term sense within the existing legal and attitudinal framework and in the longer term context of varying the legal and political framework within which bargaining takes place, such as changed legislative provisions to protect or limit Aboriginal rights or to enhance or reduce the scope for environmental protest. In this process, developers seek to influence the political framework within which development bargains will be struck, and it is in their interests to emphasise the gains from resource development and to stress the limited nature of the social costs. The States, for their part, have an interest in minimising the federal share of the rents and maximising development: consequently they often form implicit—if not explicit—coalitions with developers against the federal government.

Although by the early 1970s the development States had started to move to increase their shares of the rents, they came under pressure from a different source to do this later in that decade. Major demands on State budgets for infrastructural and service expenditures for the second resources boom, later in the 1970s (notably gas and alumina/aluminium in Western Australia, and coal and alumina/aluminium in Queensland and New South Wales), and pressures on government budgets as the general economic recession developed, led to a more critical approach to development proposals. This was only partly offset by the relaxation in 1978 of Loan Council guidelines, which permitted large State borrowings to finance the provision of infrastructure. Taxation (explicit or implicit) and advances of capital from resource developers were increasingly seen as important revenue sources in some States. At the same time the need to provide attractive incentives to invest in the main resource States was judged to be less pressing.[15] The other States, however, also started to put more emphasis on resource development, both for reasons of supply security in the case of energy resources, and in the hope of achieving financial and other benefits from resource exploitation and processing.

Differences between State and federal government objectives have a number of implications. Competition between States may strengthen the developers' bargaining position, though for most mining this is ruled out by the uniqueness of mineral deposits; thus for iron ore and natural gas in Western Australia this has not been an issue, though it may have been for New South Wales coal and for bauxite and alumina processing. Nevertheless, developers seem to have used effectively the fear of competition for their capital from other States as well as from other countries to increase their share of the rents. This they have achieved by increasing in the minds of governments the level of 'normal' profit necessary to make it worthwhile for the developer to participate in the development. Where governments had to be seen to be committed to development for political survival—and were judged in relation to the commitment of other States—this was not difficult, and in any case governments might otherwise have given insufficient weight to the importance of such competition. Where development was electorally regarded as desirable, however, competition between State and federal governments may have increased the level of development but at some national cost in terms of allowing 'greater' opportunities for private interests to prevail in general economic development, particularly in minerals.[16]

Since the concern of governments has shifted from a largely uncritical objective of maximising development, even in a period of high unemployment, to one where the objective is to gain, through taxation in various forms, a good share of the rents, competition between federal and State governments may, as has been argued from the Canadian experience, increase the overall community gain as against that of the developer.[17] On the other hand it may also lead to more than simply the rent being collected, at some national cost (disincentive effects). This is more likely when rent-collecting mechanisms, such as freight rate charges and export levies, do not vary as rents vary. In circumstances such as the cyclical economic downturn of the early 1980s, this could penalise useful development.

The objectives of the State and federal governments are reflected in their resource policies. We need, therefore, to consider some of these specific policies—resource taxation, foreign investment, export policies, environmental policies and Aboriginal rights—in the light of the earlier discussion.

Resource Taxation

It has been observed that governments could either look to obtain benefits from resource development through linkages arising autonomously, in which case taxes were likely to be kept low or, if such external benefits were not considered sufficient, they might judge fiscal linkages (through taxation) to be appropriate.

It is a common argument that the resource-rich States, notably Queensland

and Western Australia, overestimated the indirect benefits likely to flow from resource development and in consequence tended not to bargain strongly for a clear sharing of the resource rents until the late 1960s or 1970s. Moreover, government provision of infrastructure and services may have meant that, in Western Australia at any rate, resource development was being subsidised rather than providing a net benefit, at least in the early years. This is less clear for the Pilbara iron ore developments—where, under the 1960s agreements, the companies were to provide their own industrial infrastructures—than for the North-West Shelf gas project and perhaps, as has been argued, for bauxite.[18]

In an isolated resource development project, in which infrastructures have no use other than in association with that development, a net national gain arises only if the national benefits are sufficient to cover all costs, including infrastructure costs. The position for social infrastructures is less clear, since governments would normally provide those in some form in any case. It is difficult to calculate what proportion of the infrastructure costs are 'project' costs and what represent 'normal' calls on government budgets because of the difficulty of making judgments about possible alternative uses, about the costs of social infrastructures, and about how social, as distinct from industrial, infrastructures are defined. Cost recovery of industrial infrastructure is clearly not, however, a way of gathering rents unless the infrastructure has other uses. Given the isolated nature of Australia's resource development, State financing of industrial infrastructure in most major resource developments would involve a subsidy.

The level of royalties actually collected confirms a view that either the States' bargaining position is weak or that available rents are low. As can be seen from Table 4.2, except perhaps for Victoria (where the figures largely reflect Bass Strait oil royalties), State royalties are in general not high. State mineral royalties for Queensland rose from less than 1 per cent to 4.5 per cent of the value of production in 1974/75 (reflecting the Queensland government's tenfold increase in most mineral royalties in 1974), and have stayed at around 4 per cent since; despite a 7.5 per cent royalty on most iron ore exports, Western Australian royalties have hovered around 4–5 per cent since 1969/70, the first year for which separate published figures are available. In New South Wales royalties on some minerals are profit related, and receipts, as well as being slightly higher on average, are more variable.

Mining is taxed by State and federal governments in various other ways apart from the company taxes common to all corporate enterprises. In New South Wales and Queensland, in particular, infrastructure financing and charges have been important, as have federal levies on oil and coal. The precise level of effective taxation revenue gained through these indirect methods is unclear. Emerson and Lloyd suggest that, when subsidised infrastructure and input provision are taken into account, as well as implicit taxes on profit, the Australia-wide effect could be either negative or positive.[19] The Commonwealth Grants Commission in 1981 observed that the Western Australian taxable effort was less than the national standard (the new basis for its recommendations for revenue sharing), and Western Australia subsequently raised a number of local

Table 4.2 State government mineral royalty collections (ad valorem equivalent)

	NSW (%)	Vic. (%)	Qld (%)	WA (%)	Tas. (%)	SA (%)
1968/69	2.95	na	0.74	na	na	na
1969/70	3.38	2.96	1.05	4.84	0.41	2.05
1970/71	4.46	7.43	1.83	5.27	0.40	2.22
1971/72	2.11	8.48	1.12	5.20	0.39	2.16
1972/73	1.87	7.98	0.81	5.44	0.42	1.71
1973/74	2.53	8.71	0.69	5.70	0.30	1.90
1974/75	4.91	8.05	4.49	4.80	0.29	1.79
1975/76	3.32	8.19	3.81	4.52	0.45	1.95
1976/77	4.17	8.40	4.40	4.75	0.69	2.11
1977/78	4.04	10.79	4.66	4.26	0.90	2.80
1978/79	2.49	9.77	4.25	4.41	0.78	2.39
1979/80	5.62	12.17	3.66	3.91	0.63	2.41
1980/81	6.33	12.01	3.94	4.40	na	2.97
1981/82	4.09	9.76	3.93	4.09	0.81	3.19

Notes: The ad valorem equivalent rate is the actual royalty payment expressed as a percentage of the ex-mine (or wellhead) value of output excluding the royalty payment. The mineral value of production (ex-mine) is taken from ABS statistics. Mining royalties are taken from the Reports of Auditors-General for the various States. The figures for Victoria include royalty payments on petroleum—the first royalty payment on petroleum was made in May 1969. The increase for Victoria between 1979/80 and 1980/81 is due to the operation of the Commonwealth government import parity pricing structure for crude oil.
na Not available

service charges (such as transport and electricity) to offset lower federal grants. A large proportion of the Queensland coal freight charges was taken by the Commission, however, to reflect the exploitation of a taxable rent capacity.[20] Of the three components of the Queensland government's rail freight charges— capital costs, operating costs and excess rail freight—the last is explicitly a tax and the first has become so in cases where capital costs of rail construction have already been met, since the capital charge continues. The excess rail freight is negotiated separately for each project, with rates apparently set higher on mines closer to the coast.[21] Freight charges are, for various reasons, a tax mechanism preferred by the State government to royalties, and Stuart estimates that in 1980/81 the freight 'profit' component on coal was $70–110 million, compared with total coal royalties of $35 million.[22] Capital and other charges are also levied on coal projects.

In practice Queensland also raised its royalties on bauxite in the mid-1970s despite earlier agreements with the developers, but royalties still constitute a relatively small proportionate charge. In Western Australia some degree of flexibility in tax payments was provided by an ad valorem rate on iron ore, one of the limited number of non-specific royalties in Australia. (Another important one was the royalty on offshore petroleum after 1967.)

Generally, however, taxing mechanisms, including rail freight charges, employed fixed rates and therefore were not effective in adjusting the tax upwards when the rents grew rapidly. The Queensland rail freight charges were fixed in agreements signed in the 1960s and they captured none of the added rent that came with energy price rises, though it should be remembered that this lack of flexibility was a common feature of commercial and industrial practice before the early 1970s. The learning process was not all one way. For the Utah coking coal operation in Queensland the government appropriated some of the rent through a condition in the mining lease that the associated steaming coal production be provided at cost to the government; with increased coal prices and production levels this became a substantial royalty or rent component, apparently of considerable benefit to Gladstone's electricity consumers. In the case of rail freights, the Queensland government subsequently varied the agreements to provide for escalation of rates. When rents fell in the early 1980s, however, these 'profit' margins tended to remain unchanged, the tax rate being adjusted downwards.

As suggested earlier, with competition from the federal government, particularly in imposing levies on exported coal and oil, a larger share of the rents appears to have been taken from resource development; it has been argued that fear of a larger federal tax led to the increased level of excess rail freights in Queensland.[23] For the high-quality coking coals now subject to the coal export levy, levy receipts are higher than the royalties received in either Queensland or New South Wales. Similarly the federal government's levies on oil production provide returns very many times higher than the federal or State royalties.

These various forms and levels of taxation constitute a tax system that conflicts substantially with the requirements of efficient taxation.[24] In that sense governments cannot be sure that they have been effective in gaining a substantial share of the rents—and no more than the available rent—nor have they managed resource development, through an efficient tax system, in a way likely to maximise the rents available for distribution between developers and governments. In addition, the equity of distribution of the revenue collected by some of the taxing mechanisms may also be in doubt; rail freight profits, for example, are likely to subsidise country freight rates and urban transit charges (and inefficiency in the rail system).

There has been considerable discussion of more efficient profit-related tax mechanisms for resources, usually in terms of a resource rent tax. Such a tax would avoid the disincentive effects on production and investment of royalties that apply equally to marginal and intramarginal production. The Northern Territory considered such a tax favourably for some time, but the States have generally dismissed the idea, though usually in the context of a federal imposition of such a tax. An earlier federal government rejected proposals for a resource rent tax put forward particularly for uranium, but the intention to levy a resource rent tax on offshore oil has since been announced. As a taxation mechanism profit-related taxes have advantages over royalties and production-related taxes, though they do not remove the need to bargain over what are considered to be 'normal' profit levels.

In certain circumstances, a profit-related tax is more efficiently combined with a tender system for allocating mine leases. There have been a few examples of leases being auctioned in this way, one in New South Wales and several, including the Winchester South coal lease, in Queensland: for this latter lease, a gradually increasing super royalty—rising over twenty years' life of the mine—was offered by the successful bidder. In a number of other cases, as in the allocation of New South Wales coal leases, front-end payments are negotiated, but that seems to be a less efficient way of operating the bargaining process than through open tender.

The existing tax structure tends to penalise efficient mines in years when prices (and presumably rents) are low, and undertax them in good years; it does offer some stability in State financial receipts, but at the cost of instability for the developers. If the States' objective were to maximise the revenue from resource development, they would perhaps gain from a federal tax-collecting system which redistributed the revenue to the States. A cooperative arrangement would increase both government revenues and aggregate economic efficiency. While the present forms of taxation (which are not neutral in their effects) are in use, however, reliance on federal taxing mechanisms may not be the best course, since the federal export levy is even less efficient than the Queensland freight charge.[25]

A cooperative system based on a relatively neutral profit-related taxing system could be more effectively operated by the federal government, with tax distribution being determined on political grounds. Yet to assume that the States' objectives are simply to maximise the revenue gain from resource development not only overlooks the fact that the States (and the federal government) have other objectives (stability, equity, independence, status), and their own ideas about how to achieve them; it also begs the question of the nature of the federal system discussed earlier.

Those who argue that the community's realised share in the overall rents over the whole of an economic cycle is less than is possible acquire some support from the capital gains made in resource enterprises and the front-end sums paid for leases that are auctioned rather than allocated. The non-neutrality of the taxing system also suggests that the level of rents available for taxation may not be as high as is feasible. This depends not only upon how managerial efficiency is affected by the taxation system, but also on the controls applied to foreign investors and to the marketing of resources.

Foreign Investment

The large capital needs of the Australian economy and the large capital sums and high technology needed for resource development have customarily been seen as predominantly available from overseas investors; both State and federal governments have consequently put considerable effort into developing an attractive environment for such investment in Australia.

The foreign investment issue raises questions not only of its direct economic costs and benefits but also of its indirect costs, such as loss of resource sovereignty and constraints on the ability to pursue national interests. Directly economic questions about foreign investment include those of the sharing of development proceeds. A generous taxation approach may attract investment but reduce Australian returns, or give foreign capital an undue competitive advantage over Australian capital. The treatment of foreign investment for federal taxation purposes can therefore affect the attractiveness of Australia as an investment outlet. It can also enable foreign investors to underprice Australian competitors in overseas markets, thus probably lowering total Australian market returns. Foreign investors have, in any case, a number of potential advantages over domestic investors, though they are not always able to take advantage of them. These include, for example, tax-minimising mechanisms such as transfer pricing payments for products, capital goods, loan funds, management services or technology. At the same time, although some of the apparent disadvantages have greater public salience, many potential benefits—capital, technology, expertise, market links—are associated with foreign investment.

The important question is what price the community needs or is willing to pay for foreign investment. Until the late 1960s, given the preeminence of the development objective, governments seem to have taken the position that the price they were paying was either not high or was worth paying. In the 1960s, however, signs that the community's desire for development was not unqualified and that it was putting a higher price than before on the associated loss of national sovereignty raised the social costs involved. In response governments gradually introduced controls on the rate of inflow of foreign capital.

Restricting the share of non-domestic ownership of mineral and energy resources does two things. It avoids some concerns at the limited direct benefits from foreign investment by ensuring that at least some of the rents are received by Australian residents; and it shifts the balance in favour of local ownership by raising the price to be paid by foreign investors, thus overcoming some of the concerns of the resource nationalists.[26] The rapid increase in foreign ownership and control of the mining sector up to the early 1970s that stimulated wide public concern has been largely stopped. In mining, foreign ownership (some 51 per cent) and control (some 58 per cent) have declined marginally from 1974/75 levels. In mineral processing, Australian control (56.6 per cent) has increased, although ownership (slightly under 54 per cent) has fallen slightly.

The development States in particular have tended to value more highly the benefits of foreign investment and give a lower weight to the social costs involved. Moreover, as already indicated, they distinguish much less between overseas capital and capital from Sydney or Melbourne—all being seen commonly as 'foreign'. From a purely national viewpoint, therefore, foreign investment may well have taken place 'on terms more advantageous to the investor than otherwise would be the case'.[27] A State viewpoint is likely to differ. Consequently State governments (particularly in Queensland and Western Australia, and more recently the government of the Northern Territory) have not accepted as readily the need for control, and the two main development States have attempted from time to time to exert political pressure at the federal level to have the regulations relaxed. New South Wales, on the other hand, introduced in 1970 a requirement for majority Australian ownership of mineral developments. Foreign ownership and control of the mining sector remains particularly high in Queensland and Western Australia. In Queensland, foreign ownership was some 82 per cent in 1974/75; under new definitions, including naturalising companies, foreign ownership of mining was some 73 per cent in 1981/82 (and some 70 per cent for mineral processing). In New South Wales the level was relatively low until the 1970s, particularly in the coal industry; foreign ownership has increased significantly in the coal industry, but is limited ultimately by both federal and State controls.

Constraints on foreign ownership and control by the federal government are consequently seen in the main development States, and in the Northern Territory, as limiting State development objectives. Since Australia's attractiveness as a mining investment outlet is high, however, any effects have probably been more marked on the processing sector (for example, petrochemicals, bauxite refining and steel mills) than on mining itself. Yet, although the costs may not have been high, the satisfying of nationalist economic demands may have passed some of the rent to local shareholders, leaving less potentially available for the States in other forms. This could have been overcome in part if governments had taken an equity position in the development, but this practice has not been followed to any significant extent in Australia.[28]

Export Policies

It has been noted that the benefits to Australia from resource development depended in part upon how these were shared with the consumer. Formal State and federal objectives have at times been strongly directed towards strengthening Australia's bargaining position with respect to consumers, although policies actually implemented have reflected the conflicts with other objectives that are entailed.

These conflicts are not only between State and federal governments. Federal governments have been reluctant to intervene in markets without the support of the industry, though the degree of industry support may reflect State government attitudes. Thus federal governments traditionally intervene in agricultural marketing and in the marketing of some minerals, such as uranium, tin and tungsten, but have been reluctant to do so in iron ore and coal and most non-ferrous metals because of lack of industry support.

A non-competing purchaser, as Japan has tended to be for iron ore, coking coal and, more recently, steaming coal, is normally in a position to gain most from trade with a competing supplier. In some commodities Australia has attempted to limit this disadvantage by applying export controls and by encouraging collective rather than competitive export negotiations. In practice, until the early 1970s the States were also often interested in achieving a coordinated export bargaining position through export controls. A strong federal move (though less clearly a strong actual policy) to this effect in the early and mid-1970s was followed by pressures, from Western Australia and Queensland in particular, to constrain the federal government's use of its export control powers, partly for fear of greater federal involvement in their mining industries.

State governments also perceive themselves as gaining at the expense of other States at times through the achievement of long-term sales contracts and the associated investment, which permits the maintenance of the high production levels on which the revenue receipts depend. State interests are not always seen as being served by a coordinated selling policy, any more than are those of individual developers.

Just as investors can pass the rents they receive to the foreign consumer, thereby gaining larger markets but at the expense of other exporters, so a failure to extract rents from a domestic producer gives scope for that producer to undercut in export markets and thus lower overall price levels. It has been argued that a failure to appropriate much of Utah's rent has enabled that company to be a weak seller in the export coal market.[29] Yet, in the buyers' market for coking coal of 1981 to 1983, low charges applicable to Utah-mined coal may simply have enabled that company to accept lower prices so that its taxable rent has been lower; other Australian exporters would have had to follow, but it is the absence of a coordinated selling policy in the presence of a coordinated buyer that is the crucial factor. Some market share gain may have been achieved overall in relation to sales from suppliers in other countries, and assessments of the balance of advantage would need to take both factors into account.

The extent to which federal policies could improve the trading position of resource exports thus depends not only upon State objectives and policies but also upon the nature of the competition from non-Australian suppliers and upon the general characteristics of the market. Even with a general competitive advantage over competing suppliers, failure to gain the rents from favoured domestic exporters would not mean that, in general, economic Australian projects would not be able to operate profitably, though, since total supply is likely to be greater, marginally profitable mines would then become unprofitable.

The objectives of high rates of resource development in the States (and mostly but not always, at the federal level) and the setting of conditions specifying minimum development rates, as in New South Wales coal agreements, or the effective provision, as in Queensland freight charges, of financial disincentives to reducing production levels, are likely to lead to lower export market prices. On the other hand, production-related taxes discourage both production and investment in marginal mines and so have a price-raising effect. It may be that the worsening of the terms of trade effect is likely to be the greater, but the evidence is not clear.

State–federal conflicts have arisen in other contexts, such as the federal objective of energy supply security which delayed approval for exports of Western Australian natural gas. This was not just a conflict between a development State and the federal authorities over exports; gas-consuming States such as New South Wales also had an interest in conserving the largest possible domestic reserves of natural gas.

Environmental Objectives and Policies

The exploitation and use of resources have increased their impact on environmental resources. At the same time, the community's willingness to accept this use of environmental resources has declined, whether the matter for concern is air or water pollution or the destruction of wilderness areas. The social costs have increased in consequence, and governmental objectives and policies reflect these changes, if at times very imperfectly.

Where environmental costs have been considered too high, steps have been taken to internalise these social costs to development, exploitation or use by way of environmental regulations and charges. To the extent that they have not been internalised they continue to constitute an implicit, though not clearly determinate, subsidy to resource development. Developers, naturally, press for a low level of environmental control in order to avoid such costs by persuading governments either not to impose controls, since developers pay the costs involved, or to persuade the community that the environmental costs are unimportant; environmentalists take the opposite position.

Public perceptions of environmental costs may differ, however, from region to region, and different levels of government, in responding to those perceptions, may be responding to different community interests. The federal government may react to a wider community concern by using its export powers, as it did over the mining of mineral sands on Fraser Island. Queensland, being more concerned with the direct regional benefits, balanced differently the costs and benefits of that resource development project. National and State interests also diverged over the likely benefits from the project, the national loss probably being small, since other mineral sands operations benefited through higher export prices from the absence of Fraser Island production. Whether there was any significant loss to Queensland depended upon what the government's share of the rents would have been (or how large the non-fiscal linkages would have been) had the development proceeded. Similar regional differences over the costs and benefits of resource development occurred between Tasmania and the rest of Australia over the Franklin Dam. The decision on the Franklin Dam, as with Fraser Island earlier, has changed the bargaining framework, in the short term at least, by raising the perceived political cost of federal intervention in environmental matters.

Policies Towards Aborigines

Because resource development tends to be in outlying areas, it frequently impinges on areas important to Aborigines through present or past settlement. Federal and State attitudes differ on Aboriginal interests and the willingness to allow those interests to be affected in order to obtain the wider benefits of resource development. They have also changed over time, in part according to changed perceptions of what Aboriginal interests are, including the Aborigines' rights to be involved in the management of resource development or to benefit from its taxation. A number of writers have referred to the frontier mentality, which sees the wilderness (and its inhabitants) as something to be tamed and civilised.[30] Support for Aboriginal land and other rights is perceived by the development regions as opposed to this ethos. Again, like the concerns for the environment, such concerns are seen as limiting development and as mainly entertained by the urban populations of south-eastern Australia, who are judged to be uninterested in the problems of resource development.

Federal governments and, at times, some State governments have made moves to strengthen the position of the Aborigines by changing the legislative framework, and various legislative provisions, federally as well as in South Australia and New South Wales, have been enacted for this purpose. These have not always been effective, either in the Northern Territory[31] or in the face of Western Australia and Queensland opposition, amounting at times to moves in the opposite direction. Generally these provisions reflect a priority for the social benefits of preserving Aboriginal cultures higher than the priority given to that objective by developers and the resource development States. The extent to which State and developer coalitions can prevail was shown, however, in the 1980 Noonkanbah incident in Western Australia.

State and federal governments each have many objectives with respect to resources—development, revenue collection, resource conservation, processing, domestic ownership and control, management of the environment and of Aboriginal interests—not all of which are consistent one with another. The federal government has other interests, some held in common with resource-deficient States—supply security and a national sharing of the benefits of resource development, usually through the distribution of revenue—and some specific to it, such as macroeconomic management objectives and the pursuit of international diplomacy.

Because of the interest differences that are reflected in different weightings of common objectives, or that lead to the pursuit of different objectives in different jurisdictional areas, resource policies will often conflict. The overlap of powers implies that these conflicts will commonly lead to inconsistencies, both among the policies themselves, and between the policies and concepts of efficiency, defined in the static orthodox economic sense, and the national interest defined from the viewpoint of the federal government.

The overall significance of these inherent conflicts is difficult to determine. Not only would the resource development States not see orthodox economic efficiency as necessarily in their interests, but all governments have more than just economic efficiency as objectives. (Efficiency can in any case be defined in broader terms, depending on the envisaged role of governments). Moreover, the States would not view the national interest in the same way or with the same priority as federal governments. Thus a federal government interest in ensuring that most rents are received domestically may have less weight for resource-developing State governments. They may not consider such policies to their benefit, not just because they may feel disadvantaged with respect to other States, but because they differentiate less than federal governments between the two senses of foreign (overseas and elsewhere in the Commonwealth).

Stevenson has argued that the Australian federal system operates to the advantage of the resource-developing States by comparison with a unitary government.[32] He has also argued that resource development has reversed the apparent trend towards centralist government.

Whether that is so or not, the federal government has since been competing more vigorously for direct revenue, federal–State financial arrangements have been varied, and the federal government has extended its influence over domestic ownership and control. There have nevertheless been substantial realignments in State–federal relationships as well as between States, and these have important implications for resource policies.

First, the potential for a consistent and stable set of overall policies is limited, since no federal policies are likely to be able to meet all the needs of the conflicting interests involved. Second, the process of change is still under way and, indeed, is likely to be continually with us. While this makes it difficult to point to likely developments, either in State–federal relationships or in their policy implications, the conflicting interests and the constant bargaining processes at various levels militate against major changes that might interfere unduly with the underlying market forces. Third, since the various parties are engaged in a continuous process of bargaining, it is also difficult to put much weight on the statements of positions, attitudes and policy objectives of any of them.

5 The mineral exploration and production regime within the federal system

MICHAEL CROMMELIN

Ownership of Onshore Mineral Resources

In Britain, the United States of America and Canada there is extensive private ownership of mineral resources. This position has its origins in the English common law, which presumes that the owner of land is entitled to all that lies above or below the surface of his land (*cujus est solum, ejus est usque ad coelum et usque ad inferos.*) Minerals are regarded as part of the land in which they naturally occur, and thus pass into private ownership upon Crown grant of the land unless they are specifically reserved from the grant. The only exceptions to this general rule are the 'royal metals', gold and silver, which (by virtue of the royal prerogative, recognised by the courts in 1568[1]) remain subject to Crown ownership notwithstanding the grant to a private landowner of the land in which they naturally occur, unless that ownership is relinquished by 'apt and precise words'.[2]

Accordingly, the legal regime governing mineral exploration and production in these countries is, to a significant extent, made up of private leasing and licensing arrangements between landholders and mining companies.

The Australian colonies inherited this common law;[3] until the last quarter of the nineteenth century, the position in Australia was that private landowners were usually entitled to all minerals within their land other than gold and silver. Afterwards, however, the Australian colonies adopted the policy of reserving all minerals from Crown grants of land.[4]

At first this policy was not applied retrospectively; minerals already in private ownership were not affected. This produced a complicated situation in which mineral ownership depended upon the date on which the relevant land passed into private ownership. In more recent times, however, Crown mineral ownership has been significantly extended by the expropriation of certain minerals which passed into private ownership before the policy of general reservation was adopted. With regard to petroleum, all Australian States have declared that petroleum in place is owned by the Crown without excpetion, regardless of when any land containing petroleum passed into private ownership.[5] Victoria and Tasmania have done likewise with regard to uranium and thorium.[6] In 1981, New South Wales expropriated all privately owned coal in that State[7]—a move which provoked some political controversy, as deposits of privately owned coal were very extensive. South Australia (in 1972[8]) and Victoria (in 1983[9]) dealt with the issue on a broader basis by expropriating virtually all privately owned minerals in those States.

The result is an established norm of Crown ownership of minerals in Australia. Exceptions remain, but they are relatively minor.

Federation in 1901 left mineral ownership undisturbed, in the hands of the Crown in right of the various States (State governments). The Commonwealth acquired ownership of minerals in the Northern Territory upon acquisition of that Territory in 1910, but transferred that ownership (other than in relation to uranium) to the Northern Territory government upon the establishment of self-government in 1978.[10]

The importance of State government ownership of minerals in Australia is twofold. First, it means that governments, rather than private landholders, determine the legal regimes governing mineral exploration and production. Second, it has constitutional significance, a matter taken up below.

Onshore Mineral Exploitation and Production Regimes

Notwithstanding the norm of government ownership of minerals in Australia, it has been the usual practice of State legislatures to provide for the development of these resources by private rather than public enterprise. Regimes permitting mineral exploration and production by private enterprise fall into three broad categories: the claim-staking system; the discretionary leasing/licensing system; and the system of government agreements.

The claim-staking system was introduced in the middle of the nineteenth century in response to the gold fever in New South Wales and Victoria. This regime adopted many of the customs and practices of immigrant miners from Devon, Cornwall and California. The basic principle was that of possessory right. The holder of a document known as a miner's right (obtainable by all upon payment of a modest fee) was entitled to enter and take possession of unoccupied Crown land and to mine for gold on it. Land acquired in this way was known as a claim, and the miner remained entitled to his claim as long as he worked it. This regime, later extended to private land and to minerals other than gold, was aptly described as the 'free miner' system.

This system has been on the wane throughout the twentieth century in Australia, and it was never adopted for petroleum. Nevertheless, it remained an important feature of mineral legislation in Western Australia until 1982, and miners on a large and small scale exploited it in the Western Australian mining booms of the 1960s and 1970s. Nowadays, however, to the extent that it has been retained in mineral legislation, it is intended to cater for the needs of small-scale prospectors.

The free miner system has gradually been supplanted by a system of discretionary leasing and licensing. Mineral leases and licences also date back to the nineteenth century. Unlike claims, however, leases and licences cannot be obtained as of right; they lie in grant rather than in possession, and grant depends upon the favourable exercise of a discretion, usually vested in a government minister.

It is important to recognise, however, that State governments and their ministers are entirely dependent upon statutory authority for their powers to deal with mineral exploration and production titles (leases and licences). This is a consequence of State constitutional provisions, which vest the entire management and control of Crown lands (and minerals) in the legislative branch of government. Furthermore, the courts have insisted that when State legislatures attach procedural requirements to the exercise by ministers of statutory powers to grant mineral leases and licences, those requirements must be strictly observed.[11]

The discretionary leasing and licensing system governing mineral exploration and production in Australia is not uniform. Each State and the Northern Territory has its own regime for minerals other than petroleum and a separate regime for petroleum. New South Wales and Tasmania each has yet another regime for coal. Accordingly there are some sixteen different regimes in operation.

Nevertheless, it is possible to discern some common features in these regimes. The basic model is that of a two-stage system, with one form of title available for mineral exploration (usually known as an exploration licence or authority to prospect) and another for mineral production (usually known as a lease or production licence). The exploration title may cover a large area, up to several thousand square kilometres. The production title is seldom larger than several hundred hectares. However, it is unusual to find any statutory limits placed upon the numbers of exploration or production titles that may be held by any one person or company.[12]

In most cases, an application for an exploration title may be lodged upon the initiative of the applicant. It is not necessary for the minister to invite applications. The grant of an exploration title is a matter of ministerial discretion, with few statutory guidelines to control the exercise of that discretion. Typical provisions of an exploration title require the expenditure by the holder of specified sums of money upon mineral exploration, payment of a modest rental, and relinquishment of designated percentages of the title area at specified intervals. The right conferred upon the holder of an exploration title to explore for the mineral or minerals for which the title is granted is usually exclusive.

One crucial issue is whether the holder of an exploration title who discovers minerals within the land subject to his title has the right to obtain a production title in respect of that discovery. Here an interesting dichotomy emerges between petroleum and other minerals. In the case of petroleum the answer is usually affirmative,[13] but as regards minerals other than petroleum the answer, until recently at least, has been negative.[14] In 1982, however, Western Australia broke ranks with the other States on this issue by conferring on the holder of an exploration licence a statutory right to obtain a mining lease, even without a discovery.[15] Whether other States will feel obliged to follow the Western Australian example remains to be seen. In any event, the question of why petroleum is generally favoured in this way is intriguing. Perhaps the answer lies in the fact that petroleum operations have not yet given rise to the acute land-use conflicts that have occurred in relation to the production of other minerals such as rutile, titanium and zircon (the beach minerals). Alternatively, it may be that a strong desire to attain self-sufficiency in petroleum production has given governments a particular reluctance to place obstacles in the path of petroleum exploration.

Production titles are also granted as a matter of ministerial discretion, unless the applicant is the holder of an exploration title and is given a statutory right to obtain a production title. The duration of production titles is comparatively long (typically 21 years), and there is often a statutory right to renewal. State government levies are made in the form of rentals and royalties. The holder of a production title is allowed considerable freedom to determine matters such as scale of development and rate of production, although the minister may make the title subject to special conditions designed to deal with environmental problems.

One further point may be noted. The Northern Territory[16] and Victoria[17] have recently introduced three-stage title systems for minerals other than petroleum, in place of the traditional two-stage system. A new form of title (known as a retention or development lease), available between the exploration and production stages, is designed to provide for evaluation and feasibility studies after discovery but before mine development. The mineral industry has expressed strong support for this innovation.

Surprisingly, perhaps, most major mineral developments in Australia in the past 30 years have not proceeded by way of discretionary production titles. Instead, there has been a unique legal regime for each of these projects. This has been achieved by negotiation of an agreement between the project developer and the relevant State government, followed by statutory endorsement of that agreement. This approach has been particularly favoured in Western Australia[18] and Queensland,[19] although examples of it may also be found in South Australia,[20] New South Wales[21] and Victoria.[22] So far it has been confined to the development stage of mineral operations.

In concept this regime of government agreements (with statutory endorsement) is reminiscent of the era of the petroleum concession in the Middle East. The content of such agreements is too variable for description: in some cases the parties merely adopt the general discretionary title system with little modification (perhaps to duration of the title, area, rent and royalty); in others a new form of title is devised.

State Control of Mineral Developments

Ownership of the minerals within their boundaries allows the States to control mineral exploration and production in two ways: by direct participation in exploration and production, either alone or through joint ventures with private enterprise; and by manipulation of the terms of the exploration and production regimes governing mineral operations by private enterprise.

Examples of direct State government participation in mineral exploration and production in Australia are relatively few: the State Electricity Commission of Victoria (coal); the Electricity Commission of New South Wales (coal); the Gas and Fuel Corporation of Victoria (petroleum); and the South Australian Oil and Gas Corporation Pty Ltd (petroleum). Nevertheless, the scope for such participation in the future may be considerable.

The South Australian Oil and Gas Corporation provides an interesting case study. This company was incorporated in 1977, pursuant to the South Australian *Companies Act* 1961, with two shareholders: the Pipelines Authority of South Australia (a South Australian statutory corporation controlled by the State government) and the South Australian Gas Company (a public utility holding the franchise for natural gas distribution in Adelaide). The South Australian government, through the Pipelines Authority of South Australia, obtained effective control of the company through a right to appoint a majority of its directors. The company was formed for the particular purpose of acquiring from the Commonwealth an interest in the Cooper Basin petroleum fields. The Commonwealth had earlier purchased this interest from one of the private participants, Delhi Petroleum Pty Ltd, but following the dismissal of the Labor government in 1975 the Commonwealth decided to divest itself of this interest. Incidentally, the South Australian government was in a good position to ensure that the Commonwealth did not sell the interest to anyone else, since section 42 of the South Australian *Petroleum Act* 1940 (as amended) required the consent of the South Australian Minister for Mines and Energy to any assignment of an interest in a petroleum title.

It appears that the South Australian govenment had two main objectives in acquiring this interest in the Cooper Basin petroleum fields. First, it wanted access to information in the possession of the private participants regarding the size of petroleum reserves in the region. As a participant in the joint venture, the South Australian Oil and Gas Corporation was entitled to such access. Second, it wanted to quicken the pace of petroleum exploration in the region, in the hope that the discovery of additional natural gas deposits would avert a threatened crisis of gas shortages in Adelaide after 1987. Again, direct participation in the joint venture offered the means. A commonplace provision of mineral exploration joint venture agreements is a 'sole-risk' clause, which allows any party to undertake additional exploration at its own expense with substantial rewards to the sole-risk party in the event of successful exploration. The provisions of the sole-risk clause thus allowed the South Australian Oil and Gas Corporation to fulfil the government's objective of accelerating exploration in the Cooper Basin.

This case study is instructive in its demonstration of how State governments may, through direct participation in mineral exploration and production, use the provisions of the statutory title system and the private contractual framework to achieve public policy objectives. It seems possible that in some cases this approach allows the States greater flexibility of action than the alternative of legislation amending the leasing and licensing regime. At the same time it raises difficult questions. How can legislative supervision of the executive branch of government be achieved in such cases? And how can a minister avoid the conflict of interest inherent in the two roles assigned to him, that of participant (through a government corporation for whose actions he may bear ultimate responsibility) and that of regulator of the industry as a whole (through the exercise of the statutory powers vested in him regarding the discretionary leasing and licensing regime)?

Direct participation in mineral exploration and production may also offer the States a significant constitutional advantage, through the as yet ill-defined protection against Commonwealth taxation afforded by section 114 of the Constitution to property of any kind belonging to a State.

The manipulation by private enterprise of the terms of the exploration and production regimes governing mineral operations provides a more familiar example of State control of mineral developments within State boundaries. Clearly, discretionary power to grant mineral exploration and production titles may be used to influence the timing and extent of investment in this sector of the economy. Likewise the power to determine expenditure commitments undertaken by mineral explorers is an important control lever. Again, the requirement for ministerial consent to the transfer of an interest in a mineral exploration or production title is a control device with significant economic implications. The actual provisions of a leasing and licensing regime, and the way in which these provisions are used in practice, clearly have a direct effect on the allocation of resources to mineral exploration and production, which in turn influences the economic value of mineral deposits and the capacity of governments to derive revenue from them.[23]

It is here too that State government ownership of minerals assumes constitutional significance. Section 90 of the Constitution makes the power to levy duties of excise exclusive to the Commonwealth Parliament. The High Court has decided that most taxes upon goods are duties of excise.[24] Hence the capacity of a State to levy taxes upon minerals produced within its boundaries is severely constrained. Nevertheless, to be a duty of excise a levy must be a tax: 'a compulsory levy by a public authority for a public purpose'.[25] The area rental charged in relation to mineral exploration and production titles and the royalty levied upon mineral production are not taxes (and thus cannot be characterized as duties of excise), provided that they represent the sale price of rights to explore for and to produce government minerals. In other words, as long as the States ensure that they link their mineral levies to the acquisition and exercise of mineral exploration and production rights and thus distinguish them from taxes (perhaps a fine distinction, but nonetheless vital), they escape the ever-expanding reach of section 90 of the Constitution. However, not all States appear to have been as careful here as they might have been.

A Canadian example further demonstrates how mineral titles may be used to preserve State control of mineral exploration and production in the face of encroachment by Commonwealth legislation. Under the Canadian Constitution the power to regulate interprovincial trade and commerce is given exclusively to the central government. Any attempt by a provincial parliament to legislate on this matter would presumably fail. Nevertheless, Alberta has sought to control the export of natural gas from the province by means of provisions inserted in the petroleum and natural gas lease, which is cast in the form of a determinable grant. Should a lessee fail to comply with provincial restraints upon the export of natural gas, his rights to produce the gas terminate automatically.[26] In practice, at least, this has proved an effective device. So far the Australian States have not resorted to anything comparable,[27] but the opportunity is there.

Commonwealth Control of Mineral Developments

The division of legislative, executive and judicial power between the Commonwealth and the States effected by the Commonwealth Constitution is described in detail by Cheryl Saunders in chapter 2. It is clear that the Commonwealth has extensive power to influence mineral developments in Australia. It is sufficient here to confine discussion to a few examples.

The significance of the power of the Commonwealth to control exports was demonstrated by the case of *Murphyores Incorporated Pty Ltd.* v. *The Commonwealth,*[28] one of the many skirmishes that occurred in the battle for Fraser Island. Murphyores and another company held mining leases on Fraser Island, granted by the Queensland government under the provisions of the *Mining Act* 1968 (as amended). Under the leases the companies were entitled to produce zircon and rutile, the principal markets for which were overseas. Accordingly, although the companies were entitled to conduct mining operations on Fraser Island, the commercial feasibility of such operations was dependent on obtaining approval for the export of zircon and rutile concentrates. Regulation 9 of the Customs (Prohibited Exports) Regulations made under the Commonwealth *Customs Act* 1901 (as amended) prohibited the export of the concentrates unless an approval in writing was issued by the federal Minister for Minerals and Energy and produced to the Collector of Customs. In 1974 the company sought the Minister's approval for the export of concentrates to be produced from their mining operations on Fraser Island, and on 13 December 1974 the Minister indicated that approval would be forthcoming on certain conditions.

However, four days later the Commonwealth *Environment Protection (Impact of Proposals) Act* 1974 came into force. On 12 July 1975 the Minister administering this Act directed that an inquiry be conducted into

> all of the environmental aspects of the making of decisions by or on behalf of the Australian Government in relation to the exportation from Australia of minerals (including minerals that have been subjected to processing or treatment) extracted or which may hereafter be extracted from Fraser Island in the State of Queensland.

An inquiry was undertaken, although the companies chose not to participate in it. The Minister for Minerals and Energy indicated that he would consider the report of the commissioners who had conducted the inquiry before making his decision on the application by the companies for export approval.

The companies then began proceedings seeking to restrain the commissioners from presenting their report to the Minister administering the Act, and to obtain a declaration that the Minister for Minerals and Energy was not entitled in considering any application for export approval to take account of any report of the commissioners or any environmental aspects of the mining operations on Fraser Island. The main contention advanced by the companies was that the discretion conferred upon the Minister for Minerals and Energy to waive the prohibition of exports of mineral concentrates was confined to considerations of 'trading policy'. Otherwise, it was argued, the legislation giving the discretion would exceed the constitutional power to legislate with respect to trade and commerce with other countries, since that power did not enable the Commonwealth Parliament to regulate and control the environmental aspects of mining, even if carried on for the purpose of export.

However, this proposition obtained no support in the High Court, which confirmed that the trade and commerce power enabled the Commonwealth Parliament to prohibit, regulate and control the import and export of goods. It was of no moment that the exercise of this power in these circumstances effectively prohibited mining operations on Fraser Island that had been authorised by the Queensland government. Although it was conceded that 'the control of the Plaintiffs' mining operations and of their effect upon the local environment [was], no doubt, essentially a matter for the state',[29] this in no way precluded Commonwealth intervention as long as that intervention lay within the scope of Commonwealth legislative power. Thus the Commonwealth was not inhibited by the lack of a direct power to legislate with respect to mineral operations and environmental protection. Effective control of these matters was obtained indirectly by use of the trade and commerce power.

More recently, the decision of the High Court in the *Franklin Dam* case [30] has demonstrated that the Commonwealth government has the capacity to extend the power of the Commonwealth Parliament into virtually any field by incurring treaty obligations in relation to it. Constitutional limitations upon this capacity are of minor consequence. Moreover, the power of the Commonwealth Parliament to regulate the activities of both foreign and domestic corporations engaged in mineral operations (provided such operations are conducted with a view to sale of the product) is very extensive indeed.

These examples show how Commonwealth power may be used in an essentially negative way in relation to mineral operations, to prohibit such operations or to subject them to Commonwealth regulatory requirements. However, these powers also have a positive aspect. It is well established, for example, that the Commonwealth Parliament can legislate under the trade and commerce power to set up a corporation to engage in interstate and overseas trade and commerce,[31] and Commonwealth executive power to establish such bodies is no less extensive.

The ill-fated Petroleum and Minerals Authority is worth remembering here.

In 1974 the Commonwealth Parliament sought to establish this body by legislation: the *Petroleum and Minerals Authority Act* 1973. However, the High Court struck down this statute, for procedural rather than substantive reasons; the requirements of section 57 of the Constitution (dealing with enactment of legislation at a joint sitting of the two Houses of Parliament) had not been satisfied in relation to this statute. The prompt response of the Commonwealth government was to incorporate the Petroleum and Minerals Company of Australia Pty Ltd in the Australian Capital Territory, with the intention that the company would take over the assets and perform the functions of the defunct statutory authority. However, a change of government put paid to this plan, leaving unresolved a host of important constitutional issues. One was whether Commonwealth executive power was sufficiently broad to permit the formation of a company to engage in mineral exploration and production in the States. Assuming an affirmative answer to that question, another was to what extent this Commonwealth entity would be bound to comply with the provisions of State statutes in the performance of its functions.

Once again, this example demonstrates to the States the significance of their mineral ownership. Whether or not the States can control a Commonwealth mineral exploration and production company through legislation, they have the capacity to restrict the activities of that company within their borders by refusing to grant it the necessary exploration and production titles, and by refusing consent to the assignment to it of interests in existing titles.

One further head of Commonwealth legislative power deserves mention: the power to make laws on taxation. Clearly this power allows the Commonwealth Parliament not merely to derive revenue from mineral operations, but also to exert an indirect influence over mineral exploration and production by creating incentives and disincentives for specific activities. However, that may not be all. In the *Victorian Pipeline Tax* case, [32] some members of the High Court suggested that the Commonwealth taxation power may also be used to render inoperative State taxing statutes.[33] This radical proposition, if confirmed, further erodes the capacity of State parliaments to derive revenues from mineral production, a capacity already limited by section 90 of the Constitution. However, it could hardly be said that a Commonwealth law on the sale of mineral exploration and production rights is a law on 'taxation'. In other words, there is further reason for the States to ensure that their levies upon mineral operations do not have the legal character of taxes.

Jurisdiction over Offshore Resources

Offshore petroleum exploration has been conducted in Australia for 25 years. At first there was no legislation directed specifically at offshore operations. Exploration rights were required under the petroleum legislation of adjoining States.

However, doubts were soon expressed about the capacity of the States to grant offshore petroleum rights. In 1962 negotiations began between the

Commonwealth and the States regarding offshore jurisdiction. Two years later the seven governments announced that 'a national solution to the problem of offshore oil exploration and exploitation was necessary'.[34] It was decided that there should be an agreement between the Commonwealth and the States on joint legislative arrangements over the whole offshore seabed in relation to petroleum operations. It took a further three years to conclude the details of that agreement and the appropriate legislation. On 16 October 1967 the Commonwealth and the States executed the

Agreement relating to the exploration for, and the exploitation of, the petroleum resources, and certain other resources, of the continental shelf of Australia and of certain territories of the Commonwealth and of certain other submerged land.

At the heart of the Agreement lay the desire of the seven governments to set aside their competing jurisdictional claims without derogating from them. However, if offshore petroleum operations were to proceed, it was necessary to provide a method of granting exploration and production titles that would be valid regardless of the eventual outcome of the jurisdictional issue. Further, it was felt that offshore petroleum operations should, as far as possible, be subject to a common legal code.

The device employed for achieving these objectives was described as 'mirror legislation'. In the Agreement, the seven governments undertook to legislate in identical terms on offshore petroleum operations, and to refrain from amending such legislation without prior unanimous agreement. The principal Commonwealth statute enacted in accordance with the Agreement was the *Petroleum (Submerged Lands) Act* 1967. State statutes of the same name were also passed in that or the following year.

A major achievement of the Agreement was the delineation of the 'adjacent areas', one belonging to each State and coastal territory. The Commonwealth legislation extended to all adjacent areas, and each State statute applied to the adjacent area belonging to its land territory. In this way, two statutes (one Commonwealth and one State) purported to govern all offshore petroleum operations conducted in the adjacent area of a State. Conflict was avoided by framing the two statutes in identical terms so that rights and obligations had two possible sources. The security of offshore petroleum titles was divorced from the issue of jurisdiction by the granting to each applicant of two identical titles (one Commonwealth and one State) for each offshore area.

Although the Agreement provided for the enactment of a common legal code for offshore petroleum operations, it also provided for the separate administration of that code in each of the adjacent areas. In the adjacent area of a State the administration of both the Commonwealth and the State statutes was carried out by the State minister, described as the designated authority. The Agreement required consultation between the State and the Commonwealth before the exercise by the designated authority of the more important powers conferred by the *Petroleum (Submerged Lands) Acts,* but it appears that such consultation was minimal at times of stress in Commonwealth–State relations.

The attempt to set aside the question of offshore jurisdiction was unsuccessful. In 1973 the Commonwealth Parliament enacted the *Seas and Submerged Lands Act* 1973, asserting Commonwealth sovereignty over the territorial sea and Commonwealth sovereign rights to explore the continental shelf and to exploit its natural resources. Predictably, this Act was challenged by all states. In *New South Wales* v. *The Commonwealth* (the Seas and Submerged Lands case),[35] the High Court upheld its validity. A majority of the Court decided that the seaward boundaries of the States were constituted by the ordinary low-water mark, except in the case of any bodies of water within State boundaries before federation. It followed that the Commonwealth was entitled to exercise the rights derived from international law over the territorial sea and the continental shelf.

The immediate effect of this decision was to confirm that the legislation governing all offshore petroleum operations was the Commonwealth *Petroleum (Submerged Lands) Act* 1967, rather than the various State statutes. Otherwise, the position remained unchanged. The Commonwealth statute continued to be administered separately in each of the adjacent areas by the several designated authorities.

The States, however, were most dissatisfied with this result. Their dissatisfaction was increased by further decisions of the High Court casting doubt on the capacity of State legislation to operate seaward of State territorial limits.[36] Accordingly, discussions took place between the Commonwealth and the States at various Premiers' Conferences with a view to reaching a political accord regarding offshore jurisdiction. At the Conference held on 29 June 1979, the governments concluded such an agreement.

The 1979 Agreement modified the 1967 Agreement in a number of important ways. First, the States and the Northern Territory were to be given legislative power over the territorial sea and property rights over its seabed. Second, offshore petroleum operations outside the territorial sea were to be regulated by Commonwealth legislation alone, consisting of an amended *Petroleum (Submerged Lands) Act*. Third, arrangements for administration of the Commonwealth legislation were to be revised. While day-to-day administration would continue in the hands of the designated authority, the more significant powers were to be vested in a newly created joint authority for each adjacent area, made up of the federal minister and the State minister. Fourth, offshore petroleum operations in the territorial sea were to be regulated by State and Northern Territory legislation alone, although the common mining code was to be retained as far as practicable. Fifth, offshore exploration for and production of minerals other than petroleum were to be governed by arrangements based on those applicable to petroleum.

In 1980 the Commonwealth Parliament enacted a vast body of legislation to give effect to this Agreement.[37] Subsequently the States and the Northern Territory enacted legislation relating to petroleum exploration and production in the territorial sea.[38] Most of this legislation came into operation on 14 February 1983.

In summary, the present position on offshore mineral exploration and production is as follows. Each State and the Northern Territory has its own legislation, which is applicable to petroleum operations in its territorial sea. The Commonwealth has the *Petroleum (Submerged Lands) Act* 1967 (extensively amended in 1980), which is applicable to petroleum operations in all the adjacent areas, now redefined to exclude the territorial sea. The State and Territory legislation is closely modelled upon that of the Commonwealth, with the result that in substance there is a single legal code governing offshore petroleum exploration and production. However, administration of this code is highly fragmented. For the purposes of administration, there are eighteen distinct offshore areas: seven stretches of territorial sea (one for each State and one for the Northern Territory) and eleven adjacent areas. Four of the adjacent areas relate to Commonwealth territories; one is administered as if it were part of the Queensland adjacent area, while the other three are administered directly by the Commonwealth. For each of the remaining seven adjacent areas (one for each State and one for the Northern Territory) administration is divided between a joint authority (the federal minister and the relevant State or Territory minister) and the designated authority (the relevant State or Territory minister).

The Commonwealth Parliament has also enacted legislation relating to exploration for and production of minerals other than petroleum beyond the territorial sea,[39] but it has not yet brought this legislation into operation. It is expected that the States and the Northern Territory will prepare similar legislation applicable to the territorial sea.

The Offshore Petroleum Exploration and Production Regime

The *Petroleum (Submerged Lands) Acts* establish a two-stage system of offshore petroleum titles, the first stage represented by the exploration permit, the second by the production licence. To simplify administration, the various offshore areas are divided into graticular blocks, each measuring five minutes of latitude by five minutes of longitude. The area of blocks varies from 60 square kilometres in southern waters to 80 square kilometres in the north.

The power to grant exploration permits is vested in the joint authority. The allocation process is discretionary. The first step is for the designated authority to invite, by public notice, applications for permits over specified blocks. Each application must be accompanied by particulars of the proposed work program, proposed expenditure, technical abilities and financial resources of the applicant. Where an application is made for a block that previously formed part of a production licence or location (a term explained below) there is provision for a limited degree of competitive bidding, as applications must also specify the amount that the applicant is prepared to pay for the permit. Nevertheless, the discretion of the joint authority is very wide; there is no requirement that the highest bidder be awarded the permit. A permit is granted subject to such conditions as the joint authority thinks fit and specifies in the permit. Of great

importance are those specifying the work program and expenditure commitment. These are determined in practice by negotiation between the joint
authority and the applicant before the permit is granted. When there are several
applicants for a particular permit, the proposed work programs and expenditures may be very important in determining which applicant is successful.

The duration of a permit is six years. In addition, a permit may be renewed
for successive periods of five years, as of right, if the holder has complied with
the conditions and requirements of the *Petroleum (Submerged Lands) Acts*. Upon
each renewal, however, a permit holder must surrender at least half the number
of blocks covered by the permit.

There are two methods by which a production licence may be obtained. A
permit holder who discovers petroleum within the permit area is entitled as of
right to the grant of a licence in respect of the discovery. The procedure by
which the licence area is selected is rather complex. The permit holder is
entitled to nominate a block to form the centre of a location to be declared in
respect of the discovery well. A location is a group of nine blocks, three blocks
square, containing the discovery block. Once a location has been declared, the
permit holder is given an option in the selection of the licence area. The first
course open is to apply for a licence covering any five of the nine blocks in the
location, in which case the standard royalty rate of 10 per cent is charged. The
second course is to apply for a licence over more than the five blocks, when the
applicable royalty rate, lying between 11 per cent and 12.5 per cent, is
determined by the joint authority. Any blocks within a location not selected to
form part of the licence area must be relinquished.

The second method of allocating production licences involves competitive
bidding and applies to blocks which previously formed part of a location or
licence. If the joint authority is of the opinion that there is petroleum within the
blocks, it is entitled to use this procedure. Both cash bonus bidding and royalty
bidding are allowed. However, the joint authority has the discretion to accept or
reject any bid.

A production licence is granted subject to such conditions as the joint
authority thinks fit and specifies in the licence. However, one important
condition is specified in the *Petroleum (Submerged Lands) Acts;* this is an annual
expenditure requirement, calculated at the rate of $300 000 per block. However,
the value of any petroleum produced from the licence area in the preceding year
may be deducted from this figure.

Commonwealth–State Division of Powers:
Offshore Petroleum Developments

Under the new arrangements for administration of the offshore petroleum
regime, the States and the Northern Territory have the capacity to control the
timing and extent of petroleum exploration and production in the territorial sea,
whereas the Commonwealth has the capacity to exercise this control in the
various adjacent areas. The Commonwealth has gained this control in the
adjacent areas by the transfer of the more important discretionary powers

conferred by the *Petroleum (Submerged Lands) Acts* from the designated authority to the joint authority. Although each joint authority is made up of a Commonwealth minister and a State minister, the Commonwealth minister is given a casting vote in the event of disagreement.

One further feature of the offshore petroleum regime must also be mentioned: the provision for revenue sharing between the Commonwealth and the States. The 1967 Agreement required the sharing of royalties between the Commonwealth and the States on the basis of 4 per cent to the Commonwealth and the remainder (between 6 per cent and 8.5 per cent) to the States. In addition, the States were entitled to all further revenues derived from offshore petroleum operations, such as rentals and any payments made upon acquisition of permits or licences when competitive bidding was employed. Surprisingly, perhaps, it would appear that this arrangement continues under the 1979 Agreement; certainly royalties are to be shared on the same basis. The published terms of the 1979 Agreement do not indicate whether the States and the Northern Territory remain entitled to all revenues other than royalties, but it seems reasonable to assume that the 1967 Agreement is unaltered in this respect. If so, it could provide a significant source of revenue to some States if the opportunity were taken to allocate certain selected blocks by competitive bidding.

The provision for royalty sharing has an interesting dimension. Royalties are calculated as a percentage (between 10 per cent and 12.5 per cent) of the wellhead value of petroleum production. Obviously, determination of wellhead value is a crucial matter. Section 9 of the *Petroleum (Submerged Lands) (Royalty) Act* 1967 states that the value of petroleum at the wellhead is to be determined by agreement between the licence holder and the designated authority, or, in default of agreement, unilaterally by the designated authority. However, the designated authority is obliged to act in this matter in accordance with directions given by the joint authority. So far it seems that determination of the wellhead value of petroleum has presented some problems. Agreement was reached between the Bass Strait producers and the Victorian designated authority only after negotiations stretching over a period of more than ten years.

However, it is the relationship between royalties and other government levies that is of greatest interest. The Commonwealth crude oil levy presently operates at a marginal rate of 87 per cent in relation to the most prolific petroleum reservoirs in Bass Strait, which raises the question of whether account is taken of the crude oil levy in determining wellhead value for royalty purposes. The answer seems to be positive, with the result that wellhead value (and thus the Victorian share of royalties) is considerably smaller than it would otherwise be. However, it is far from clear that this is a necessary result. The *Petroleum (Submerged Lands) (Royalty) Act* 1967 refers to 'the value at the well-head of any petroleum', rather than to the value of that petroleum to the producer. Further, this issue will emerge again in a different guise if the Commonwealth proceeds with its plan to replace the crude oil levy with a petroleum rent tax.

Ownership of onshore minerals by State governments provides the States with an opportunity to control mineral exploration and production within State boundaries through a range of instruments otherwise denied to them. It also provides a means by which the States may derive revenue from mineral production, notwithstanding the severe limits placed by the Commonwealth Constitution upon their capacities to levy taxes. Offshore the Commonwealth occupies a predominant position with respect to mineral exploration and production, at least beyond the territorial sea. For historical and political reasons the States continue to participate in the administration of the Commonwealth petroleum regime, and they also share in petroleum royalties and some other revenues. In contrast with the onshore position, however, they enjoy their offshore status at the will of the Commonwealth.

6 Mining taxation issues in the Australian federal system

KEN WILLETT

There is a veritable hotchpotch of State and Commonwealth government imposts on the Australian mining sector (including petroleum). Mining taxation arrangements have evolved in an ad hoc fashion without cooperation or consultation between the States or between the Commonwealth and the States, and even the arrangements of the Commonwealth and of individual States have tended to develop in the same way.

Inevitably, therefore, some very important questions have been raised in recent years in relation to mining taxation. This chapter identifies and discusses the main fields of debate, and evaluates existing and proposed mining taxation arrangements. Specific issues addressed include the highly distortionary nature of existing arrangements and their shortcomings in terms of their power to distribute revenue equitably between the resource sector and the community; the controversy over the resource rent tax and similar systems; and the importance for successful mining taxation policy of the existence of efficient tenement allocation arrangements, and the neglect of this critical point in previous discussions of mining taxation reform.

Objectives of Mining Taxation Policies

Australian State and federal mining taxation systems are major instruments of resource management and economic development policy. The broad objective of such policy should be to maximise the contribution of mineral resources to the long-term welfare of the relevant jurisdiction. This objective has several sub-objectives: to ensure equitable distribution of mining returns between mining enterprises and the people by maximising the long-term welfare effects of mining taxation revenue; to minimise economic inefficiencies in the use or allocation of resources; to facilitate economic growth that is in the best interests of the jurisdiction; to ensure that mineral revenue liabilities are met, while keeping costs to the government and the enterprise at a reasonable level; and to facilitate a stable flow of revenue over time. These sub-objective—are useful criteria for evaluating the various royalty and taxation measures, but judgments must be made about their weightings within each system, as no one system is superior in terms of all requirements.

In the 1950s and 1960s State and federal governments placed great emphasis on attracting mining investment in order to promote economic development. More recently the Commonwealth and some of the States have realised that appropriating rents for respending within the local economy can assist economic development, and that sacrificing mining taxation revenue to attract investment can be self-defeating in the long term. Economic development is better achieved by policies designed for the purpose than by hidden subsidies through low royalties or other mining taxes.

The mining taxation arrangements most compatible with the growth objectives of the States and the Commonwealth would be those that fully exploit the revenue-raising opportunities of the mining sector without encouraging inefficiency or reducing incentives for mining enterprises. In other words, the economic development goal can be subsumed in the equity/revenue and economic efficiency objectives. The economic efficiency objective would tend to maintain incentives, while satisfaction of the equity objective would help to ensure that the community generally would benefit from mining-based growth.

In the 1950s and 1960s the concept of the economic rent of minerals was virtually unknown, or its significance was not understood, and this is still the case in some areas. Thus the opportunities it offers for the redistribution of rents from the mining sector to the community without unduly affecting incentives have been recognised only recently, and in many cases slowly. Until recently, moreover, most policymakers and advisers have shown little interest in the adverse economic efficiency effects of royalty, de facto royalty and mining taxation arrangements. In the States, in particular, the emphasis has been on keeping royalty and de facto royalty systems simple and avoiding royalty arrangements that produce fluctuating revenue and complicate the preparation of the budget. This is partly explained by a failure to grasp the significance of resource allocation issues relative to administrative and revenue stability issues, particularly at high royalty rates.

Obviously, State and Commonwealth governments can have very different perceptions of the reference group to which the criteria relate. A given State will be more interested in an appropriate distribution of the benefits from mining between its own resource sector and its people than in the distribution between the mining sector and Australians generally or between individuals in other States. Similarly, States may be competing for mining investment and operations, leading to a conflict of growth objectives in which national economic efficiency receives little consideration.

Evaluation of Mining Taxation Arrangements

In this section a number of mining taxation arrangements are evaluated by the criteria outlined above. It is assumed that the underlying tenement system has no effect on the yield from mining taxation. The implications of this assumption have been largely ignored in discussions of mining taxation, and the consequences of relaxing this assumption are analysed in the following section.

Ad valorem and specific royalties, export coal duty and Queensland 'excess' freight rates

An ad valorem royalty represents a percentage of the gross value of production, and a specific royalty is a charge per unit of physical production. These and various combinations of them are by far the most commonly applied royalty systems in Australia.

These royalties do not allow for net value differences between units of ore within each mineral deposit. Thus they discourage the production of ore units yielding a surplus less than the royalty levied on those units. In other words, they cause a mining enterprise to leave behind some ore that would be profitable in the absence of the royalty. It is also known that, to the extent that barriers to entry to and exit from the industry exist, these royalties may induce changes in the timing of extraction as well as in overall recovery.

Specific and ad valorem royalties also fail to allow for net value differences between deposits. The less economically attractive a deposit, the more likely it is that a specific or ad valorem royalty will prevent development of that mine because too much ore has been rendered uneconomic. Likewise, the higher the royalty rate, the higher will be the quality and quantity of ore left behind. Finally, the higher the royalty rate, the more likely it is that the royalty cost will cause the abandonment of an existing mine or prevent the development of a new mine.

In addition, these royalties discourage risk taking because they reduce the probability of achieving each possible level of positive net present value and increase the probability of achieving each possible level of negative net present value. Hence they tend to skew the frequency distribution of net present value in a negative direction, thus discouraging investment and exploration, and the size of these adverse effects will increase with the royalty rate. Furthermore, these royalties do not reduce the expected net present value of each mining project by the same proportion and can therefore alter the ranking of possible mining investments, so that projects could be deferred in favour of projects that would be less attractive in the absence of the royalty.

Specific and ad valorem royalties cannot yield significant revenue without adverse effects on the size and composition of the industry, and so, in the long term, they erode the base for royalty revenue. This is inconsistent with the equity/revenue objective. The main strength of a specific royalty is that it is easily administered. Ad valorem royalties are harder to administer because of the need to identify fair market prices, but easier than systems that allow deductions for costs.

Specific royalties are completely unresponsive to a changed revenue-raising climate. If specific royalty rates are not raised, their real value may be eroded by inflation. Royalty revenue does not change automatically if mineral prices and profits soar, and the revenue-raising opportunity may have disappeared before the royalty rate can be altered to exploit the situation. In addition, frequent adjustments to royalty rates create uncertainty and discourage investment, which may also lead to erosion of the tax base. Revenue from ad valorem royalties moves with mineral prices and output, which may avoid the reduction of real revenue by inflation but causes revenues to fluctuate.

The export coal duty and Queensland's 'excess' rail freight rates are de facto specific royalties, and the above comments generally apply. However, one major difference between these and specific royalties is that the 'excess' rail freight rate automatically escalates with certain railway costs while a normal specific levy remains fixed until deliberately changed.

Crude oil levy

The crude oil levy on 'old oil' is a modified ad valorem tax to appropriate a very high proportion of the economic rents or net value realised from crude oil and commingled condensate from fields discovered on or before 17 September 1975. The excise rate per barrel has varied over time with the import parity price of crude oil. The marginal excise rate also varies in discrete jumps with the volume of production, from 5 per cent of the import parity price for production in the range 50–100 million litres a year to 87 per cent for production in excess of 600 million litres a year. As from mid-1984 a levy has also been applied to onshore and offshore oil (outside the territorial sea) discovered after 17 September 1975, for which production licences had been issued before 1 July 1984. The levies applying to this 'new oil' are much lower than those for 'old oil'. The marginal excise rate ranges from 10 per cent of import parity for output in the range 500–600 million litres a year to 35 per cent for production in excess of 800 million litres a year. From the end of 1984 a levy on 'intermediate oil' was introduced. This is oil from fields discovered on or before 17 September 1975 but undeveloped as of 23 October 1984 and specifically excluded from the application of the resource rent tax on offshore petroleum. The marginal tax rate ranges from 15 per cent of the import parity price for output in the range of 300–400 million litres per year to 55 per cent for output above 800 million litres per year. From the standpoint of any particular field, therefore, the crude oil levy operates like an ad valorem impost. From the standpoint of the industry as a whole, it operates as an ad valorem impost that increases with one factor (field output) that tends to lower average costs, but is unaffected by the other factors that influence costs.

The variability of the excise rate was designed to avoid closing small fields that were in production when the levy was introduced, but the crude oil levy will cause oil to be left behind in producing fields. For example, in the case of 'old oil' fields in the over 600 million litres a year range (such as Barrow Island) it would not pay the producer to extract any oil with a marginal cost of production in excess of 13 per cent of the import parity price. The crude oil levy may also induce changes in the timing of extraction, just as a pure ad valorem royalty does.

While the crude oil excise takes into account one factor (output) that influences net value differences between fields, it ignores others. Because the production categories do not reflect cost categories closely enough, there are some 'old' deposits that have not been brought into production. The intermediate oil category was introduced to assist some of these. Similarly, some 'new' deposits may be discovered that would be viable without the 'new oil' levy but not with it. The onshore 'new oil' levy will discourage risk taking in the same way as specific and ad valorem royalties. Exploration and investment can be expected to contract and the long-term revenue base to decline.

The crude oil levy has the attractions of being easy to administer and of providing an early and steady stream of revenue over time, but these advantages are minor compared to its disadvantages in economic efficiency and long-term revenue.

Proportional accounting profits royalty or tax

An accounting profits royalty or tax base is derived by deducting exploration, operating and borrowing costs and asset depreciation allowances from revenue. The Commonwealth income tax system is a proportional accounting profits tax with a rate of 46 per cent. The only comprehensive proportional accounting profits royalty in Australia is the recently introduced Northern Territory system, which applies at a rate of 18 per cent to mines established after 1 July 1982. Other proportional accounting profits-based systems are combined with ad valorem systems and apply only in selected cases.

Unlike specific and ad valorem royalties, an accounting profits royalty or tax base allows for net value differences between deposits because the base varies with costs as well as prices. Moreover, it allows for differences within a particular mine in quality or economic attractiveness of units of ore.

Given the level of investment in a mine, a proportional accounting royalty or tax takes a constant proportion of the difference between price and marginal cost of each unit of ore. Thus the royalty on a marginal unit of ore will be zero. Moreover, when prices and costs change over time, an accounting profits royalty or tax remains a constant proportion of the difference between marginal costs and prices. Consequently, marginal and supra-marginal ore will not be rendered commercially unattractive by the royalty or tax. However, the system will affect decisions on exploration outlays and investment to establish new operations or increase recovery from existing operations, rendering some prospects commercially unattractive. There are a number of reasons for this.

First, there is no existing or proposed accounting profits tax or royalty in Australia that provides full loss offsets. Losses from exploration and operations are not refunded at the same effective rate as profits are captured by the royalty or tax, so that the distribution of possible outcomes is negatively skewed. This discourages investment and risk taking.

Second, accounting depreciation allowances do not allow for the true decline in the value of assets because of their arbitrary nature and the effects of inflation. This can affect asset ranking and investment decisions, and can also distort decisions about asset life. Selection of a set of true economic depreciation scales that would overcome these problems is impractical.

Third, because of uncertainty, most firms face limited debt–equity ratios, particularly for major projects. Such investments would need to be financed, at least in part, by retained earnings or new share issues. Moreover, it is unlikely that exploration activity would be financed by borrowing. An accounting profit royalty therefore falls on 'normal' returns to equity capital associated with exploration and other new investments. This discourages exploration and investment.

Fourth, the royalty base often includes some return, not covered by specific deductible payments, to the synergistic effects of the efforts of skilled managerial and technical teams. Where this occurs, efficiency and bold entrepreneurial activity are discouraged.

Despite these shortcomings, an accounting profits system is less likely to damage resource development incentives than ad valorem or specific royalty systems, which make no allowance for costs or negative cash flows, and tax returns to all inputs (although they do tax returns to managerial and technical ability less heavily than an accounting profits system yielding similar long-term revenue). Having a less damaging effect on incentives, an accounting profits system erodes the long-term tax base less than those other systems, making it superior to them in terms of the equity/revenue objective.

An accounting profits arrangement does involve significantly greater administrative problems and costs than the other systems, but this disadvantage must be kept in perspective. At high rates, the long-term revenue gains from less erosion of the royalty base would easily outweigh the extra administrative costs. Such a system also tends to defer revenues and to yield more volatile revenues than the other systems. However, the budgetary inconveniences of this are outweighed by the potential long-term revenue gains.

Progressive accounting profits royalty of tax

The New South Wales Government applies a substantial progressive accounting profits royalty to the Broken Hill lead, silver and zinc mines and a much smaller one to the Cobar copper and zinc mine. This type of royalty need not be discussed in detail here. It is enough to point out that it is inferior to a proportional accounting profits royalty in terms of the criteria of economic efficiency, equity/revenue, administrative efficiency and revenue stability.

Pure economic profits or net value royalty

A company income taxation scheme proposed by Cary Brown and Vernon Smith effectively exempts the supply price of or required rate of return on capital, and taxes only 'pure economic' or 'above normal' profits accruing to firms as windfall gains, monopoly profits or economic rents.[1] Brown and Smith, and others, have argued that this tax does not affect the allocation of resources. It is also said to be neutral even if applied to a single economic sector or private firm.[2] Consequently it has been suggested that it could be used as a royalty scheme to levy the economic rent of minerals in a neutral fashion.[3]

Under a pure economic profits system the royalty base is net cash flow, positive or negative, in each period. If the net cash flow is negative in any period, including the exploration and development phases, the rebate is equivalent to the royalty rate multiplied by the negative net cash flow. When net cash flow is positive, the Treasury collects revenue equal to the positive cash flow multiplied by the royalty rate. In calculating net cash flow, conventional depreciation and borrowing cost deductions are not allowed because the immediate write-offs permit full deductions for exploration and capital expenditure and effectively exempt the supply price of or required rate of return on capital from the royalty. This form of royalty is like government equity participation in exploration and mining activity, with a shareholding equal to the royalty rate but without the voting and other privileges of a shareholder.

A pure economic profits system allows for variation between the net values of units within a deposit by taking a constant proportion of each of those net values. Material that is supra-marginal (net value exceeds zero) remains supra-marginal, and material that is marginal (net value equals zero) is not rendered sub-marginal. This remains the case when prices or costs change, because the tax adjusts automatically. The system also allows for quality differences in ore between deposits: it takes the highest revenue from the most economically attractive deposits; a deposit that would be supra-marginal or marginal without the tax is not rendered commercially unattractive by the tax; a marginal deposit earning just enough revenue to cover full costs, including minimum required returns to capital, effectively pays no royalty; and deposits that would be worth mining after price or cost changes without the royalty remain economically viable when the royalty is imposed.

The neutrality of the pure economic profits royalty extends to the rate of output. Since the royalty takes a fixed proportion of net present value, it does not alter the timing that maximises the net present value of the deposit. In theory the system is neutral with respect to investment decisions as well, including decisions concerning the screening, ranking and timing of investments.

An expected zero or positive net present value of a project before the royalty is not altered by the royalty, and the net value royalty reduces potential net present values, positive or negative, in the same proportion (equal to the royalty rate). Consequently, the dispersion of the frequency distribution of possible outcomes, as well as the expected value (average), is reduced by the same proportion, and worthwhile projects are not rendered uneconomic by the royalty. Furthermore, the system reduces the expected net present value and limits the probability distribution of all projects or investments by the same proportion, and so does not change the ranking of projects subject to the royalty. Finally, the optimum timing of development investment is not affected by the economic profits royalty, since the royalty takes a fixed percentage of net present value.

Despite the positive economic efficiency attributes of a pure economic profits royalty, this system is not perfect. Distortions could arise at very high rates of royalty plus other taxes (say above 70 per cent). Because of the applicability of rebates at the royalty rate for negative cash flows, the government would provide much of the exploration investment and take much of the return above operating costs. There would be little incentive for efficiency, since returns to managerial and technical ability would be levied by the royalty to the extent that they were not a deductible cost, and the economic rent could be partly dissipated by ill-advised expenditure and poor management. The royalty rate must therefore be low enough to provide incentives for efficiency; but relatively high rates will be necessary to compensate for the immediate expensing of capital outlays and exploration expenditures through the negative cash flow rebates while still providing an appropriate share of the economic rent for the community.

The revenue yield of a pure economic profits royalty is likely to be highly volatile. Not only would revenue fluctuate with changes in prices, operating costs and output, but it would also be significantly affected from time to time by the provision of rebates at the royalty rate for new exploration and other investments. Thus royalty revenues could switch from a high positive to a high negative figure quite quickly, particularly when the industry is in a strong expansion phase, and then back again. This casts doubts on the acceptability of the system in a State budgetary context.

A pure economic profits system involves problems in revenue and cost determination similar to those for an accounting profits system. However, it does not require the specification and administration of a system of depreciation allowances and exploration deductions, because all these costs are expensed. Moreover, tax avoidance problems from manipulation of debt–equity ratios to increase interest deductions would not arise because interest is not deductible under a net value system. These attributes would reduce administrative costs and difficulties as compared with an accounting profits system. Nevertheless, significant administrative resources could be involved in administering the system of cash rebates at the royalty rate for such expenditure, particularly since high rates would be necessary to collect adequate revenue, and the incentive to incur dubious expenditures would be greater than with an accounting profits royalty. This would raise the administrative difficulties and costs.

Overall, however, a pure economic profits system would probably be less costly to administer than an accounting profits system. It would cost more to administer than a specific ad valorem system, but again this needs to be kept in perspective. The advantages for efficiency of a net value system over specific and ad valorem systems increase with the royalty rate, and are immense at high rates. The advantages would include higher levels of output, employment, investment and exploration. Because of its non-distortionary character, the long-term revenue potential of this system would be very much higher than those of the other systems. Revenue gains could be expected to be well above the extra administrative costs.

Resource rent tax/royalty system

A variant of the pure economic profits royalty that is purported to be politically more acceptable is the resource rent royalty or tax. This system was designed to simulate the relative neutrality of the pure economic profits royalty without the requirements for the government to make payments when net cash flows are negative.[4]

In contrast to the pure economic profits royalty, which allows rebates for negative cash flows in the period incurred, the resource rent tax provides for negative cash flows to be carried forward with interest at a particular threshold rate of return for deduction from future cash flows. A resource rent tax system defers royalty payments until all exploration expenditure and development investment directly related to a project has been recouped, along with a particular threshold rate of return on capital invested (as measured by discounted cash flow methods). After that, positive net cash flows are subject to royalty. Payments in the form of interest, dividends and repayment of provision of capital are not deductible, and receipts of interest, dividends and capital funds are not assessable.

A resource rent system may be either proportional or progressive. A proportional system uses only one threshold rate and one royalty rate. The Commonwealth government has introduced such a scheme for offshore petroleum projects operating under licences issued after 1 July 1984 in waters outside the territorial sea. The threshold rate is the long-term bond rate plus 15 per cent and the tax rate is 40 per cent. A progressive system uses more than one threshold rate and more than one tax rate. When an investor has recouped his entire investment in a project, together with interest equal to a second and higher threshold rate, subsequent positive cash flows attract a higher tax rate.

When a project incurs losses that are not covered with interest in later years or when unsuccessful exploration expenditures are not recovered immediately or with interest in later years, a resource rent system, unlike a net value royalty, does not provide the equivalent of full loss offsets at the royalty rate. Without full loss offsets, the frequency distribution of net present values would be skewed negatively by the tax. Consequently, the expected (average) net present value of some investments could become negative. Investment in exploration and development would be discouraged to some extent, and ranking of investments within the industry could be affected.

Various schemes could be used for accommodating unsuccessful exploration expenditures (those not directly related to a project) in the resource rent tax structure. One scheme would be to provide exploration expenditure refunds at the royalty rate (as in the case of the pure economic profits royalty), which would provide full exploration loss offsets. Another scheme would allow transferability or sale of exploration deductions to other projects, which would approximate to a full exploration loss offsets scheme, particularly when there were enough resource rent tax payers to provide a competitive market for unsuccessful exploration expenditure deductions. A third scheme would allow unsuccessful expenditures to be carried forward with interest at the threshold rate and offset against revenue from a firm's next successful project.

The Commonwealth government's offshore petroleum resource rent tax does not allow for unsuccessful exploration expenditures apart from those within a permit containing a production licence that pays a resource rent tax. Instead, a higher threshold rate has been set than would be appropriate if full exploration loss offsets applied. This is an unsatisfactory arrangement because exploration will still be deterred by the lack of full loss offsets, while the higher threshold rate will distort investment decisions and exclude some petroleum rents from the tax base.

Unless the threshold rate of return is set equal to the relevant supply price of capital, a resource rent royalty scheme will to some extent adversely affect investment decisions. Setting the threshold rate too high may encourage overinvestment and increase the capital–labour ratio, employment and output at the expense of tax revenue, because some returns in excess of those required to induce investment are exempted from tax. Setting the threshold rate too low would deter investment and reduce employment and output because part of the return required to induce investment would be taxed, and short-term gains in revenue would probably be followed by long-term losses.

The appropriate threshold rate may vary between investors, investments and different phases of a project, so a different rate or set of rates would be required for each project. Detailed knowledge of the probability distribution of investment outcomes and of investors' attitudes to risk and other factors affecting the supply price of capital would be necessary to set the rates in each case. This would be further complicated by the fact that investors' identities would not be known before exploration. Unless threshold rates were set before exploration began, uncertainty would increase and investment be discouraged. Clearly a single threshold rate would not be appropriate for all projects and types of investment. On the other hand, the amount of information required to tailor the threshold to each case means that setting of project- and investment-specific thresholds would be impracticable.

Selection of appropriate threshold and royalty rates will also be difficult because the royalty and threshold rates are interrelated. This results from the tendency of these schemes to skew the frequency distribution of net present values negatively, thereby raising the appropriate threshold rate of return. Adjustment of the royalty and/or threshold rate is required to minimise this distortionary effect. In addition, there is the unresolved theoretical issue of how to calculate the threshold rate of return when resource rent tax is applied before company income tax. It is clear that the relevant concept is the cost of capital, but despite considerable debate among economists concerning the cost of capital over the past decade, the matter has not yet been resolved.[5]

Like a pure economic profits royalty system, a resource rent royalty scheme at very high rates would damage the incentive for efficient management. The incentive to realise the net value of minerals would be blunted and the incentive for ill-advised and wasteful expenditure enhanced. Projects covered by resource rent tax systems with very high rates might appear relatively unattractive to efficient firms but quite attractive to inefficient enterprises.

Another argument against a resource rent tax scheme relates to the progressive system (multiple royalty and threshold rates). It is generally considered that such a system is more likely to damage incentives for efficient management than a proportional system (a single rate of tax) because of the higher marginal tax rate. Moreover, a progressive system is more likely to discourage risk taking if deductions for unsuccessful exploration expenditures are associated only with the lower tax rate while high returns are taxed at a higher rate. Such lack of symmetry would skew the probability distribution of outcomes negatively and discourage exploration. It has been argued that a progressive system could be tailored to reduce the practical importance of the inevitable distortions arising from the impossibility of setting a single threshold that is exactly right for all investment.[6] However, it is not clear precisely how this would be done.

A resource rent tax scheme would perform like the pure economic profits system with respect to both the total quantity of minerals recovered and the rate of recovery.

Clearly, a resource rent tax system is not neutral towards investment decisions, but if skilfully applied it will distort incentives to invest and explore much less than conventional ad valorem, sliding-scale ad valorem and accounting profits royalties, particularly at high rates. In the long term, therefore, it will affect the tax base less and be a superior source of revenue.

On the grounds of economic efficiency and long-term revenue a resource rent royalty is inferior to a pure economic profits system because it distorts incentives to explore and invest to a greater extent. Moreover, the revenue base of the resource rent tax is smaller to the extent that the supply price of capital increases (that is, increments of capital are available only at successively higher costs). Setting the threshold rate at the marginal supply price of capital to encourage supply of higher priced capital allows a significant amount of net value to escape from the royalty base, because for many investments the threshold rate of return allowed before royalty applies is higher than the actual supply price of capital. Of course, if the (lower) resource rent tax threshold is kept down to ensure that full net value is included in the royalty base, the royalty falls partly on target rates of return, and therefore investment is discouraged and the long-term royalty base eroded. In contrast, a pure economic profits royalty would automatically include the full net value in the royalty base.

With a resource rent tax system, tax or royalty is not payable until outlays on exploration and investments have been recovered with interest at the threshold rate(s) of return, and some years may elapse before tax or royalty is payable by a project. Morever, subsequent investments can reduce or eliminate the royalty liability of individual mines from time to time. This characteristic of resource rent tax may give rise to political and budgetary concerns for governments, especially if mineral revenues are large relative to total government revenues and the resource rent tax applies to only a small number of projects.

The revenue yield of a resource rent tax is likely to be less stable than that of an accounting profits royalty, for two reasons. First, the existence of thresholds will add to volatility, and the presence of more than one threshold and tax rate would tend to accentuate this. Second, the immediate deductibility of exploration and other investment could cause revenues to fluctuate significantly between years.

A resource rent tax would involve similar administrative problems to those of a pure economic profits royalty or an accounting profits royalty. In addition, the higher rates necessary to derive adequate revenue from a resource rent royalty would lead to more administrative difficulties than are entailed in an accounting profits system, as in the case of a pure economic profits tax. In other respects, administration and compliance problems will differ.

Carrying forward undeducted costs with interest in the case of a resource rent tax is more complex and would probably cost more to administer, and to comply with, than the facility of the pure economic profits tax to offset losses fully. On the other hand, it is likely to involve lower administrative and compliance costs than the conventional depreciation methods that would apply under an accounting profits tax. The overall administrative costs of a resource rent tax are likely to be lower than those of an accounting profits system and higher than those of a pure economic profits system. While the administrative costs of a resource rent tax will be higher than those of an ad valorem or specific royalty, these costs need to be considered in the context of the higher long-term revenue yields from a resource rent tax. These will outweigh the extra administrative costs by a very substantial margin at high rates of tax/royalty.

A Neglected Issue: The Effects of Tenure Policy on the Allocation of Resources and Royalty/Tax Revenue

Most discussions of mining taxation policy have implicitly assumed that the underlying tenement system is allocationally neutral and has no effect on the yield of mining taxation arrangements. Notable exceptions are Gaffney's classic contribution on the economics of mining taxation; the *Green Paper on Mining Royalty Policy for the Northern Territory*; and a paper by Nellor et al that was prompted by the *Green Paper*.[7]

The conditional first-come-first-served and work-program bidding systems that have traditionally been used in Australia and many other parts of the world to allocate tenements can adversely affect the allocation of resources and the yield of profits-based royalty and tax systems. For example, Commonwealth income tax yield may be reduced by the operation of State and Commonwealth tenement systems, and Commonwealth resource rent tax on offshore petroleum could be reduced as a result of a work-program bidding system established under Commonwealth legislation. The conditional first-come-first-served and work-program bidding systems are analysed below, along with lump-sum (cash bonus) bidding, which has been used extensively in some parts of the United States and Canada to allocate petroleum tenements.

Lump-sum bidding has been proposed by some Australian economists as a substitute for all other types of royalty and de facto royalty systems.[8] It has been advocated as part of a combined system with a resource rent royalty by other economists.[9] The Australian government has proposed that such a combined system be applied to offshore petroleum.[10] Swan has suggested that it would be preferable to combine lump-sum bidding with an economic profits royalty.[11]

Conditional first-come-first-served system

In the Australian States and the Northern Territory, exploration licences are usually allocated on a first-come-first-served, subject to a commitment to undertake an exploration program considered satisfactory by the administering authority, and to a fixed period with compulsory relinquishment of portions of land over time. Security of tenure is dependent initially on compliance with the work-program and relinquishment provisions, and ultimately on discovery of an ore body.

The suitability of the program is generally assessed by the authority on the basis of such criteria as quality, quantity and timing of proposed exploration work, financial capacity, expertise available to the applicant and past performance; that is, tenements are allocated on the basis of administrative discretion rather than market forces. When conflicting applications are received, a choice is usually made on the same criteria as are used to assess a single application. Here the traditional method of allocating exploration licences takes on the character of work-program bidding.

Clearly the system does not provide secure tenure during the exploration and discovery phase of a venture, and this insecurity distorts the allocation of resources in three ways. First, uncertainty is increased, which discourages exploration to some extent. Second, the system indues preemptive exploration, which distorts the timing of exploration expenditures Third, certain conditions attaching to tenure may make marginal exploration prospects unworthy of attention.

The case of perfectly secure tenure before as well as during the development phase provides a benchmark for evaluation of the conditional first-come-first-served system in relation to the timing of exploration expenditure. A firm would wish to keep exploration and discovery outlays to a minimum, and to incur them as late as possible without jeopardising the ideal time for commencement of mining. This would eliminate avoidable expenditures such as interest on earlier exploration outlays and maximise the economic rent realisable from exploiting the deposit, which would be the best possible result for society as well as for the firm.

The ideal timing of exploration can rarely be achieved in practice because of uncertainty about the results of exploration. Nevertheless, given perfectly secure tenure it will always be in the firm's commercial interests to approach the ideal as closely as possible. The less uncertainty, the more closely the firm can approach the ideal timing—the more knowledge there is about an area and the more attractive it appears, the more accurately a firm can anticipate the best timing. But under a conditional first-come-first-served system an enterprise can obtain only temporary and conditional tenure over suspected mineral-bearing lands. The licence holder will realise that if exploration in compliance with the covenants is undertaken and deposits are discovered, the enterprise's chances of holding on to the deposits are greatly enhanced.

If an area is highly prospective, so that the expected economic rent of minerals is high but only a low to moderate proportion of this is likely to be captured by royalties, the expected rewards for exploration are high relative to the returns available from alternative uses of capital. In these circumstances, under a conditional first-come-first-served system there is powerful pressure on the firm to preempt the potential resource by acquiring exploration rights as soon as possible. The firm is then forced to explore in order to retain title, regardless of its commercial judgment about the most efficient timing of activity. In theory, a firm can begin preemptive exploration as soon as the expected discovery value of a target exceeds the exploration and discovery costs. Preemptive exploration reduces the potential economic rent from the resource through interest forgone on early exploration outlays. If preemptive exploration did take place as soon as expected discovery value exceeded exploration and discovery costs, the entire economic rent of minerals in the tenement would be dissipated.[12] In highly prospective areas, these economic efficiency losses will be high.

Moreover, in highly prospective areas firms will effectively be competing with other applicants on the basis of work program. Then the conditional first-come-first-served system takes on the character of work-program bidding. The analysis below of the latter system indicates that this would reinforce the reduction in the realisable economic rent of the resources.

If royalty and tax arrangements are likely to capture most of the potential economic rent, the incentive the tenement allocation system provides to misallocate resources is greatly weakened. In these circumstances the economic efficiency costs described above will be low. However, to the extent that the royalty/tax system exempts returns to exploration investments, the incentive to misallocate resources tends to be preserved and the revenue base destroyed. To varying extents such returns are excluded from the tax base by a pure economic profits system, a resource rent system, and the mining/petroleum company income tax and any accounting profits system that treats exploration similarly. A pure economic profits system and a resource rent tax system with full exploration loss offsets excludes them completely by providing subsidies calculated at the royalty rate for exploration outlays in the period during which they are incurred. The resource rent tax proposal, which allows exploration outlays to be carried forward at the threshold rate of return until they can be deducted from positive cash flows, is less effective in excluding returns to exploration capital from the tax base. Accounting profits taxes and royalties exempt such returns only to the extent that sufficient income is available for immediate expensing of exploration outlays. The effect of these various arrangements is that firms can advance exploration outlays to establish secure tenure with zero or limited royalty/tax penalties.

Conventional revenue- and tonnage-based royalties that disregard costs would avoid the tendency to preserve the resource misallocation and revenue base dissipation arising from the conditional first-come-first-served system if the rates of royalty could be set high enough to capture the potential economic rent. However, the other severe distortions caused by revenue- and tonnage-based systems at high rates of royalty mean that rates must be kept low or moderate.

When an area is not particularly attractive from the exploration viewpoint, the incentive to misallocate resources through preemptive exploration is greatly weakened. However, the conditional first-come-first-served system distorts resource allocation in other ways in these areas. If work or expenditure covenants inserted in exploration licences by the administering authority are too demanding, firms may be discouraged from taking out or renewing exploration licences in marginal areas. This could be partly overcome if the administering authority could set covenants in line with the prospectivity of each area. However, if covenants were to be set with an appropriate degree of sensitivity, significant administrative resources would be required. Compulsory relinquishment of proportions of land under exploration licences, at rates determined by the administering authority, can also discourage exploration of marginal areas that are sacrificed in order to hold more promising ground. To overcome this problem, relinquishment arrangements would need to be sensitive to the varying degrees of attractiveness of different areas. Once again, this would be virtually impossible to achieve with a scheme relying on administrative discretion.

It is clear that expenditure covenants and methods of inducing or forcing relinquishment that rely on administrative discretion are likely to have adverse effects on the allocation of resources to exploration in the case of less attractive areas. Since marginal areas *ex ante* can become above-marginal areas *ex post*, royalty/tax revenue also can be lost.

In view of the popularity of the conditional first-come-first-served system among government administering authorities in Australia, it must be asked whether it has any positive economic features.

Its only economic advantage is a propensity to correct inefficiencies arising from external economies produced by exploration. When a firm undertakes detailed exploration, its results provide valuable free information to other explorers, but a firm will ignore these benefits when formulating its exploration program. Moreover, firms may tend to wait for others to explore adjacent areas before committing their own funds, and exploration expenditures may therefore be smaller and incurred later than is socially the best. A conditional first-come-first-served system that increased exploration and advanced the timing of exploration outlays would tend to offset this inefficiency.

In highly prospective areas this advantage is likely to be overwhelmed by the inefficiencies and revenue losses arising from preemptive exploration. In relatively unattractive areas the advantages (in terms of correcting externalities) of a conditional first-come-first-served system are likely to be greater than in highly prospective areas and the disadvantages are likely to be less. Thus it is not clear whether or not there is a significant case against the conditional first-come-first-served system on the grounds of economic efficiency for relatively unattractive lands.

A conditional first-come-first-served system is costly to administer because of the numerous conditions of tenure and the significant level of administrative discretion involved. There are no real winners under this system, apart from the suppliers of goods and services used in exploration and the public servants who benefit because a larger bureaucracy is needed than under a tenement allocation system relying solely on market forces.

Work-program bidding

In the past, work-program bidding has been used to allocate offshore petroleum tenements, and in some cases onshore petroleum and mineral tenements. Work-program bidding combines elements of a market system (in that programs are submitted competitively) with considerable administrative discretion (in that applications must be assessed by multiple criteria and in that enforcement creates problems).

Under a work-program bidding system, areas available for exploration are divided into separate tracts and explorers are invited to submit applications detailing intended work programs and technical and financial capabilities. Applications are assessed by the same criteria as applications under the first-come-first-served system, and tenements are generally allocated to the proponent of the program judged to be 'the best'. Conditions as to terms of tenements and gradual relinquishment of area are also applied.

If retention of tenure after allocation is strictly conditional on adherence to work bids, and if those administering a work-program bidding system place great weight on the quantity of work offered, bidders will attempt to estimate how much they can promise to spend on exploration and still expect to cover the minimum required rate of return on capital. Clearly, the present value of the expected economic rent from the tract could be diverted to the work program without bringing the expected rate of return below the required minimum.

An applicant will be willing to offer 'gold-plated' programs and/or more intensive activity on the tract than is necessary for development in order to capture the tract and the associated economic rents. Consequently, this system tends to dissipate the potential economic rent from mining, thus reducing the value of the resource to both the community and the miner. A large proportion of the royalty/tax base under profits-related royalty or tax arrangements would be destroyed because the cost of the additional capital and labour diverted to the tract to capture the economic rent will be included in deductible costs in the royalty/tax calculation.

If administering authorities place great weight on particular types of exploration or on early exploration when assessing programs, firms will be encouraged to change the proposed content and timing of programs from that which would accord with their commercial judgments and maximise the value to the community of the resource development. These distortions lead to inefficient use of resources, and will be manifested in partial or total dissipation of the economic rent and a consequent reduction of profits-related tax or royalty bases. Such alterations to the content of programs dissipates economic rent and revenue from a profits-based tax or royalty by increasing costs. The greater the expected net present value of minerals in an area, the more willing the explorer will be to change the content of his program in order to capture the title.

Inducing early exploration extends the period between exploration and development and thereby increases the interest forgone on exploration outlays. This reduces the realised economic rent and the size of profits tax and royalty bases that permit immediate exploration expenditure write-off. If the expected net present value of minerals in an area is high, there is a strong incentive to undertake to explore before the most efficient time in order to capture title. In theory, a firm could be induced to start preemptive exploration as soon as expected discovery value exceeded expected discovery-oriented exploration costs, and the revenue from a profits tax or royalty with immediate exploration expenditure write-off provisions would be entirely dissipated.

It is sometimes argued that the tendency of the work-program bidding system (and of the conditional first-come-first-served system) to induce earlier than normal exploration outlays is a good thing because it results in earlier development of resources. However, earlier exploration does not mean earlier development. After all, it is well known that prematurely discovered resources can remain undeveloped for years, sometimes for decades. Given secure post-discovery tenure, a rational firm will not wish to exploit a deposit until the net value of the resource stops rising more rapidly than the relevant discount rate. This is commercially and socially the best possible timing, and it will not be altered by forcing earlier exploration.

The only favourable resource allocation effect of a work-program bidding system is a tendency to offset the inefficiencies arising from the external economies produced by exploration, which were discussed earlier. However, this advantage will be swamped by the disadvantages arising from dissipation of the economic rent, particularly in highly prospective areas. In general, the inefficiencies and associated revenue losses caused by the work-program bidding system will be more substantial in highly prospective areas than in less attractive areas, simply because the potential economic rent that is translated into a subsidy on more, earlier or differently structured exploration and development is higher in the case of highly prospective areas.

If areas allocated through work-program bidding turn out to be less attractive than anticipated, enforcement of work programs can render them uneconomic and development will not proceed. This is because, when an area falls short of expectations held when the program was formulated, the costs of the additional or different work offered to win the area may no longer be sustainable and may cause the return to the investment to fall short of the minimum required rate. In these circumstances, taxes or royalties will be lost.

The work-program bidding system is likely to make individuals in the States and mining firms worse off than they would otherwise be, since by dissipating the economic rent from mining it reduces the flow of benefits to both groups. As with a conditional first-come-first-served system, those who gain are the suppliers of goods and services and the public servants who benefit from the need for a larger bureaucracy.

Maintaining the credibility of a work bidding system requires a strong commitment to the enforcement of work programs. Without effective enforcement, work-program bidding would become a method of allocating tenements to those who make the most unrealistic or dishonest promises.

The administering authority needs to be able to evaluate in advance who is bidding realistically and who is not, otherwise the overoptimistic or dishonest bidders win and the realistic or honest bidders lose prime tracts. The necessary vetting system is likely to be very costly to administer. However, the more effective the enforcement, the higher the losses of efficiency and revenue. Commitments to work programs have been difficult to enforce. Overly ambitious programs have been offered to obtain tenure, and firms have subsequently walked away when the areas did not live up to expectations. Often, programs have not been enforced in order to avoid abandonment of the area by the explorer. Bidders usually have very plausible arguments to support requests not to be held to their promises, but acceptance of these arguments undermines the credibility of the system as a method of allocating tenements. Work commitments can be enforced only as long as the expected net present value of an area exceeds the present value of the outstanding commitments. Beyond that point, enforcement partly or totally dissipates the economic rent from a profits-based tax or royalty.

Lump-sum bidding

Under a lump-sum bidding system tenements are allocated through the market mechanism. Another feature of this system is that tracts are granted relatively free of conditions, thus providing significant security of tenure. Private sector experts estimate what an area is worth and bid accordingly. Tenements are allocated on the basis of the size of cash payments offered. This system eliminates the strong element of administrative arbitrariness that characterises the conditional first-come-first-served and work-program bidding systems.

For many years lump-sum bidding has been used extensively in parts of the United States and Canada to allocate rights to explore for and extract oil and gas. Since 1976 coal tenements on United States federal lands have been allocated only by lump-sum bidding, and this has so far been the only method of allocating oil shale tenements in the United States.

The level and timing of exploration, development and mining activity will be solely dependent on commercial factors. Lump-sum bidding does not distort exploration, mine development or operating decisions relative to the ideal, because these decisions will be independent of the successful bid and will not determine whether or not secure tenure is obtained. Nevertheless, payment of a lump-sum to secure a tenement ensures a strong psychological commitment to the land through sunk costs attuned to the expected value of the area.

Of course, to the extent that a lump-sum bidding system is modified by administrative interference to provide for short tenement terms, minimum work programs, relinquishment of portions of the tenement, and so on, the modified system will tend to involve the same economic efficiency costs as are associated with the conditional first-come-first-served system.

A basic idea underlying lump-sum bidding is that, in general, firms with superior overall combinations of skills and other resources will submit the highest bids. This is desirable from society's viewpoint, since it means that the land will be explored and developed in a way that uses resources efficiently.

Lump-sum bidding is more than a method of allocating tenements. It is also a flexible means of capturing what the industry is prepared to pay for the right to explore and mine. Unlike royalty systems, however, its base is the expected net value of minerals *in advance* of discovery and mine development, rather than some concept of realised value. Given perfect competition and perfect knowledge of the potential value of mineral-bearing lands, the successful lump-sum bid will be equivalent to the present realised net value of minerals. In reality, the winning bid will fall short of this figure to an extent depending on the impediments to competition, on risk and uncertainty, and on the inadequacy of risk-sharing devices. The effectiveness of lump-sum bidding as a tenement allocation system will also depend on these factors. However, they are not sufficiently important to cause the rejection of lump-sum bidding in favour of another system, particularly when certain modifications are made.

In relation to impediments to competition, analyses of experience in the United States (where lump-sum bidding has been used for many years) indicate that competition for tenements has been strong enough to protect the public interest.[13] There is little doubt that competition in Australia would be strong in highly prospective areas and would weaken with declining prospectivity. If there is concern that competition could be adversely affected because lump-sum bids constitute a barrier to entry for small firms, allowing joint bidding by small firms would improve the situation. Use of sealed rather than oral bidding would help to combat collusive practices, stimulate a competitive environment and encourage firms to make their maximum bids. Setting minimum bids, reserving the right to reject any or all bids and excluding large firms from joint bidding with other large firms would also help to prevent collusive arrangements.

The influence of risk and uncertainty on the effectiveness and revenue yield of lump-sum bidding requires a little more explanation. A background sketch of the significance of risk and uncertainty for efficient resource allocation is presented below, along with a brief discussion of the implications of this for policy on lump-sum bidding and royalty arrangements.

In the absence of perfect and complete contingency claim markets, risk taking is likely to be less than is desirable on the grounds of economic efficiency. For the mining sector, aversion to risk is likely to be reflected in reduced exploration and mining investment. Nevertheless, a wide and imaginative range of market-type risk-sharing arrangements has evolved within the private sector and between the private and public sectors in partial compensation for the lack of formal contingency claims markets. The availability of such arrangements substantially corrects the socially deficient level of risk taking.

The presence of risk and uncertainty does not mean that lump-sum bidding is less effective than the conditional first-come-first-served or work-program bidding systems in allocating tenements, because those systems must also operate under this constraint. Great risk and uncertainty would, of course, be reflected in low bids, but firms with favourable geological expertise should be better placed to win the area than others. However, it should be remembered that lump-sum bidding provides much greater security of tenure than any other tenement allocation system. In addition, lump-sum bidding may be varied in a number of ways to allow greater risk sharing and consequent inducement to further risk taking. Joint bidding permits risk sharing within the private sector, which is highly desirable for small firms without the resources to spread risk internally over a wide range of activities.

If lump-sum bidding is used as a complete substitute for royalty as well as a tenement allocation system, mining firms have to bear all the risks associated with exploration, development and extraction. Because they are generally risk-averse, the expected value to government (after allowing for risk to government) of revenue can be increased if the government allows some risk sharing with industry. This can be achieved by combining a lump-sum bidding system with a normal royalty, because payment of a royalty is conditional upon the discovery of deposits and upon certain characteristics of any subsequent mining operation. The degree of risk sharing depends on the level of the royalty rate and the nature of the royalty system.

Combined lump-sum bidding and royalty system

A combination of lump-sum bidding with a high royalty rate entails more risk sharing than a combination with a low royalty rate, because the up-front, lump-sum component of the government take will be less in the former case. Specific and ad valorem systems entail the least risk sharing, while profits-based royalties share risks to a much greater extent because the amount of royalty is conditional on both prices and costs. An accounting profits royalty will share risks less than a resource rent royalty, which in turn allows less risk sharing than a pure economic profits royalty.

Governments are likely to be risk-averse, and those in Australia have shown little inclination to go beyond profits-based royalties and undertake exploration and mining themselves. In fact they have shown little interest in sharing risks even as much as a pure economic profits royalty system does. It follows that the arrangement that maximises the expected utility of State government revenue is likely to lie between (but not include) the extremes represented by a lump-sum bidding system alone and an economic profits royalty with perfect tenure other than lump-sum bidding.

Considerations of resource allocation and administration favour a lump-sum bidding system on its own because of its non-distorting nature and its low administration costs. Government concerns about the revenue adequacy of lump-sum bidding alone, and company concerns about the dissatisfaction of governments with *ex ante* payments only when realised returns exceed expected returns, favour relying solely on a royalty/tax regime. On the basis of the analysis of alternative royalty arrangements elsewhere in this chapter, it can be deducted that the best trade-off between revenue, resource allocation and administration considerations is a system combining lump-sum bidding and a resource rent royalty. Unfortunately, the best mix of lump-sum bidding and resource rent royalty, which will be determined by the royalty and threshold rates, cannot be identified precisely, because it is not clear whether mining companies or governments are likely to be more risk-averse; because the relative abilities of mining companies and governments to spread risks are unclear; and because the extent of the resource misallocation caused by a resource rent royalty, which in turn affects the long-term royalty base, is difficult to quantify. These conclusions are similar to those of Emerson and Lloyd.[14] They are also consistent with the pioneering work of Leland on combined lump-sum bidding and royalty arrangements.[15]

Lump-sum bidding in combination with a resource rent royalty is superior on the grounds of revenue/equity, economic efficiency and administrative efficiency to either a conditional first-come-first-served or a work-program bidding system with the same royalty system. In highly prospective areas, this superiority is substantial. The following reasons may be adduced for the superiority of a combined lump-sum bidding and resource rent royalty arrangement.

In the first place, lump-sum bidding supplements royalty revenue, particularly in highly prospective areas where the potential economic rent is likely to be well in excess of general royalty liability. Second, it does not adversely affect decisions to explore, invest and extract, thus enhancing the long-term royalty base. Third, it corrects the problem of severe dissipation of the royalty base that is likely to arise in highly prospective areas under tenement allocation systems relying on administrative discretion. Fourth, it allows the royalty rate to be kept moderate, which maintains distortions at more tolerable levels while ensuring that the overall government take is attuned to what the industry is prepared to pay. Fifth, as knowledge of the geology and potential of an area increases and interest in it improves, bids are likely to move closer to the realisable economic surplus from minerals minus royalty, this improving the flow of benefits to the people of the relevant jurisdiction over time. Sixth, a lump-sum bidding system is a very simple method of allocating tenements. Since it uses market forces rather than administrative discretion, it involves much lower administration costs than conditional first-come-first-served and work-program bidding systems. Seventh, a combined lump-sum bidding and resource rent royalty system is likely to reduce the risk that the government will impose additional charges if an area attracting low lump-sum bids subsequently produces a bonanza. Conversely, a combined system protects the government from unduly low returns from such an area without the necessity of changing the rules of the game after the event. (Of course, it must be remembered that conditional first-come-first-served and work-program bidding systems are also susceptible to government changes in the rules after substantial discoveries are made.)

In relatively unattractive areas, the advantages of lump-sum bidding in combination with a resource rent royalty over a conditional first-come-first-served system in conjunction with a resource rent royalty may not be significant. This is because bids for such areas will probably be small and the problems of economic efficiency and erosion of the royalty base associated with the conditional first-come-first-served system are not likely to be severe.

There is no mining taxation scheme in Australia, existing or proposed, that is superior to all others in terms of the criteria of equity/revenue, economic efficiency, economic development, administrative efficiency and revenue stability. While the traditional specific and ad valorem royalty systems have administrative advantages and produce less volatile revenue flows than systems based on accounting profits, pure economic profits and resource rent royalty tax, it is argued that this is outweighed by the equity/revenue and economic efficiency advantages of the various profit-related systems at moderate and high rates of royalty/tax.

Among the profit-related systems the ranking from best to worst in terms of minimising both distortions and administrative costs is a pure economic profits royalty, a resource rent royalty and an accounting profits royalty. In terms of revenue stability considerations, the order is reversed.

It has been demonstrated that mining taxation policy is closely related to tenement allocation policy. Indeed, it has been shown that, in highly prospective areas, the existing conditional first-come-first-served and work-program bidding systems could greatly undermine the extent of the equity/revenue and efficiency advantages of profits-related systems over ad valorem and specific systems. The introduction of lump-sum bidding in combination with profits-related royalty/tax systems would correct this position and avoid the distortions arising from the very high rates of royalty/tax that might be set to achieve ambitious equity/revenue objectives. In relatively unattractive areas, however, the advantages of lump-sum bidding over the existing systems of allocating tenements are unlikely to be significant.

The pressure of evidence is towards the view that the best—possibly the only —starting point for useful reform of mining taxation in Australia is the creation of efficient and acceptable mechanisms for consultation and cooperation between Commonwealth and State governments regarding royalty/taxation and tenement allocation systems. Proper resource taxation reform would need to be undertaken within the broader context of reform of the Australian taxation system as a whole and revision of the assignment of taxation responsibilities between the Commonwealth and State governments.

7 The mining industry in the federal system

JOHN D.S. MACLEOD

This chapter sets out to document the extensive series of trade-offs that are negotiated between mineral resource companies and all three levels of government in Australia—trade-offs that have not always been readily apparent to observers of the significant growth of this sector of the economy over the past couple of decades. The reasons for this obscurity are many: the scattered nature of the industry, far from the major cities; a necessary degree of confidentiality between government and developer; and the diversion of attention to aspects thought to be of greater importance. It is hoped that a more balanced view of the developments may be obtained by outlining the range and importance of these trade-offs.

The principal aim is to emphasise that the States play an active role in encouraging resource developments and maximising the benefits they provide. In particular, the role of new mineral projects as catalysts for other local and State developments is stressed. In this regard the States (and, to a lesser extent, local governments) share the resources generated by the industry. The various ways in which this has been achieved have changed markedly over the past twenty years, and this chapter attempts to describe some of these changes.

It is clear that mining has been unique in many ways, but the reasons for this uniqueness are not always so obvious. It is not the intention, however, to question existing practices, nor to put forward alternative (perhaps more efficient) methods of achieving these ends. The evidence shows that 'bootstrap development' is, as it has always been, a successful strategy in Australia (The term 'bootstrap development' is derived from the metaphor 'to haul oneself up by the bootstraps'. It suggests a process that is self-starting and generates its own impetus.)

When the interaction between governments and the mining industry in Australia is examined, the balance of evidence lies heavily with the interventionist functions of governments. Their contributions to the industry are also documented here so that readers may form their own judgments.

At the outset it is important to be clear in the use of the term 'mining'. The strict lexical meaning, as defined and used by the Australian Bureau of Statistics, is very narrow: the physical digging up or quarrying of resources from the earth. This is a restrictive definition, and for the purposes of this paper 'mining' covers not only the extractive process but the dedicated transportation of resources, refining and smelting, research and development, the exploration industry and, where it is an integral part of the operation, the social and industrial infrastructure.

Mining is one of Australia's oldest industries: we were exporting coal years before we exported wool. The industry's turbulent history, therefore, covers a period before federation and a major growth period in the 1960s and 1970s which fundamentally altered its structure and orientation. Many in the industry think longingly of the days before federation—the flow-on effects of the profits generated from Ballarat, Bendigo, Kalgoorlie and the fabulous Broken Hill fields are widely recounted. Those approaches contrast markedly with the current views, which start with the assumption that governments can spend these resources more wisely and effectively than can shareholders or other stakeholders (such as employees or suppliers). Some even quote the pre-federation claim that the taxes required to finance a federal system would be equivalent per capita to a dog licence fee. Some dog and what licence! We might indeed wonder at the number of licences alone.

Looking back over the history of the industry, an economist would observe some recurrent features—some good, others perhaps not quite so obviously positive. Most outstanding have been the periods of intense activity and stimulus to development, associated with heavy inflows of capital—and of personnel in the early stages—and marked disruption requiring painful adjustment in much of the rest of the economy. Mining has, of necessity, been an outward-looking, internationally competitive industry marked by its independence of so-called government 'support'. Its irregular surges of development have heightened speculative investment interest in Australia, frequently leading to excesses. The flow of earnings from the industry has nurtured many new industries in other sectors of the economy, and it is important to recognise that these range from the very largest (steel and oil) down to the smallest family corner shops.

From its inception, and particularly in the early gold period, the popular image of mining has been of an industry generating large profits, and hence it has attracted all three levels of cash-starved governments. At its most primitive stage this derived from the role of government as an issuer of title to a mining property. The security arising from the title remains an essential factor in the high-risk exploration sector of the industry. Upon this base the feudal concept of royalties, or payment to the Crown for the material extracted, was constructed.

In examining the implications of the federal system for the industry, it is convenient to divide the subject into three phases: exploration, mining, and refining and processing.

Exploration

This is the front end or high-risk end of the industry. In a business where every ore body has a limited life, successful exploration in new areas and exploration of the ore body as it is mined determine how, and for how long, the miner stays in business. This gives exploration activity a cutting edge unique to the industry—the amount of unsuccessful expenditure and the long gestation periods (for example, Mt Isa) are especially notable aspects. As in other industries, it is essential to remain at the forefront of technological development, but it is also necessary to find replacement economic ore bodies. This represents a double research and development effort.

The high-cost, high-risk nature of mineral exploration and mineral development in Australia is seldom appreciated by those outside the industry, including economists. Barriers to entry are very low, so that the industry includes sole operators with minimal capital resources right through to the largest companies with exploration budgets which would make many non-mining managements cautious. Consider, for example, the private mining exploration expenditure in 1981/82 of $A600 million and compare that with the total private research and development expenditure in the same year of $288 million (some $50 million or more of which is mining).

Another way of looking at the risk aspect has been documented in the forthcoming work of Mackenzie and Bilodeau,[1] who estimate that the average cost of discovering an economic metal deposit in Australia in the period from 1955 to 1978 was $38 million (expressed in 1980 dollars), and that to be 90 per cent certain of making an economic discovery the explorer must be prepared to spend $87 million. In 1983 terms this is about equivalent to the market capitalisation of the ninetieth largest company listed on Australian exchanges (a business the size of Clyde Industries or Pioneer Sugar).

Another feature, an unusual one for Australia, is the technological leadership and world-scale resources employed. Advances in the techniques of exploration by satellite are but one example of the position at the very frontier of technology occupied by the Australian industry.

The exploration phase of the industry is very much a State rather than a federal matter. Even foreign investment guidelines tend to be different for exploration investment, thus maximising exploration effort in Australia. But it is in the State sphere that the first example of differences between State and national priorities occurs—to many, of course, State interest is synonymous with national interest.

One aspect of federal taxation relating to exploration is important in connection with barriers to entry: the fact that mineral exploration expenditure may only be offset against mining income (*not* against dividends) for company tax purposes. This favours existing mines but, as has been amply demonstrated over the past couple of decades, is not an insuperable barrier.

The part played by the States through their mines departments should be emphasised. Grassroots exploration, in the main, is a neutral stage of government control: most Australian States place a high value on exploration (whether by the individual prospector or the large company) as a means of outlining the mineral resources of the State. This earliest phase confines the public sector's role to title issuance and record keeping and sorting out rival claims, plus a number of work commitments designed to maximise exploration effort. This statement is not intended to play down the importance of the contribution of mines departments—the maintenance of detailed historical and geological records, for example, is of great importance to the exploration industry.

The States employ a wide variety of ways to influence exploration in accordance with government policy. Some examples of this diversity are:

1 restrictions on the amount of land that may be held under exploration title;
2 relinquishment requirements;
3 expenditure commitments ($x per km^2, with a minimum sum specified);
4 refusal to issue titles for the minerals where it is policy to discourage exploration (for example, uranium and brown coal);
5 reservation of areas for small-scale explorers (for example, Coober Pedy and the Western Australian goldfields);
6 developmental conditions to be entered into (these may be just those covered by the general law, or, at the other end of the spectrum and in relation to major discoveries, as in Western Australia, may require a State agreement);
7 land rights or land reservation;
8 access rights (for example, for farmers in New South Wales and Western Australia).

Once an ore body (economic or otherwise) has been discovered (even in its most preliminary form), the role of the States changes dramatically as the possibility of a new development, whether large or small, begins to attract political attention.

Public sector involvement in these two phases of exploration varies, especially in regard to net expenditure, but in general it may be described as minimal. One exception that should be noted is direct exploration expenditure by the States—coal in New South Wales is an example—but the total sums involved are fairly small. Much has been made in federal budget documents, for example, of the 'aid' to the industry of the activities of the Bureau of Mineral Resources—mapping is frequently quoted as an essential input to exploration—strangely, more obvious 'aid' functions to other sectors, such as the various agriculture, manufacturing, transport and labour economics bureaus in Canberra, are not described as 'industry assistance' to the relevant industries.

But the key field of State preeminence is the issuance of title and the maintenance of a well-understood system that ensures the security and sanctity of continuing title. The federal government, except in the territories, plays a negligible role in this. Few explorers, whether on a large or a small scale, are prepared to risk large front-end exploration expenditure unless the rules of title are clearly understood and are seen to stand the test of time at the outset. In particular, the explorer wants to be assured of the right to develop any discovery he may make. It needs to be appreciated that this security of title must also be seen to extend well into the future to provide time for the proving, feasibility, and research and development (if necessary) of the particular ore body. This latter phase can, and frequently does, require a minimum period of ten years.

One procedure much favoured in economic literature is the auction system of granting leases—either for territory as yet unexplored or, in a few coal examples, where preliminary geological exploration has been completed at State expense. Australian experience of such auctions requires further proving: at present there are too few examples of successful tenderers actually proceeding to profitable production, nor is there enough evidence that government would abide by such auction agreements in the event that the area proved especially valuable.

When the exploration moves into its final proving-up stage, State and then federal policy issues come to the fore, and the lengthy process of negotiation to determine how the rents are to be distributed begins. As a rule it is only at this stage that potential terms and conditions of mining licences become known. The overriding sovereignty of the State as the owner issuing rights to mine must not be overlooked, nor should the States be seen as either passive in this phase or driven solely by rational economic motives. It is here that the regional, social, economic and environmental ambitions of individual States first appear and the Commonwealth begins to be involved. The tough terms and conditions imposed by States in renewing exploration permits or granting licences to mine need to be understood.

A whole host of other federal–State issues arises in the exploration phase: examples are environmental provisions, Aboriginal rights, national parks, and exploration areas that straddle State borders.

Mining

After exploration has delineated a body of ore, the State and to a lesser extent the federal authorities become active in the negotiations about development. The terms agreed need to be outlined before worthwhile feasibility studies can be made. In most cases, and contrary to the assumptions of many, it is rare for a project to be an obvious bonanza, so that the decision to mine or not to mine can depend to a considerable extent upon the outcome of these negotiations.

At this stage the development, if it is of any size, becomes highly politicised and trade-offs begin between economic efficiency and political objectives. Politicians, driven by a desire to be re-elected, begin to associate 'development', especially if it is a remote location, with progress, job creation and so on, and start to assume a high profile. This applies to government and opposition parties alike, with no obvious difference between political parties. Local government also plays a significant role in this process, since local ambitions are often more keenly honed than State or federal aspirations. A local football field or contributions to regional roads (whether used by developers or not) have become minimum demands.

The negotiations concern the right to mine the body of ore and the terms and conditions applying to that right. Questions must be resolved concerning the scale, location, methodology and timing of the mining operations, as well as such matters as the royalty arrangements and other taxation issues, further processing and local purchasing obligations, who provides the social and industrial infrastructure and at what cost, and what the social and environmental impacts are likely to be. At the federal level negotiations will need to cover the Foreign Investment Review Board, environmental impact, exchange control, customs, export controls, and much more.

This list is growing, and the longer the list, the longer it takes to reach agreement. The situation has now been reached where the time taken to reach agreement and to conduct the associated studies is measured in years, not months, and thus Australia's competitive position is, in many cases, seriously endangered. Western Mining frequently quote the example of Kambalda, where the first treated ore left the mine only eighteen months after the first drill intersection, thus establishing a valuable early cash flow; that was in 1966 and 1967. With Roxby Downs, the corresponding period is likely to be thirteen years—in the first eight of these years, expenditure has totalled a huge $90 million, and it is estimated that another $60 million remains to be spent just to complete the feasibility study. Should the go-ahead then be given, another $1500 million will need to be invested before the first revenues flow to the developers. These governmental requirements arise at the same time as the developer is finalising design, financing, sales and so on. Early generation of cash flow allows developers to secure a place in markets and to minimise capital requirements, thereby enabling smaller (sometimes Australian) companies to undertake developments.

Royalty arrangements have changed significantly in recent years. The profit-related royalties from Argyle or Roxby Downs bear little resemblance to their counterparts of ten or twenty years ago.

The extent of these negotiations, and the powers of all three levels of government, tend to be widely underestimated, especially in the economic literature. Looking at only one aspect—say the royalty arrangement—is not likely to give a complete picture of the way the 'rent' is captured by government; it seldom measures the regional perception of benefits from new mining developments. An economist's calculation of rates of return to a project, to a region, to a State and to the nation adopts a much wider perspective.

Much of the mining development of the past two decades has occurred in the outlying States of Western Australia and Queensland. For a number of reasons these States were relatively underdeveloped until the early 1960s, with only small portions of their mineral resources adequately explored, and they understandably sought faster growth and a greater share of national development; they also saw themselves as disadvantaged by comparison with New South Wales and Victoria. New mining developments provided an opportunity for strong political effort to redress some of this perceived imbalance—much along the lines of manufacturing development in South Australia under Thomas Playford some 30 years ago. For this policy to succeed, political considerations must override economic considerations. Some examples will illustrate the point.

Development of the 'outback' or remote regions has a great attraction for many Australians—witness, for example, some of the costly regional development failures stemming from concepts of 'balanced' regional development. Thus the discovery of vast deposits of iron ore in the remote north-west, close to Indonesia, resurrected the dream of populating this huge area. Pearling, gold mining and pastoral activities had failed to sustain earlier hopes. The discovery of iron ore not only raised hopes of ports, airports, towns and other infrastructure, but propagated a much more ambitious dream, that of processing on a large scale in Western Australia. Here was the opportunity for a number of trade-offs for the right to mine that were subsequently seem as extremely successful examples of 'bootstrap' development.

The first such trade-off concerned the social and industrial infrastructure: should it be provided by the government or the private sector, as in most other developments throughout Australia, or by the mining company? The answer in the Pilbara development was the latter, and the result was a huge capitalisation of the projects, partly because social and industrial infrastructure outweighed mine expenditure by three to one. The outcome has been several large country towns and some of the biggest and most internationally competitive transportation systems in Australia. The existence of these important trade-offs should not be forgotten when resource rent considerations come to the fore decades afterwards. Not the least significant of these trade-offs have been the breaking of State monopolies in several areas of infrastructure provision and (a somewhat less enthusiastically received outcome) the demonstrated superior efficiency of modern systems, which stands in stark contrast to the performance of State monopoly infrastructure systems.

Infrastructure trade-offs occur across a wide range of services—railroads, energy, water, or local rates: the list is very long. In most cases the initial assumption of governments is that mining projects can stand much higher charges than other industries in remote locations. A classic example is coal railway freights in New South Wales: why should they be so much higher than, for example, wheat rail freight rates in the same State?

Another trade-off—one that is much less visible—is in the area of preferential purchasing from State suppliers. Local and state suppliers have natural competitive advantages in such contracts, so the reference here is to efforts over and above such natural competitive advantages. Some idea of the distribution of orders was provided in a study carried out by W.D. Scott[2] for Hamersley Iron, in which expenditure was tracked on a $304 million expansion in 1977/78. Of this amount, around 11 per cent was supplied from overseas; of the remaining $272 million, no less than $202 million was spent in Western Australia. More recently it has been estimated that some 80 per cent of the Argyle pipe expenditures will be made in Western Australia: the press release by the Premier, Mr Brian Burke, announcing the go-ahead said that ' . . . ADM would be *required* to use Western Australian suppliers and contractors wherever possible' (author's emphasis).

Such high State expenditures must be treated with some reserve: the capacity use of supplier industries at the time of tender, for example, will influence the competitiveness of tenders. However, the shares gained by Western Australian and Queensland suppliers for projects in those States represent capacities far in excess of the previous manufacturing strengths of those States. It is only necessary to fly into Perth to observe the sizeable number of new manufacturing plants designed to service the major mineral developments. The securing of these orders to supply (and maintain) the mineral projects is closely supervised by State officials and politicans, and the benefits for the State then tend to be exaggerated into national benefits.

A further and more recent expression of narrow State interest and developmental ambitions concerns the location of head offices. States see these offices as requiring and developing considerable service input in such areas as design, purchasing, marketing, accounting, legal and financial expertise, and research and development. They also recognise that Melbourne and Sydney have superior facilities in these fields, in part because of a concentration of head office locations there. States are keen to see their service industries strengthened as a basis for other local industries, and they view mining company head offices as a means of achieving this. The location of head offices in Perth or Brisbane not only builds local skills but materially expands national and international connections for all businesses and governments in those cities.

A special feature of the mining industry is closure and the costs and regulations associated with it. Mine closures are quite common, as the economic life of the ore body is inevitably limited. The provisions for closure costs in those years when the end is in sight present some taxation difficulties. Increasingly strict environmental requirements—for example, in the closure of a uranium mine—involve mostly local and State authorities in terms of expenditure, but Commonwealth authorities in connection with taxing procedures.

Refining and Smelting

A decision to proceed downstream into refining and smelting raises many additional issues for all three levels of government.

First, refining and smelting are more glamorous than mining. They are more capital-intensive, employ more people, have higher value added and are generally thought to have more forward and backward linkages. Since the weight or volume of output in relation to value is lower, freight costs play a less significant part in determining the ability to deliver competitively in all major world markets—for ore and to a lesser extent for concentrates Australia has a competitive advantage in Asian markets, but is less favourably placed in the big markets of Europe and the eastern seaboard of the United States. The final product, however, as distinct from ores and concentrates, tends to encounter protection in world markets. Here the Commonwealth has the overriding authority in arenas such as the General Agreement on Tariffs and Trade or in bilateral discussions.

This element of glamour is equated in some eyes with national pride—consider, for example, the importance of possessing a steel industry or an international airline—and politicians will go to considerable lengths to secure new refining and smelting industries.

The location of a mining operation is determined primarily by the geographic position of the ore body, but the siting of refining and smelting industries is governed by different considerations; transport costs and the availability of energy and other infrastructure are important influences upon the choice of location. Refining and smelting plants are located primarily on the Australian coast, with none in capital cities. The choice between States for location has depended upon a number of factors, principally energy cost, energy availability, ports, other transport and communication facilities, and access to markets. These factors have some geographic distribution points that have favoured New South Wales in the past. There are other federal–State political factors that bear on this problem; coastal shipping is perhaps the best example of a legislated inefficiency which acts to limit the most favourable decisions on location.

State governments go to some lengths to attract processing industries, especially in those States with few mineral resources of their own—examples are the zinc and aluminium smelters in Tasmania, the Port Pirie lead smelter and the Portland aluminium smelter. Thus the location of processing industries may be determined by the presence of superior facilities, by local processing requirements, or by the existence of government incentives. The processing obligations imposed on iron ore and diamond producers by the Western Australian government as a condition of the right to mine the ore are two examples of State pressures. Both Queensland and Western Australia have made considerable strides in the processing of bauxite into alumina and then into aluminium as a result of such pressures.

In recent years much effort has been devoted to measuring the impact of new projects on the economy, and these studies have attempted to differentiate between regional, State and national returns, as well as returns to investors in the project. Most of these studies have concerned the aluminium industry, but they are by no means confined to developments in that industry.

Foreign Investment

Foreign investment has been built up into a major issue for the mining industry over the past two decades. It might be asked what is so different about mining—why not motor cars, merchant banking, advertising, accounting, or chemicals? Mining has been at the forefront of the debate ever since General Motors Holden's profits dwindled, and mining is now singled out for special treatment, whether favourable, as in the case of some exploration, or unfavourable, as in the case of uranium.

The special attention paid to foreign involvement in mining probably stems from two distinguishing factors. The first is the cargo cult aspect of physically digging up pieces of rock and exporting them, which is a highly emotive issue. The second concerns the size of the mining investment; individual developments, whether in the 1960s or the present, dwarf most other investments in the economy in terms of dollars invested. Of course the financial scale—the size of the individual project risk—is one reason for the foreign participation in the first place. The capital market in Australia has not had the capacity to handle and diversify this risk, and in fact the financing can be handled by only a few of the world's largest banks in syndicate with other banks.

The requirement to finance most mining developments offshore is a fact widely accepted by those studying foreign investment in Australia. Gradually the differences between equity and debt and between ownership and control have come to be appreciated. With respect to the equity side of the minimum ownership requirement of 50 per cent, the Australian investor has long indicated other preferences. Those preferences, which are reinforced by the financial system that has been established to cater for them, are clearly to give priority to housing and then to property, plus a marked liking for high-risk gambling (the TAB and the lotteries, for example). These investments are characterised by superior after-tax investment performance and, in the cases of housing and property, high long-term gearing, frequently provided on subsidised terms by a financial system designed to cater for them.

The debate in Australia has come to recognise the important distinction between ownership and control underlying the naturalising/naturalised concept that arose from developments in the mining industry. Thus, a clear definition of 'control' has been formulated. The naturalising concept has a high degree of bipartisan support and has helped to defuse the 'foreign' investment issue, as did the requirement for a minimum Australian participation in a mining project of 50 per cent. The ability of Australians to reach a consensus on this emotive issue stands in marked contrast to the Canadian experience.

The foreign investment powers have been largely administered by the Commonwealth, with only minor (and short-lived) attempts by the States to form different policies, but differences of opinion on the subject between the three levels of government remain acute. Opportunities for local development are frequently seen as being hindered by restrictive attitudes in Canberra. Interestingly, 'foreign' in this context can mean interstate ('Eastern'), within the State ('Southern'), or overseas. In the overseas context, the most difficult aspect has been how to accommodate the ownership ambitions of the major Asian customers when European and North American investors were the pioneers and high risk takers.

The two most important developments under this heading have been the successes of the naturalising program and of a number of large 'buying back the farm' exercises. The naturalised/naturalising program involves most of the major non-Australian mining companies (with the exception of the large oil companies): the list includes CRA, MIM, Aberfoyle, Rennison and Argyle. The 'buy-back' list is also large—Delhi, Burmah and Peabody, with the plum Utah about to be finalised. Indeed, the process has gone further; important examples are the purchase by an Australian subsidiary of a large stake in the parent United States company, and the purchase by another company of a large foreign group of mines.

The real outcome of this long but successful effort to increase Australian ownership and control is yet to be fully appreciated. The changes in this area, plus the considerable expansion of the mining industry, have produced something unique to Australia: a group of companies that are large in global terms, are at the forefront of technology and research and development, are beginning to build downstream marketing investments offshore (aluminium in

Japan and zinc and lead in Europe being the best examples), and yet require and receive no government assistance or support. Such companies have the potential to exert a significant influence on the nature and size of private sector performance in the years ahead.

National Interest

The foregoing discussion raises the question whether the national interest is maximised if individual State (or local) interests are maximised. It is easy to point to examples: the setting of exchange rates and the continuance of exchange controls work heavily against export- and import-competing industries; excessive protection for Victorian and New South Wales manufacturing industries may maximise benefits in those States to the disadvantage of others; national foreign investment policy frequently appears inconsistent with State preferences; and export control powers and exchange control powers can be powerful federal weapons with a strong influence over individual State developments.

Another example is provided by the history of the iron ore industry in Western Australia over the past five years or so. It has not been difficult for Western Australians to see the development of another iron ore mine in the Pilbara as a highly desirable proposal. Such a mine would provide new jobs, expand capacity and lead to increased royalty payments once production started. It could also seriously weaken the marketing stance of existing Australian producers by inducing lower prices or lower tonnages (or both), which could reduce taxable profits for all producers. Thus, while the State would benefit, the national treasury would receive lower taxation revenues.

A further example came to light with the publication of the weak—but damaging—Fitzgerald report.[3] Among other things, the report made it clear to the mining industry that neither governments nor voters were in a mood to wait for taxation revenue to be generated by tax-paying enterprises with a unique set of characteristics—vast, visible, highly capitalised projects with a set of depreciation provisions for tax purposes that matched the peculiar characteristics of the business.

Government Conflicts

A difficulty in the federal–State taxation sphere has appeared recently—a difficulty not specific to resource industries but apparently of importance in State government thinking. Over the past decade or so it has gradually become evident that, under the existing royalty regime, the economic life of the ore bodies being worked is limited. The future of the city of Broken Hill and the companies concerned, plus the associated smelters in New South Wales, South Australia and Tasmania, provides an example. Broken Hill mining company royalties plus company taxes have frequently taken around 70 per cent of profits in recent years. Offers to change the royalty basis, however, have been delayed until a formula can be worked out to ensure that such a reduction is *fully* reflected in a longer life for the mines; 'fully' means that 46 cents in every dollar of royalty relief does not go back to the federal government in the form of additional company tax.

A more recent feature common to federal and State governments is that of governments as direct participants in mining ventures. Governments may become minority equity investors (for example, the government of Western Australia in Argyle diamonds or the federal government, through the Atomic Energy Authority, in Mary Kathleen Uranium), or they may be direct operators, as in the mining of coal by State electricity authorities. In the latter case, governments have become extremely vulnerable when industrial action threatens a disruption of electricity supplies, and there have been examples of significant concessions to those employed in the coalmining operations. Unfortunately, such concessions quickly flow on to all coalminers, many of whom work for industries dependent for sales not on a domestic monopoly but on tough, highly competitive world markets. It is in this way, among others, that employees receive a share of 'rent'.

Another federal–State difficulty arises from the monopoly powers of infrastructure suppliers. Sometimes these State bodies are forbidden to purchase such services from interstate suppliers, even when economic rationality so dictates.

Little reference has been made here to the environmental and Aboriginal aspects of this federal–State resource development debate, because the subject has already been extensively documented elsewhere, and because emotive arguments advanced by 'single-issue' proponents rarely include any evaluation of the economic implications.

Mention should be made of the Commonwealth's international obligations and their impact on resource projects. The main example is perhaps participation in commodity groupings (copper, bauxite, iron ore), or in the commodity stabilisation programs, of which the best known is that for tin. An essential feature of a workable commodity price stabilisation (read 'maximisation') scheme is the power of the manager to limit output. The allocation of these output cuts within the framework of a federal system requires careful attention. Should cuts be made across the board? Should consideration be given to regional employment and social conditions? Should the economics of the projects or companies be taken into account? How may a potential new entrant be accommodated? These are but some of the problems associated with the implementation of a price stabilisation scheme in a federal system.

In marketing, Commonwealth and State governments have generally displayed a marked desire to 'help' the producers—who frequently seem to be ill-informed, short-sighted, incompetent or, worst of all, in competition with each other. The outcome of such government involvement varies from marginally helpful to disastrous (for example, zircon, domestic copper prices, iron ore pellet contracts, bauxite prices, coal marketing). Buyers have been quick to seize on such government involvement to point out the unreliability or lack of competiveness of Australian suppliers—they are in competition with other world suppliers, who are not always asked to bear special levies, additional freights or the effects of overlapping federal–State fiefdoms.

One other interesting development is the imposition of federal levies on output. The export levy on coking and steaming coal is an extraordinary levy on an export product; the reasons for singling out coal are not altogether clear, but the procedure needs to be noted. This industry has also suffered another extraordinary levy—a research levy—which is apparently another example of the attitude that 'Canberra knows best'. The results of this bureaucratic action have still to be documented, and as yet we do not know whether any scale efficiencies (or inefficiencies) exist in this area. The imposition of research levies on the exports of a single industry raises the question of why market imperfections are perceived in that industry. Those who advocate such schemes sometimes point to the low level of research and development expenditure in the industry, but they usually fail to ask why that should be so: could it be that profits over a sustained period have been grossly inadequate? The 1983 Minerals Industry Survey,[4] for example, shows that the average rate of return on funds employed over a seven-year period was a meagre 9.4 per cent a year.

This analysis presents a picture of some of the special State (and intrastate) issues that resource developers must face. Extra effort by developers is required to understand differing State requirements, to appreciate intending policy shifts (including the policies of opposition parties) and yet, at least in the case of major projects, to satisfy Commonwealth objectives as well. The system has a number of weaknesses—but it also has some strengths. Perhaps the main weakness is the duplication of federal and State regulations, which tends to slow down decisionmaking; the main strength probably lies in the variety of national interest, which tends to strengthen entrepreneurial forces in the mining industry.

8 State and federal attitudes to foreign investment and its regulation

F.G.H. POOLEY

Foreign capital has played an integral part in Australia's economic development since European settlement in the eighteenth century. Over the past 30 years or so net capital flows have financed a transfer of real resources to Australia, as reflected in the balance of payments current account deficit, which has provided approximately 10 per cent of the resources directed to gross capital formation in Australia.[1] This supplement has been equivalent to, on average, about 2–3 per cent of gross domestic product annually, and a somewhat higher proportion in recent years.

Although foreign investment has long been a significant element in Australia's economic development, it is only fairly recently that a comprehensive approach to the screening of foreign investment proposals has evolved.[2] Before the 1970s there was basically an 'open door' approach to foreign investment, although specific restrictions were applied to particular sectors of the economy. A movement towards a comprehensive approach to foreign investment began during the late 1960s, when there was growing community concern about, in particular, the extent of foreign ownership and control within the Australian economy. At the close of that decade the Commonwealth government expressly reserved the right to prevent foreign takeovers that would be contrary to the national interest.[3] Subsequently, in 1972, the Commonwealth gained this power with the enactment of Australia's first general foreign takeovers legislation.[4]

The first comprehensive statement of foreign investment policy was that by the Labor government in September 1975.[5] Two important aspects of the approach outlined in that statement were the introduction of the *Foreign Takeovers Act* 1975, which enhanced the scope of the review process, and the introduction of specific Australian equity requirements in new mineral projects. Projects proceeding to development were expected to have no more than 50 per cent foreign equity and no more than 50 per cent of the voting strength on the company's board of directors held by foreign interests.

The Liberal government also issued a comprehensive statement of foreign investment policy in April 1976.[6] This retained the broad thrust of the approach announced in 1975 but created the Foreign Investment Review Board to advise the government on the administration of foreign investment policy. Since then the policy has been reviewed on a number of occasions but, although there have

140

been a number of developments in the light of experience and changing circumstances, the fundamental features of the policy have remained unaltered.

The evolution of foreign investment policy in Australia has reflected changing community perceptions and concerns. In economic terms, foreign investment policy has sometimes been viewed as a 'second-best' policy where alternative and more direct measures may not have been in place. The essential rationale of foreign investment policy has been, nevertheless, to achieve a balance between the economic benefits which Australia has been able to gain from foreign capital on the one hand, and the need to be able to respond to community sensitivities about the extent of foreign ownership and control within the Australian economy on the other. If this balance were not sought, and foreign ownership and control were perceived to be rising to a level unacceptable to the Australian community, there could be pressures for policy changes which could ultimately inhibit the potential for foreign investment to contribute to economic growth in the long run.

It is apparent from all this that the past decade has seen a considerable measure of agreement at the political level concerning the approach to foreign investment, and this has been reflected in statements by the Labor government since it came to office in March 1983.[7] These statements have affirmed the government's recognition of the economic benefits of foreign investment and its acceptance of the broad thrust of the policy elaborated by the previous (Liberal) government.[8]

In a statement issued on 23 December 1983 the Treasurer, the Hon. Paul Keating, said:

Policy on foreign investment, which is basically concerned with longer term direct investment, will continue to be based on 'twin pillars'. First, a recognition of the significant contribution that foreign capital can make to the development of Australia's industries and resources. By providing access to additional overseas resources, foreign investment provides scope for rates of growth in economic activity and employment to be higher than would otherwise be the case. At the same time these economic benefits of foreign investment have to be balanced against the recognition of continuing community concerns that the degree of foreign ownership and control should be kept within acceptable bounds. The second important pillar of policy is thus the affording of adequate opportunities for Australians to participate in the development of our industries and resources. In the future administration of policy, the Government intends to give more emphasis to the existing requirements that Australians be given adequate opportunities to participate as fully and effectively as practicable in the development of Australia's industries and resources.

The government decided not to establish specific Australian equity guidelines for all sectors of the economy, nor to require majority Australian equity in new projects or businesses.

The specific foreign investment policy guidelines applying to the natural resources sector and to rural properties remain, although future proposals for investment in large tracts of rural land (defined as those involving 100 000 hectares or more, or having a value of $1 million or more) will be required to provide for an effective Australian–foreign partnership or have economic benefits of national or regional significance.

Examinable Proposals

Proposals subject to examination are:

1   proposals falling within the scope of the Foreign Takeovers Act;
2   all proposals to establish a new business or project, irrespective of size, in industries subject to special restrictions—finance, insurance, the media, civil aviation, and uranium and activities relating to uranium;
3   proposals to establish new businesses in other sectors where the total amount of the investment is $5 million or more (including diversification into activities not previously undertaken directly in Australia and new projects in mining and other natural resource industries);
4   direct investments by foreign governments or their agencies (excluding investments related to their official representation); and
5   proposals to acquire real estate and real estate development projects.

   The Foreign Takeovers Act is concerned with the acquisition of companies or businesses operating in Australia by foreign interests, and with agreements and arrangements relating to Australian companies to which foreign interests are parties. The Act requires non-residents, corporations or businesses controlled by non-residents, and Australian companies in which non-residents have a substantial shareholding, to notify the government of proposals to acquire, or alter, a substantial interest in a company. A substantial foreign interest is defined for the purposes of foreign investment policy as an interest of 15 per cent or more in the ownership or voting power of a corporation or business by a single foreign interest, either alone or together with associates, or an interest of 40 per cent or more in aggregate in the ownership or voting power of a corporation or business by two or more foreign interests and their associates, if any.

Australian Participation

The provision of opportunities for Australians to participate in proposed investments to be undertaken by foreign interests is an important element of foreign investment policy. Australian participation is generally sought to the extent appropriate to the particular commercial and other circumstances of each proposal, although specific equity guidelines have been applied in respect of natural resource development projects, and, in certain circumstances, in respect of the acquisition of rural properties, the non-bank financial sector and real estate developments.

Naturalisation

Foreign investment policy has also provided a naturalisation framework, under which predominantly foreign-owned companies may choose to increase the level of Australian participation in their Australian operations. This process is an entirely voluntary one for the companies which choose to participate in it. To achieve naturalised status, a company must be at least 51 per cent Australian-owned; its articles of association must provide that a majority of its board members be Australian citizens; and there are general understandings between the company, major shareholder interests and the government about the exercise of voting powers concerning the company's business in Australia. A company may achieve naturalising status if it has 25 per cent Australian equity, provides for a majority of Australian citizens on its board, and publicly undertakes to increase Australian equity to 51 per cent subject to agreed undertakings between the company, major shareholder interests and the government concerning, among other things, practical arrangements for meeting the last of these conditions. Participating companies have been expected to naturalise all, or at least the predominant parts of, their Australian operations.

Companies that elect to participate in these arrangements are entitled to certain benefits while they are naturalising. They may be accorded prior credit for achieving majority Australian ownership, thereby facilitating their participation in certain new projects and ventures subject to Australian participation guidelines.

Natural Resources

Foreign capital has played a significant role in the development of the minerals industry during the past two decades as the industry has assumed an important role in the Australian economy, and particularly in the export sector. In the three-year period preceding 1982/83, during which Australia experienced a surge in resource-based investment, the prominent involvement of foreign interests was reflected in the considerable number of new, large-scale development projects approved under foreign investment policy.

The provision by overseas investors of large blocks of capital that could not all be supplied from domestic sources highlights the importance of foreign capital in Australian mineral developments. Mineral exploration also involves a substantial element of risk which may not be attractive to a considerable proportion of potential Australian investors. They may also be less attracted than overseas investors by the delay in receiving returns on investments undertaken in mineral developments involving long lead times. Another aspect of the case in favour of foreign investment is the access it provides to technology and other skills and to markets. Of course, these characteristics are by no means the sole preserve of foreign investors and may be possessed, to varying degrees, by Australian companies.

The development of Australia's natural resources has been closely linked with developments in the international economy. In 1982/83 the impact of domestic and international economic conditions, including the weakening of international energy prices, was reflected in a sharp reduction in estimates of prospective expenditure associated with proposals approved by the government under foreign investment policy. With a decline of $1400 million in expected expenditure associated with mineral development proposals, the prospective investment associated with proposals for the establishment of all new businesses in Australia in 1982/83 amounted to only $500 million, compared with $2100 million in 1981/82 and $2600 million in 1980/81. (While these estimates clearly reflect the trend in foreign investment in the industry, it should be remembered that they are subject to considerable reservation: they represent no more than an indication of the plans of both foreign and Australian investors at the time their proposals are but before the government.)

Foreign Ownership and Control of the Mining Industry

It may also be of interest to note the extent of foreign participation in the mining industry. Past estimates by the Australian Bureau of Statistics have shown that in 1974/75 foreign ownership of the mining industry was 51.8 per cent,[9] while in 1976/77 foreign-controlled enterprises were estimated to account for 59 per cent of the industry's total value added.[10]

The results of a further survey published by the Australian Bureau of Statistics in September 1983 indicated that overall foreign ownership of the mining industry, which stood at 51.2 per cent, had changed little from the earlier level, while that of mineral processing had increased by about 7 percentage points to 46.3 per cent.[11] In respect of direct (as distinct from portfolio) foreign ownership of the mining industry (which is, of course, the primary focus of foreign investment policy), there was a fall from 40.9 per cent to 35.7 per cent between 1974/75 and 1981/82. It should be noted that the latter figure does not reflect the fact that various projects that have been approved with at least 50 per cent Australian equity have only just come into production or will come into production in the future.

As for control, recent estimates published by the Australian Bureau of Statistics have delineated three categories: outright foreign control, joint foreign–Australian control, and control by naturalised and naturalising companies. Overall, foreign control of the mining industry was put at 58 per cent, but almost half of this fell outside the category of outright foreign control. Foreign control of mineral processing was estimated to be 43.5 per cent, of which all but a small fraction represented outright foreign control.

Foreign Investment Policy in the Natural Resources Sector

The application of equity participation guidelines to mineral development projects has been a significant feature of Australia's foreign investment policy. For many, and for international observers in particular, such guidelines have distinguished Australia's approach to the regulation of foreign investment. From a domestic perspective they have been an important means of ensuring that the style of development of Australia's resources is consistent with the community's needs and aspirations.

Resource Development

Under the existing policy, proposals for the establishment of new businesses or projects in the mining (other than uranium), agricultural pastoral, fishing and forestry sectors that involve a total investment of $5 million or more and are not contrary to the national interest have been allowed to proceed only if there is a minimum Australian equity of 50 per cent, and at least 50 per cent of the voting strength on the board or controlling body of the project is held by Australian interests. These guidelines have been applied flexibly. A proposal which does not meet them may still be approved if the government judges that the unavailability of sufficient Australian equity capital on reasonable terms and conditions would unduly delay the development of Australia's natural resources. In that event, however, arrangements are sought, as appropriate, for Australian equity to be increased to at least 50 per cent within an agreed period.

Where proposals involve the acquisition of a substantial interest in an existing business or project in the natural resources sector, they are examined by the government against the criteria generally applicable to foreign acquisition of Australian businesses. Provided that Australians have been given adequate opportunities to acquire the interest, approval of the proposal would require that sufficient economic benefits be demonstrated to offset any costs, including any reduction in Australian ownership and control.

Mineral Exploration

Foreign interests are not obliged to seek Australian participation in their mineral exploration activities. However, policy has favoured a continuing and significant level of Australian investment in mineral exploration. Foreign interests have therefore been expected to seek Australian participation in projects that can reasonably be expected to proceed to the development stage, and the earliest possible introduction of Australian equity participation in ventures has been welcomed. Foreign companies are expected to inform the Foreign Investment Review Board annually of their forward exploration programs.

Foreign interests granted a mineral exploration right from the relevant State or territory are not required to seek approval under foreign investment policy to take up the exploration right. However, proposals to acquire an interest in an existing petroleum exploration right (through, for example, farm-in or farm-out arrangements) come within the scope of the Foreign Takeovers Act and therefore need to be submitted to the Foreign Investment Review Board for examination.

Mineral Processing

While there have been no specific guidelines for foreign investment in new projects or ventures in mineral processing, policy has been to ensure that maximum opportunities are made available for significant Australian participation in the ownership and control of new mineral-processing projects. In the examination of proposed projects, an appropriate level of Australian equity participation has been sought in consultation with the parties to meet this objective. In this process recognition is given to the needs of such projects for relatively large amounts of capital, and in some cases for advanced technology not at present available from domestic sources, and to other special factors which could affect the feasibility of Australian participation in a venture.

Other Issues

The major role played by the mining sector in the Australian economy in the past two decades has posed a variety of questions. These clearly extend well beyond the scope of foreign investment policy. In that context, however, some of the major issues which have been addressed publicly by the Foreign Investment Review Board include non-arm's-length pricing, foreign customer and oil company investment in resource projects, and the adequacy of the Australian capital market to finance resource-based investment in conformity with the equity participation guidelines. These issues are discussed in the relevant reports of the Foreign Investment Review Board.[12]

Rural Properties

This area of foreign investment is neither central to the discussion of developments in the natural resources sector nor very significant in terms of overall foreign investment inflows. Nevertheless, it does constitute an area of foreign investment that has given rise to some sensitivity within the Australian community and is subject to specific foreign investment guidelines. It has also been of interest to the State and Northern Territory governments, and therefore has been subject to close liaison between those governments and the Commonwealth.

Proposed foreign acquisitions of rural properties normally involve the purchase of an operating farm or other rural business, and consequently require approval under the Foreign Takeovers Act. In 1982/83 foreign investor interest in rural land remained subdued, partly reflecting the economic recession, high interest rates and prolonged drought conditions. In that year 74 proposals for foreign interests to acquire rural land for a total consideration of $37 million were approved. This compared with 78 acquisitions for $75 million approved in 1981/82, and 128 acquisitions for $88 million approved in 1980/81.

Foreign investment policy has required that rural properties sought by foreign interests must first have been advertised or otherwise offered for sale in a way normal for the industry, in order to ensure that Australian purchasers have been given adequate opportunity to bid for them.

Approval for foreign acquisitions of rural properties has normally been granted only when the purchasers have firm plans to establish residence in Australia; when the proposal offers significant economic benefits; or, where the economic benefits are small, when proposals provide for an effective partnership (usually 50–50) between Australian and foreign investors in the ownership and control of the property.

These criteria have been applied in the light of individual circumstances, with attention being given to the interest displayed by Australians in purchasing the properties in question on commercial terms. Particular attention has been given to the advice of the State or Territory concerned in determining whether or not the proposed acquisitions would lead to significant economic benefits.

Operation of Foreign Investment Policy

Foreign investment policy requires that investment proposals be examined case by case against a range of economic and other national interest criteria with a view to establishing whether the policy requirements are met. Proposals are examined by the Foreign Investment Review Board assisted by an Executive provided by the Commonwealth Treasury. The results of this examination consitute the basis of advice tendered to the Treasurer by the Board. The Board is an advisory body only; decisions on foreign investment proposals are the responsibility of the Treasurer.

Two features of the administration of foreign investment policy have been the informal basis on which foreign investors and other interested parties have been able to deal with the Board, and the scope for flexibility in the application of policy. The general approach has been to regard the policy as providing basic guidelines against which individual proposals can be viewed, rather than inflexible rules. Consistent with this approach, which has been favoured both by the regulators and the regulated, most of the review process has been established by policy statement rather than law.

The vast majority of foreign investment proposals examinable under foreign investment policy guidelines fall within the scope of the Foreign Takeovers Act. The Act provides for the notification of proposals, and gives the Treasurer the power to prevent acquisitions when he considers that a transaction would result in, or change, foreign control of the enterprise and that such control would be contrary to the national interest, provided that he does so within 30 days of notification of the proposal.

On the other hand, the Act does not attempt to define control; a variety of factors may need to be taken into account here, bearing in mind the particular circumstances of each case. The Act also does not, of course, define the national interest, which again requires judgments to be made. In these matters, as with the application of equity participation guidelines, the operation of foreign investment policy has been based on policy statements.

Foreign investment policy has emphasised the cooperation of foreign investors rather than compliance with comprehensive legislation. While this approach has appeared to work well in practice, the administration of policy has ultimately relied on powers available to the government under the banking (foreign exchange) regulations and the customs (prohibited exports) regulations, as well as under the Foreign Takeovers Act.

Constitutional Basis of Policy

Although the development of comprehensive legislation relating to foreign investment has not been pursued, the dominant role played by the Commonwealth government in relation to foreign investment has a sound constitutional foundation. The Foreign Takeovers Act is based on section 51 (xx) of the Australian Constitution, which empowers the Commonwealth Parliament to legislate on foreign corporations and trading or financial corporations formed within the limits of the Commonwealth. Section 51(i) of the Constitution relating to trade and commerce provides support for exchange and export controls.

The States are not precluded, however, from applying foreign investment guidelines given their residual powers under the Constitution. Moreover, powers provided to the Commonwealth may be exercisable concurrently at both levels, although, if there is a conflict between Commonwealth and State laws, the Commonwealth law prevails and the State law, to the extent of the inconsistency, is invalidated under section 109 of the Constitution. It should be noted that section 37 of the Foreign Takeovers Act records the intention that the Act is not to exclude any law of a State or Territory to the extent that any such law is capable of operating concurrently with the Act.

State Responsibilities

It is also relevant to note in the foreign investment context that power over land titles falls within State and Territory jurisdiction, as does authority over the exploration and production of minerals (including petroleum). Under State legislation it is usual for the relevant minister to be entrusted with very wide discretionary powers in granting mining leases. These powers extend to consideration of the extent of foreign ownership and control, and in some instances the States have used them to apply foreign investment guidelines.

A notable example of this has been in New South Wales. Both the *New South Wales Mining Act* 1973 and the *New South Wales Coal Mining Act* 1973 provide that the responsible minister may, in deciding whether or not to grant an exploration or prospecting licence or a mining lease, take into account the extent to which the controlling interest in a company is foreign.

In 1978 New South Wales introduced guidelines broadly similar to the guidelines that have applied at the Commonwealth level but seeking 51 per cent rather than 50 per cent Australian equity.[14] The New South Wales guidelines also allow scope for flexibility in their application where difficulties are experienced in obtaining majority Australian participation at the outset and the mineral venture is of exceptional value to the State or special technology is required for its operation.

Australian participation is not required by New South Wales at the exploration stage, although any changes which affect the degree of Australian participation in titles to explore or mine must be notified to the New South Wales Department of Mines. Notification of individual portfolio holdings is not required. The New South Wales government has stated, however, that any pronounced growth in foreign portfolio holdings will be discussed with the federal authorities and representatives of New South Wales mining companies on the application of Commonwealth government policy in this area.

Commonwealth–State Cooperation

Foreign enterprises are, of course, subject to the normal range of laws and regulations applied by State and local government authorities. It would be hazardous, however, to attempt a listing of State laws and policies which may bear on foreign investment as distinct from investment in general. This is not to suggest that such laws or policies have necessarily been numerous or complex; on the contrary, the general attitude of the States towards foreign investment and its role in industrial and resource development has been development-oriented and has not differed substantially from that which has operated at the Commonwealth level, although there have been some differences in emphasis. Given the lead taken at the Commonwealth level in developing a foreign investment policy, the States have not sought to spell out comprehensive policies of their own but have been prepared to cooperate with the Commonwealth by consulting with it through the Foreign Investment Review Board.

Liaison with the State and Territory authorities has been an important function of the Board. Under existing arrangements these authorities are routinely consulted by the Board in its examination of individual foreign investment proposals where proposals may be of particular interest to a State or Territory. Particular attention has been given to the advice of the State or Territory concerned in the assessment of, among other things, the extent of economic benefits which might result from a proposed acquisition or investment by a foreign interest. Following a review of foreign investment policy in January 1982, the Liberal government emphasised the consultative process in respect of proposals for foreign investment in the rural sector.[15]

The Board and its executive have sought, where possible, to hold discussions with State and Territory officials on the foreign investment policy, particularly as it relates to resources and real estate projects. The consultations have given the Commonwealth the opportunity to provide information to the States concerning the policy and its administration. They have also provided the States with an avenue through which to advance their views on policy questions and on the consultation process.

The existing arrangements for consultations with State and Territory governments concerning foreign investment proposals are kept under review by the Foreign Investment Review Board. However, the system of liaison has hitherto appeared to work to the general satisfaction of the participants, given the various constraints involved. These include the 30 day limit set by the Foreign Takeovers Act for the examination of proposals and the no less important constraint imposed by the desirability of minimising the delay to commercial processes while ensuring that the objectives of foreign investment policy are achieved.

9 Financing and charging for infrastructure

FRANCES PERKINS

Allocation of Responsibility for the Provision and Taxation of Infrastructure in the Federal System

The Commonwealth has little direct constitutional responsibility for the provision of physical infrastructure, except in federal Territories and on other Commonwealth land and through the activities of Commonwealth public authorities like Telecom and the Australian National Railway Commission. Over the years since federation, however, the Commonwealth has gradually acquired a significant de facto role in this area. It has also been active in the provision of social infrastructure like education, housing and health services, which are primarily areas of State responsibility. This incursion has been facilitated by the Commonwealth's increasing dominance over most major fields of taxation. In addition to the power to collect customs and excise duty conceded in the Constitution, the Commonwealth has gained exclusive control over income, sales and company taxes as a result of a number of High Court decisions in the Commonwealth's favour. This growing fiscal imbalance has been accompanied by an increasing tendency on the part of the Commonwealth to make revenue transfers to the States through specific purpose grants. The other major mechanism that has enhanced the Commonwealth's role in decisionmaking about providing infrastructure is the Loan Council. The Council implements the legally binding 1927 Financial Agreement controlling State and Commonwealth government borrowings and the voluntary 1936 Gentlemen's Agreement, which regulates State and Commonwealth public authority borrowings.

The States, on the other hand, have virtually exclusive constitutional responsibility for the provision of physical infrastructure, including roads, railways (except where handed over to the National Railways Commission), dams, bridges, ports and electricity generation sytems. They have responsibility for providing most social infrastructure such as education, health and welfare sevices, including welfare housing, and the maintenance of law and order. They can augment local government provision of urban infrastructure like metropolitan water supply and sewage works.

Local governments are established and operate under State legislation. Their

151

responsibilities are therefore determined by State governments, within the powers reserved for the States in the Constitution. Hence their obligations differ between States but usually include the provision of urban infrastructure such as urban roads, serviced housing sites, sewage treatment, town water supplies and recreation facilities. They also provide some local physical infrastructure such as rural roads, and social infrastructure like childcare centres, libraries, community centres and nursing homes.

The States' loss of income- and sales-taxing powers and successful legal challenges to their right to levy other potential taxes, such as on road transport, have resulted in the States' taxation base being seriously eroded since federation, to a point where their responsibilities now far exceed their capacity to raise revenue. The main taxes that the States still control are payroll tax, which was handed over by the Commonwealth in 1971, and stamp duties, together constituting more than 50 per cent of receipts. Motor vehicle registration fees, royalties ($458 million, or 7 per cent of receipts in 1981/82) and property, liquor and gambling taxes represent their other major sources of revenue. However, these revenue sources funded only one-third of the States' outlays in 1980/81 ($7.9 billion out of $23.5 billion), as shown in Table 9.1. Similarly, the local government sector raises revenue equal to only 60 per cent of its total outlays.

As a result of this massive fiscal imbalance, Australia's federal system can only function because of the large-scale revenue transfers from the Commonwealth to the State–local sector. In 1980/81, recurrent and capital grants to the States amounted to $12 billion. The Commonwealth also advanced a further $871 million through the States' Loan Council borrowing program, under which the Commonwealth raises funds on the States' behalf. In 1983/84 grants will reach $17 billion and advances $973 million. Local government received transfers worth $722 million and borrowed $545 million in 1981/82. As a consequence of growing fiscal imbalance and rising expectations regarding the standard of State government services, grants to the States rose from 3.6 per cent of GDP in 1948/49 to 6.3 per cent of GDP in 1963/64, and reached 8.9 per cent of GDP in 1981/82.

The existence of such transfers would not necessarily imply greater Commonwealth involvement in areas of State responsibility like the provision of physical and social infrastructure. However, section 96 of the Constitution enables the Commonwealth to grant financial assistance to the States on such terms and conditions as it sees fit. This has been interpreted as giving legal authority for specific purpose grants and advances. In 1920 the Commonwealth began making specific purpose grants for items like roads, and since then an increasing proportion of total revenue transfers for both current and capital purposes has been in this form. The range of capital and recurrent items receiving such grants has also expanded significantly.

Table 9.2 indicates that, as a proportion of total grants to the States, specific purpose grants rose from 21.2 per cent in 1948/49 to 36.9 per cent in 1983/84. The trend towards an increasing proportion of specific purpose grants was reversed temporarily during the term of the last Liberal–National Party government. Since most of these specific purpose grants were for social and

Table 9.1 Receipts of Commonwealth, State and local governments, 1980/81

	Commonwealth ($m)	State ($m)	Local authorities ($m)
Outlay on direct services			
Final consumption	7 478	13 569	1 122
Capital outlay (including inventory changes and advances to public financial enterprises)	1 557	6 719	1 613
Cash social service benefits	11 410	297	—
Subsidies (including grants and advances to private sector)	1 081	297	6
Interest (etc.) paid	2 734	2 597	342
Overseas transfers and advances	575	—	—
Total direct outlay	24 835	23 479	3 083
Revenue from own sources			
Direct taxes	26 482	158	—
Other taxes	11 554	5 889	1 566
Interest (etc.) received	1 838	1 185	137
Public enterprise revenue (including depreciation	1 014	689	176
Total income	40 888	7 291	1 879
Revenue surplus (+) or deficit (−)	+16 053	−15 558	−1 204
Intergovernment transfers received (+) or paid (−)			
Recurrent grants			
—from Commonwealth to States	−10 290	+10 290	—
—from Commonwealth to local authorities	−24	—	+24
Capital grants			
—from Commonwealth to States	−1 669	+1 669	—
—from States to local authorities (net)	—	−684	+684
Net advances			
—from Commonwealth to States	−871	+871	—
—from States to local authorities	—	−14	+14
Total net transfers	−12 854	+12 132	+722
Net public borrowing and other financing items	2 152	4 246	545

Sources: ABS *Year Book Australia 1983;* Commonwealth Department of the Treasury *Budget Statements 1980−81* Budget Papers Nos. 1−7

Table 9.2   Grants to the States (prices current for each year)

	1948/49 ($m)	1958/59 ($m)	1968/69 ($m)	1973/74 ($m)	1983/84 ($m)
Specific purpose grants					
Social infrastructure[a]	—	28.7	127.0	736.5	4 012
Economic infrasturcture[b]	13.8	83.0	200.8	344.2	1 703
—roads	13.8	77.8	176.1	325.7	1 221
Other	19.2	29.1	58.6	181.3	592
Sub-total	33.0	140.8	384.1	1 229.4	6 307
General revenue grants	135.4	451.5	1 049.6	2 201.8	10 773
Total grants	155.4	592.3	1 433.7	3 431.2	17 080
Specific purpose grants as percentage of total grants	21.2	23.8	26.8	35.8	36.9
Specific purpose infrastructure grants as percentage of total grants	8.9	18.9	22.9	31.5	33.5

Notes: a Education, health, social security and welfare, recreation, housing and urban and regional development
             b Roads, railways, bridges, other transport, and water resources
Sources: Jay (1975); Commonwealth Department of the Treasury *Budget Statements 1983–84* Budget Paper No. 7

economic infrastructure, the percentage of total Commonwealth grants to the States that were specifically for providing infrastructure has risen from 8.9 per cent to 33.5 per cent since the second world war. As a result, 27.5 per cent, or $4.9 billion, of the total $17.6 billion spent in these areas by the States in 1980/81 was provided by the Commonwealth in the form of specific purpose grants.

Consequently, although the Commonwealth has little direct constitutional responsibility for providing infrastructure in the States, its power to make specific purpose grants and its dominance over the main revenue sources has facilitated its steady growth in activity in this area. The States maintain that increasing the proportion of specific purpose grants seriously distorts their allocative priorities. For example in 1950/51, reflecting Country Party priorities, the Liberal–Country Party government stipulated that the States must spend 35–40 per cent of their total grants on rural roads, other than highways, main roads and trunk roads. This policy has been continued throughout the postwar years and is widely blamed for the poor condition of Australia's major highways.

There may, however, be some instances where specific purpose grants can be justified on the grounds of efficiency. These include the payment of compensation to the States for the beneficial spillover effects of their activities for other States or the country as a whole. Specific purpose grants may be necessary in such situations to ensure that an adequate level of expenditure occurs in these areas. In the case of State government provision of infrastructure in resource development regions, such expenditure may raise Commonwealth revenue collections from company tax or from oil or export levies on private developers in these areas. The export of products from such projects may also improve the national balance of payments and, by stimulating a revaluation, may benefit importers throughout the country and reduce inflation. Unless State governments receive some form of compensation for these positive external effects, their levels of investment in such infrastructure may be less than adequate. However, it is doubtful whether the bulk of the Commonwealth's specific purpose payments for economic and social infrastructure could be justified on such grounds. Most merely reflect the Commonwealth's desire to widen its power in such areas in order to further its own objectives. In some instances the Commonwealth may believe that the nation as a whole will benefit from increased expenditure in particular areas, as in the case of technical education, for example. In other cases it may merely wish to provide benefits to sectional interests from which it draws electoral support.

The second major source of increased Commonwealth involvement in providing infrastructure has been its role in the Loan Council. Under the 1927 Financial Agreement and the 1936 Gentlemen's Agreement, the Loan Council determines the size of virtually the entire public sector borrowing program. The only exceptions are borrowing for temporary purposes and defence and, since 1982, borrowing by electricity authorities. Because the States' borrowing programs are for general purpose captital expenditure, most of them are used to install physical and social infrastructure assets. While the six State Premiers and the Prime Minister constitute the membership of the Loan Council, the Commonwealth has a dominant position because it holds two votes and one casting vote, while the States hold only one vote each. Hence it is necessary for five States to vote against the Commonwealth to defeat it on decisions about the total size of the borrowing programs of the State governments and public authorities. In 1952/53, when the States did vote unanimously against the Commonwealth to increase the size of their borrowing programs, they subsequently failed to raise the total amount of approved borrowings in the domestic financial market (at the prescribed rate of interest). The Commonwealth stepped in and subscribed an additional amount, but only brought the total to marginally higher than the borrowing level it had originally proposed. In virtually every year since then, the States have been unable to raise their total Loan Council allocation on the open market, making it futile for them to vote for a larger amount than the Commonwealth is prepared to approve.[1] By giving the Commonwealth virtual control over the size of State government Loan Council programs, this development has provided the central government with a powerful tool in macroeconomic policymaking. It has also enabled the Commonwealth to determine the total amount available to the States for capital investment, most of which is used for providing infrastructure. State government Loan Council allocations, including the linked grant element, have been declining in real and even in nominal terms over the past ten years. To a certain extent this has been offset by higher real public authority borrowings.

The distribution of total State government and public authority Loan Council programs among the States in effect requires a unanimous vote of the Council. As a result the States have tended to defend their entitlements jealously. Allocations have been determined by a rigid, historically determined formula based on population, school age population and area, which favours the less populous States. Hence, State government Loan Council programs have in effect become a mechanism to achieve 'fiscal equalisation', though, unlike general revenue assistance grants, they are not continually reviewed to achieve this objective. This pattern has only occasionally been altered in favour of obviously disadvantaged States, as in 1974/75 when New South Wales received an increase in its percentage allocation. In 1982/83, for example, Tasmania's per capita allocation was 260 per cent greater than that of New South Wales. No attempt has been made to relate the States' borrowing allocations to the public investment opportunities and the economic rate of return on public investments in different States. There also appears to be no particular rationale for the practice followed since 1970/71 of giving one-third of the States' Loan Council program in the form of general purpose capital grants. It is not apparent why non-revenue-bearing capital expenditure on items like schools and hospitals, for which such grants are intended, should in each State be equal to half the State's capital expenditure on revenue-bearing investments. These mainly include physical infrastructure capable of yielding revenue, like dams, ports, housing and toll roads.

Under the terms of the voluntary 1936 Gentlemen's Agreement, the borrowing programs of public and local authorities were also brought under Loan Council control. Each State now submits a list of authorities wishing to borrow more than a prescribed amount ($1.8 million in 1983/84), indicating the borrowing requirements of each. Those seeking less than the prescribed amount are given automatic rights to do so, but must conform to the terms and conditions of loan raising stipulated by the Loan Council. However, the exception of small authorities may well have encouraged a proliferation of small public authorities and associated inefficiences. The Council then determines the amount that each larger authority can borrow, and before 1983 it also stipulated the terms and conditions on which such loans could be raised.

Since such authorities raise funds on their own behalf, the Commonwealth has a rather less dominant position in determining the overall size of their borrowing programs. However, its role is still significant by virtue of its votes and its capacity to trade off a public authority borrowing program that it considers excessive against a smaller State government program. Until June 1983, the Loan Council also determined the terms and conditions of public authority borrowing, and the Commonwealth had greater control over the actual level of funds raised in the market, because interest rates were tied to the rate offered on Commonwealth securities. As the Commonwealth has had exclusive power to borrow overseas since 1966, the States have been unable to circumvent Loan Council controls on terms and conditions, or on the total level of borrowing, by raising funds abroad.

However, Loan Council controls have been relaxed in a number of important ways in recent years. This move was initiated by a number of resource-rich States, who successfully argued that the rigid pattern of borrowing allocations and the tight overall controls would give them inadequate funds to install infrastructure required by projects associated with the resources boom. As a result, the June 1978 Loan Council meeting adopted guidelines for the consideration of special additional borrowing by the larger public authorities to finance infrastructure. Provision was also made for the authorities to borrow overseas, subject to Loan Council approval. The infrastructure program guidelines specified that such additions should be confined to exceptional projects that could not reasonably be accommodated under normal Loan Council programs, that they were for the provision of services normally provided by public sector enterprises, and that they required outlays within a relatively short time span. Approval for the addition of a project to the program required the agreement of the Commonwealth and three States, effectively giving the Commonwealth a veto power. Projects were supposed to be examined by a panel of State and federal officials to assess their viability and necessity, but in fact none of the submitted projects was rejected. However, it is doubtful whether proposals like the Dampier–Perth pipeline, the Redcliffe petrochemical project and the world trade centre in Melbourne were essential and viable projects that should have been undertaken by the public sector.

Since the start of the infrastructure program, public authorities have borrowed $2244 million for 29 approved projects. In 1980, however, the Commonwealth decided that total borrowing under the program was contributing to a blow-out in the public sector borrowing requirement, and that States might have been investing excessively in infrastructure that could have been provided by developers, in order to bid investments away from other States. Hence, the Commonwealth used its power of veto to ensure that no new projects were admitted to the program after 1979/80, and only $63.5 million was borrowed under it in 1983/84. This rapid decline in borrowings also partly reflects the exemption of the electricity authorities from Loan Council control, as several large generation projects were being funded under the program. Unfortunately, the Commonwealth did not use its veto to limit the program's size by ensuring that only the more viable projects were admitted. Instead it employed the blunt approach of admitting no new projects—a decision that caused considerable acrimony between the Commonwealth and State governments.

Despite its numerous shortcomings, the infrastructure program did initially represent an attempt to increase the flexibility of Loan Council allocation mechanisms by providing funds on the basis of opportunities for viable public sector investment, rather than according to historical precedent. It probably failed to fulfil this objective and to become a permanent fixture of the Loan Council program for much the same reason that the other Loan Council programs lack allocative flexibility: the predominance of political over economic criteria in Council decisionmaking on the distribution of the program. This is virtually ensured by its composition and the legal requirement noted previously that a unanimous agreement is required on the allocation of the program.

A potentially more significant development was the 1982 decision to exempt electricity authorities from Loan Council borrowing controls for a trial period of three years. Overseas borrowing by the electricity commissions is also now allowable but must first be approved by the Loan Council. Since the electricity commissions are the largest public authority borrowers and are expected to raise more than twice as much ($2.7 billion) in 1983/84 as the large non-electricity authorities ($1.2 billion), this move represents a significant dilution of the Gentlemen's Agreement. In 1983 it was also decided to devolve responsibility to the respective members of the Loan Council for determining the terms and conditions (interest rates and terms), though not the aggregate size, of the borrowing programs of the larger public authorities. Both these moves have resulted in a bolstering of State government control over the provision of infrastructure, after many years of growing Commonwealth influence.

Impact of the Federal System on Infrastructure Policy

The chronic imbalance between the taxing powers and functional responsibilities of the three levels of government, perceived inequalities and increasing conditionality in the distribution of transfer payments, and rigidities in the allocation of Loan Council borrowing programs have all motivated the populous and resource-rich States to try to reduce their dependence on revenue transfers and circumvent the Loan Council. The devices employed to achieve this have included leverage leasing, requiring private developers to provide infrastructure or make up-front payments in the form of providing interest-free loans, cross-subsidising infrastructure service users, levying super royalties on developers and increasing the reliance on supplier credit.

Leasing arrangements have been used for some years, with State governments leasing office space from their public authorities and public authorities leasing equipment. However, the leverage leasing scheme for the Eraring power station was far larger than that for any previous proposal and involved a considerable loss of Commonwealth tax revenue. The New South Wales government arranged for Eraring to be purchased from the State electricity commission by a group of companies and to buy back the electricity at a fixed price. The companies were not only guaranteed a nominal return of 13.5 per cent on their funds, but also expected to benefit from the investment and depreciation allowances provided for in Commonwealth company tax legislation. Hence the Commonwealth and the taxpayers were losing substantial sums to enable New South Wales to finance infrastructure outside Loan Council control. The Commonwealth responded by removing investment allowances for participants in such leverage leasing arrangements, and hence substantially reduced the attractiveness of this form of financing.

Queensland, and at various times Western Australia and South Australia, have circumvented Loan Council control, and correctly implemented the 'user pays' principle, by requiring developers with isolated projects to provide capital for major infrastructure investments, including townships, railways and port facilities. High user charges for infrastructure services and increased royalties have also been used to extract a greater proportion of infrastructure costs from developers, and even as a means of collecting resource rents. One of the reasons that the States might prefer these methods to a properly specified resource rent tax may be that they believe the latter is more likely to be fully offset by reduced general revenue assistance from the Commonwealth. High user charges may well be at least partly assessed by the Grants Commission as a factor reducing a State's 'revenue needs', but user-provided infrastructure is unlikely to be offset against transfers in this way. While user provision of infrastructure is likely to be justified in many instances, there is a danger that a range of essentially ad hoc imposts, as compared to a specific resource rent tax, will impose inefficiencies and inequities that may force more marginal producers out of business.

There has also been a trend towards a greater reliance by public authorities and State governments on supplier credit for the purchase of capital equipment like, for example, the pipes for the Dampier–Perth pipeline and most electricity generators. This credit is not subject to Loan Council control. Since such credit is usually only available from foreign suppliers and is frequently provided on subsidised terms by the suppliers' national governments, dependence on it to secure a total financing package may bias sourcing decisions against Australian producers of such equipment.

At the local government level, some councils in resource development regions have developed innovative methods to reduce the shortfall between rate collections, State allocations and borrowings and the funds required to provide large discrete urban infrastructure investments. These techniques include land developments by local councils and various schemes to increase the contribution of development projects to local government finances. In New South Wales, however, because of limitations on local council borrowing programs and revenue raising from developers, established residents have still been forced to pay higher rates to provide facilities for the incoming population, even though these new arrivals are often in considerably higher income brackets. Indirectly, this is likely to result in a transfer of wealth from established residents to developers, whose workforces are likely to accept somewhat lower wages than they would demand if they were required to pay the full cost of urban infrastructure services. Queensland councils affected by major resource developments, on the other hand, have a range of legally sanctioned means of securing grants and advances from developers for required additions to urban and social infrastructure. While the introduction of such provisions may be essential given existing restraints on the capacity of local councils to raise and borrow revenue, some of the demands made on private developers may give rise to the same equity and efficiency problems that were discussed above in relation to ad hoc State imposts.

In the less populous States, which receive particularly generous general revenue grants and State government Loan Council allocations, it is possible that such funds may be used to finance an excessive level of public investment in infrastructure. It has been argued that grants and subsidised State treasury loans to public authorities in such States could well encourage them to embark on projects with very low or negative real rates of return. Similarly, as most public authorities, including the electricity commissions, are not yet functioning commercially, the decision to release them from Loan Council borrowing controls could well result in an overexpansion of their activities at the expense of other, more productive private and public sector activities that *are* subject to market or Loan Council constraints.

When the electricity commissions were released from borrowing controls the government claimed that the move was in response to a recommendation of the Campbell Committee report. However, there is no way that the commissions as presently constituted would conform with the stringent criteria of commerciality and competitive neutrality that Campbell specified public authorities must meet before they could be released from the borrowing controls. In fact the Campbell report could just as well be interpreted as recommending the winding down and sale of public authorities like the electricity commissions (para. 26.21).[2] It could be argued that the State governments offered very low electricity tariffs to aluminium companies seeking sites for smelters in the late 1970s and early 1980s because they believed that they would be able to expand electricity generation and transmission investment with very little Loan Council restraint under the infrastructure program. When the infrastructure program was closed off and other Loan Council programs were tightened, pressure was put on the States to renegotiate electricity price contracts with major users and to devise alternative financing schemes for electricity supply and other infrastructure.

Principles of the Provision and Pricing of Infrastructure

In the absence of other distortions in the economy, the basic principle is that, if these investments are to benefit the Australian community, developers should pay the full opportunity cost of the resources used by their projects, including infrastructure facilities. In the presence of government subsidies or freeloading on existing publicly provided infrastructure, a developer may not take the full cost of such resources into account when deciding whether to invest. In this case, the project selected may not be the one with the highest social rate of return, and may displace other projects which could benefit the community more. Implementation of the user pays principle is discussed further below.

There are, however, many obvious distortions in the Australian economy. These include a legalistic wage determination system, which enables at least some wages to be raised above the social opportunity cost of labour; numerous tariffs, subsidies and taxes; and (as in all economies) the existence of public goods which cannot readily be charged for. It could be argued that in these circumstances there may be a case for paying subsidies, including the subsidised provision of infrastructure facilities and services, so long as the subsidies are directed at negating the impact of such distortions. If subsidies are designed for this purpose, however, they are best financed out of taxes or charges levied on the beneficiaries of the distortions, such as income taxes on those whose wages and salaries are too high or company taxes on tariff-protected firms. The subsidies should then be paid to all economic actors suffering from the distortion, in a form that directly addresses these distortions—for instance, wage subsidies or negative payroll taxes, or bounties for non-protected industries. Subsidies will not counteract distortions if they are distributed selectively to only a few enterprises suffering from a particular distortion (or perhaps not suffering from it at all), and/or are financed by charges and taxes on individuals and enterprises that are not benefiting from such distortions. In this situation, subsidies may generate more distortions in the allocation of resources than they overcome. The subsidised provision of project-specific infrastructure is a classic example of a subsidy that may distort resource allocation decisions by benefiting only one enterprise, or a small group of firms in an industry, rather than all enterprises suffering from a distortion. Similarly, if subsidies are financed by other infrastructure service users (such as commercial electricity customers), who may themselves be suffering from wage and tariff distortions, the inefficiencies will be compounded.

Looking first at the simple 'user pays' principle, this is more straightforward to implement in the case of developments in isolated areas, where virtually all physical, urban and social infrastructure will be project-specific and benefit only that project. In this case the public goods argument will be less tenable and, since only a few enterprises will benefit, subsidies will create further distortions. Hence there is a strong argument for user provision of all infrastructure: roads, railways, ports, housing for workers, and social and urban infrastructure. This occurred in Western Australia in the 1960s when the State government required Hamersly Iron to provide most of the infrastructure to develop iron ore deposits in the Pilbara.

It has been argued that, on equity grounds, State and local governments should provide the same social infrastructure in such settlements as they do for the residents of established areas. However, the cost and risk of providing such services in remote, single-enterprise towns is considerably higher than that of providing them in settled areas, where many enterprises underpin the local economy. This is because there is a greater likelihood that the enterprise may fail or close down before the urban and social infrastructure is fully depreciated. State and local governments may then be forced to pay off loans for such facilities without access to the royalty, levy or rating revenue that they expected would be generated by the project and its workforce. Hence equity arguments would at best justify only a contribution by State and local governments, rather than the full provision of urban and social infrastructure. These could legitimately include variable costs like salaries of teachers and health workers, as such personnel could readily be redeployed if the settlement were abandoned. If demountable schools and public buildings were provided by the government, developers could pay any relocation costs.

In settled areas, developer financing or provision of single-user physical infrastructure is also appropriate. The State may decide that it is more convenient for it to install infrastructure like railways or roads but for the developer to fully finance it. However, transport and energy generation infrastructure in settled areas will usually service a number of enterprises and individual residents. In this instance State governments may require developers to make pro rata contributions to publicly provided infrastructure for which charges cannot be levied efficiently (for example, rural roads), or set user charges to recover fully the social opportunity cost of the resources used. The latter approach would be taken in the case of electricity tariffs, rail freights or port charges. If bunching effects are expected because economies of scale dictate that large pieces of discrete physical, urban or social infrastructure be installed, developers could be required to advance interest-free (or interest-capitalised) loans. However, this will usually represent an ad hoc form of resource rent collection from the developer. Preferably, adequate borrowing authority should be granted by the Loan Council. This would relieve existing ratepayers and taxpayers from an unacceptably large borrowing burden before user charges or rates can be levied, and shift the burden of payment on to future users who will benefit from the new infrastructure.

Some excess capacity can be expected in existing social and urban infrastructure facilities in established areas, but large projects will normally require a substantial expansion of such facilities. So long as governments are confident that the expanded infrastructure will be used, and hence eventually financed, by the workforce of the project or of other local enterprises throughout its full economic life, they should be prepared to borrow from the public to finance its provision. In this situation they will expect to be able to draw on additional royalty and rate revenue in future years to pay off these borrowings. If the industry is a volatile one, like coalmining, and local or State governments believe there is a risk that loan repayments could not be met if planned developments failed, developers could legitimately be expected to shoulder or share this risk by underwriting the borrowings for multi-user physical, social and urban infrastructure, which could not be justified in the absence of these projects.

User charges levied by public authorities and government departments should, in the absence of other economic distortions, equal the social opportunity cost of resources used in producing the goods or service supplied: that is, the value of these resources in their best alternative use. Where there is a major user of a particular good or service, requiring additions to be made to the existing infrastructure stock (like aluminium smelters' requirements for electricity), the appropriate user charge is the long-run marginal cost (LRMC) of production. This is equal to the total fixed and variable costs of providing the next discrete block of infrastructure services. The LRMC not only covers the social opportunity cost of land, labour, fuel and other physical inputs used in production; it should also include a normal rate of return on the equity and loan capital employed in the provision of infrastructure services, as well as provision for depreciation on assets. The social opportunity cost of inputs may differ from their market or private cost because of the existence of imperfections mentioned previously, like government tariffs, taxes and subsidies, because of monopoly or union power, and because of the use of non-marketed goods, like publicly owned land and other resources. In New South Wales and Victoria, for example, the electricity commissions both own and operate captive mines which supply them with coal at production cost rather than at the price obtainable on the domestic or international market. This depresses the commissions' accounting estimates of their costs of production below the social opportunity cost.

Financing problems can arise from adhering to the LRMC approach to tariff setting, however, if the enterprise (public or private) is on a declining long-run average cost (LRAC) curve. Since the LRMC will be below the LRAC in this situation, marginal cost tariff setting will not enable average costs to be covered and losses will be incurred. A solution to this problem may be the imposition of a surcharge on the LRMC to ensure that all costs, including a normal return on capital, are covered. The electricity authorities at present appear to be on a rising section of their LRAC curves, however, following a long postwar period of declining costs. They could therefore expect to make healthy profits from charging a tariff equal to the LRMC. For smaller users of infrastructure services who can be accommodated within the excess capacity of existing facilities, it will be appropriate to charge a price equal to the short-run marginal cost of production. This will result in time-of-day or time-of-year tariffs when there is an uneven use of services throughout the day or year—as in the case of electricity and toll roads, for example.[3]

There is considerable controversy and an extensive literature about what constitutes a normal rate of return for a public sector project (that is, the size of the social discount rate). Depending on whether the appropriate rate is believed to be equal to the post-tax social rate of time preference (the rate of return at which people are prepared to save) or to the pre-tax social opportunity cost of capital (the marginal rate of return on capital in the private sector), a range of potential real discount rates from 2 per cent to 15 per cent a year can be estimated. In a perfect capital market with no uncertainty or tax wedge, the social rate of time preference will equal the social opportunity cost of capital. However, the financial market is imperfect and the government sector exists. Furthermore, many public authorities in Australia are carrying out commercial operations identical to those which in other countries are undertaken by the private sector (supplying road, rail and electricity services). Hence it is reasonable to argue that such authorities should be expected to earn a rate of return on assets equal to the weighted marginal pre-tax rate of return on energy and loan capital in the private sector (where weightings reflect reliance on these sources of capital). This is because if public authorities earn less than this rate of return on the funds they employ, there is a danger that they will draw resources away from more productive, private sector activities. In such circumstances, the use of the social opportunity cost of capital to calculate the social discount rate can be justified on the grounds of resource allocation. There is also a third view that the rate of return earned should reflect the proportion of funds drawn from consumption and investment activities, that is, a rate between the social rate of time preference and the social opportunity cost of capital. However, if public authorities raise funds from public security floats, it is likely that such funds would otherwise have been available to invest in alternative productive activities in the private or public sector. Furthermore, the public authority could always invest the sums raised in the private sector at the market rate of return. The resource allocation argument is, however, the most convincing reason for opting for the social opportunity cost of capital as the appropriate social discount rate for essentially commercial activities like those undertaken by such public authorities.

It has been argued that it may be appropriate for the rate of return earned on the marginal public sector investment to be lower than that earned on the marginal private sector investment, because public sector investments carry a lower risk to investors than do private sector projects. However, there is no consensus about whether public sector investments are more or less risky than private sector ones.[4] If public sector investment is carried out by semi-autonomous public authorities without an explicit government guarantee, there may not be any opportunity for them to 'even out' the losses and gains from a large number of public sector investments. Also, such smoothing may not occur if all investments are adversely affected by fluctuations in the business cycle. Furthermore, if most of the investment funds of such authorities are raised from security floats rather than from tax revenue, the risk to investors will not be reduced by spreading it over a large number of taxpayers.

Consequently, it seems likely that the appropriate social discount rate for commercially oriented public authorities in Australia will be close to the marginal pre-tax rate of return in the private sector. A pre-tax rate is appropriate because public authorities do not pay company tax. Calculations of this rate vary widely, depending on the time period over which calculations are made, whether interest payments, stock revaluation or depreciation are included in returns, and whether the denominator is valued at the historic or replacement cost of investments and net or gross of depreciation and debt. On the basis of post-war national accounts data, the Commonwealth Treasury has indicated that the crude real pre-tax rate of return on equity in the private sector has been approximately 10 per cent, and recommends the use of a sensitivity range of from 7 per cent to 13 per cent.[5] Swan correctly claims that this estimate takes no account of the riskiness of different types of projects.[6] Using the capital asset-pricing model with United States data on the divergence of returns to private electricity-generating companies from average market returns, he estimates that the appropriate real pre-tax rate of return for electricity commissions is approximately 8 per cent. This represents the rate of return that would be required if electricity generation and supply were in private hands. Swan employs a sensitivity range of 3–13 per cent (which overlaps Treasury's), but maintains that 3 per cent is too low. He argues that, in calculating the size of the Victorian State Electricity Commission's subsidy to aluminium smelters, the rate of return on capital in the private sector, rather than the social rate of time preference, is the appropriate social discount rate.

Whether governments can actually recoup their outlays on infrastructure through taxes and user charges on those who benefit from infrastructure provision will, however, depend to some extent on their taxing powers under the Constitution. This is a major potential source of divergence between ideal financing principles and the actual policies implemented by State and local governments. Similarly, such constitutional limitations may inhibit governments from using the best method of subsidising economic activities that suffer from distortions induced by wage determination, industry protection, taxation, and so on. The States have, for example, preferred not to provide direct cash subsidies to economic activities adversely affected by pricing and taxation distortions in the economy. Such transfers would impinge directly on budgets already under tight constraints because of the fiscal imbalance of the federal system. For example, it could be strongly argued that payroll tax should be abolished or even made negative at times of high unemployment, but if it were, the States would lose the major source of revenue raised on their own behalf. Nevertheless, the States would probably still be more successful in reducing distortions in the economy if they made a profit from infrastructure services and paid a subsidy on payrolls. Instead, they have resorted to a range of less than perfect, off-budget mechanisms for subsidising economic activities, one of the most important of which is the subsidisation of infrastructure facilities and services. Either because of constitutional barriers or for electoral reasons, they have also frequently failed to finance such subsidies out of taxes and charges on those benefiting from distortions. Instead, subsidies have been paid for by a variety of devices such as leverage leasing, low or negative returns on public authority investments, cross-subsidisation by infrastructure service consumers, sub-economic pricing of State-owned mineral and land resources, and the use of supplier credit. However, subsidised project-specific infrastructure and underpriced infrastructure services for selected customers, such as bulk electricity users, are likely to assist a range of activities, like protected industries, which already benefit from distortions in the economy. Furthermore, they may well fail to assist many activities, like those in the services sector, which do suffer from such imperfections. Hence they will be neither neutral nor efficient in their impact. The less than ideal financing methods used will also introduce a new range of distortions in the allocation of resources in the economy and an inequitable redistribution of income among groups like taxpayers, shareholders, employees and foreign nationals. For these reasons, subsidising the provision of infrastructure and services frequently represents an inefficient method of overcoming other distortions in the economy.

Policies on the Provision and Pricing of Infrastructure

Unlike countries such as the United States, Australia has a long tradition of publicly providing multi-user infrastructure like railways and ports, and even much single-user infrastructure, designed to benefit large projects. This policy has been used in the past as a means of opening up and developing the country's agricultural, mining and manufacturing industries more quickly than would have occurred had the pace been set only by the operation of the market. Railways have always made losses because it was accepted that they were intended to provide implicit subsidies to users (mainly farmers); water supply for irrigation and town use and rural roads were viewed similarly.[7] It is only fairly recently, since the development of Australia's mineral and energy resources has obviously achieved an international comparative advantage, that this policy has been questioned and in some cases abandoned. Policies on the provision of infrastructure nevertheless still rely crucially on the competent authority's assessment of whether or not desired development activity will be viable without subsidised infrastructure. It is not surprising that in postwar years policies concerning the public provision and pricing of electricity supplies to bulk users should have been formulated in this context. This was the case even though the electricity authorities' charters required them to break even. Subsidies therefore had to be paid for mainly through cross-subsidies from certain non-target categories of customers and by the authorities' failure to achieve a commercial return on the capital they employ.

The other major determinants of policy are the financial capacities of the relevant authorities (local, State or Commonwealth) to pay subsidies out of tax revenue or loan raisings, and the political feasibility of cross-subsidisation of infrastructure service users. Australia's federal system has considerably reduced the tax revenue and formal borrowing capacity of the State–local sector, thereby reducing the capacity for direct subsidy from these sources. Infrastructure financed by specific purpose grants, such as roads, dams and water supply projects, reflects Commonwealth rather than State priorities. State governments can also subsidise other infrastructure if they wish, but this may cause politically unpopular spending reductions in other areas. Local governments are even less able to subsidise the provision of single-user infrastructure, though they can sometimes use specific purpose road grants for this reason and may expand sewerage systems for major industrial users. Only the Commonwealth has really been in a good financial position to continue such subsidies, not only through its public authorities but also through providing infrastructure directly. The growth of specific purpose grants for infrastructure described previously is a reflection of this capacity.

Commonwealth government

Commonwealth policy on infrastructure provision has not been clearly articulated at a political level, but is reflected, for example, in its policies in the Northern Territory before and even since the introduction of self-government in 1978. The Commonwealth Treasury has also clearly outlined what it considers to be the economically appropriate policy, and the Commonwealth has generally argued that these principles should guide the States' infrastructure provision policies, so as to optimise national welfare. However, it has not necessarily adhered to these criteria when it wished to promote its own specific interests, as in the case of rural roads, dams, and infrastructure related to the resources 'boom'.

In the Northern Territory, the Commonwealth provided all planning services and social infrastructure such as schools, health services and law and order for the township of Jabiru, which was associated with the Ranger uranium project. This was formalised under the 1978 Memorandum of Understanding between the Commonwealth and Northern Territory governments, as payments were made after the introduction of self-government. The developer made some contribution to urban development and housing, as did both governments. Territory authorities are also upgrading the main road into the township. Hence there has been a significant subsidy from both the Commonwealth and the Northern Territory governments for the infrastructure associated with the project.

There has been little Commonwealth experience in the provision of resource-related social, urban and physical infrastructure in settled areas. However, the present government has agreed to provide a land lease free of charge to the developer of a 'technology park' in the Australian Capital Territory. This will presumably result in subsidised rentals for enterprises located in the park. As regards Commonwealth authority pricing, Telecom and Australia Post explicitly acknowledge that they subsidise rural customers at the expense of urban ones through both connection and user charges. However, they do not appear to provide additional subsidies for industrial and resource developments.

The Commonwealth Treasury outlined its approach to the provision and pricing of infrastructure in its submission to the inquiry of the Senate Standing Committee on National Resources into the development of the bauxite, alumina and aluminium industries. Basically, the approach accorded with the simple 'user pays' principle outlined above.

State governments

State government policies on providing infrastructure vary widely. The primary objective of the States is usually to optimise the welfare of their own electorates by either creating employment, reducing taxes or increasing incomes. In some cases groups with political leverage, like farmers, industrialists and public authority bureaucrats, may influence infrastructure policy to advance their own interests. However, the main problem for the States is how to develop policies that actually produce the best State welfare within the constraints of the federal system. One problem arises from conflicting political and community perceptions about what is the primary determinant of welfare: jobs, taxation revenue, personal incomes, quality of life, and so on. The States also lack the expertise in social cost–benefit analysis to enable them to assess coherently the costs and benefits of pursuing alternative development strategies, including the subsidisation of infrastructure for different groups in the community.

Queensland amended the State Development and Public Works Organization Act in 1981 to coordinate the provision of infrastructure and formally allocate financial responsibility for it among private developers, local councils and government authorities. Queensland experienced the social upheaval and industrial relations problems that can arise from unplanned growth in settled areas when the Gladstone alumina refinery was established in the 1970s. The other motivation for this new policy was a growing recognition by the State government that major resource and industrial projects planned for Queensland were quite commercially viable, and even included a significant rent component, and therefore did not require subsidies in the form of State provision of infrastructure.

The 1981 amendments vest overall coordination, including authority to arbitrate on responsibility for infrastructure provision, in the Co-ordinator General's Department (which has recently been amalgamated with the Premier's Department). The primary stated objective of this policy is that developers should make the maximum contribution to the costs of physical and urban infrastructure, within the constraints of project viability, so that project-related costs are not borne by State taxpayers and local ratepayers. The provisions of the legislation apply to all large development projects with a significant impact on the State economy and major infrastructure requirements. Once a project is designated a prescribed development under the Act, the Premier's Department is required to produce an infrastructure coordination plan in cooperation with the developer, local government and government departments. This specifies the infrastructure required and allocates financial responsibility for its provision. Once accepted by the government, the plan is binding on all parties, and development approval by State and local authorities is conditional on the developer's adherence to the plan.

Specifically, the Act requires the proposer of a prescribed development project to finance, though not necessarily to install:

1   all project-based physical infrastructure: roads, railways, water supply, electricity supply and port facilities;
2   all urban infrastructure required by the population increase attributable to the project: town development, water supply, waste disposal, roads, and some community services such as recreation facilities;
3   adequate housing for the construction and operational workforce required by the project. There is also a requirement to ensure that the project does not disadvantage existing residents in the rental and owner-occupied housing markets;
4   contributions to upgrading and maintaining regional roads, especially those subject to damage by project vehicles;
5   adequate apprenticeship and training schemes.

The State government is responsible only for providing social infrastructure such as education and health, welfare and law and order services. The policy has been very successful in ensuring that all necessary physical, urban and social infrastructure is provided at the right time and that the bulk of the cost is borne by developers who are benefiting from new projects. In particular, local councils have benefited from the specific power they now have under the Act to negotiate directly with developers on the augmentation or urban infrastructure, and from the provision that their agreement is required before any project is finally approved.

In New South Wales the Premier announced a new infrastructure policy to the State Parliament in September 1982. The new policy formalises the previous de facto requirement that project-based infrastructure should be provided by developers. It also requires them to contribute capital funds for urban infrastructure such as sewage treatment, water supply and serviced blocks, as well as for social infrastructure like education, health and recreation facilities for the population increase attributable to the project. The government is vested with responsibility for coordinating negotiations between developers, councils and the government. However, it is not yet clear whether this role will be interpreted as it has been in Queensland, where the government in fact acts as the binding arbitrator in such negotiations. The announced policy specifies instead that, if developers and local councils cannot agree about the cost of additional urban and social infrastructure, the developer is required to make a minimum grant of $1500 and an interest-free loan of $2000 to the council for each permanent operational employee. This contrasts with the Queensland approach, which specifies that the Co-ordinator General will intervene in such situations, and instead distances the New South Wales government from such negotiations. It seems possible that the per capita payments specified may come to be viewed as the maximum rather than the minimum liability of developers, even if councils believe that they are inadequate.

Before this policy announcement, New South Wales had a basically ad hoc approach to the provision of infrastructure by developers. The obligations placed on different projects varied, inhibiting forward planning by both developers and the responsible authorities. Frequently, infrastructure was not installed soon enough, and in some cases, such as the Newcastle coal loader, this limited the growth of resource developments and trade. During 1982, quotas had to be imposed on coal exporters in the Hunter so that congestion at Newcastle's port could be overcome. This damaged the sales prospects of several mines, particularly new Upper Hunter open cuts, as several coal export contracts could not be fulfilled. Negotiations on this issue among local councils, public authorities, government departments and developers were often carried out only after project approval had been given and coal leases granted. This undermined the basic negotiating strength of the government and introduced uncertainty into developers' financial assessments.

The requirements of the new policy in New South Wales are not as rigorous as those of Queensland, nor are responsibilities clearly defined in a parliamentary Act. However, the government's legal advice indicates that the latter is unnecessary. In announcing the new policy, the Premier indicated that developers would not be expected to meet the full cost of infrastructure, as was the case in Queensland, but that the policy 'provides a financial mechanism to relate reasonable project liabilities with the *short-term* impacts of their developments' (author's emphasis). Basically, this approach appears to reflect the belief that New South Wales resource developments will generally not be commercially viable unless at least some subsidised infrastructure continues to be provided.

The move to somewhat greater developer contributions is probably mainly a result of the financial constraints imposed on the States by the Commonwealth during the period from 1980 to 1982, rather than any radical shift in the State government's perception of the profitability of new developments, as occurred in Queensland.

The infrastructure policies of the other State governments are also essentially ad hoc, with specific provision and financing packages being negotiated for individual projects. If the governments believe that a project is fully viable, they will usually require developers to provide all associated physical and, in remote areas, urban infrastructure. Western Australia did this in the 1960s in the Pilbara, and South Australia is also requiring substantial infrastructure contributions at Roxby Downs. However, when projects, locations or marketing strategies seem unlikely to be viable without subsidies, the Western Australian and Victorian governments have been willing to provide expensive project-related and even single-user infrastructure, such as the Dampier–Perth pipeline and the transmission line for Alcoa's Portland smelter, free of charge or on highly subsidised terms. In addition, virtually all States have been prepared to offer infrastructure services such as electricity at subsidised tariffs in order to attract developments like aluminium smelters away from other States. In this instance the States appeared to believe (probably mistakenly) that they were in a buyers' market.

However, once developments are established, viable and dependent on a government monopoly for infrastructure services, State governments have not been squeamish about using this monopoly power to extract high user charges. Queensland's policy of incorporating obligations to pay high rail tariffs into the royalty and lease payment packages negotiated with developers before development approval is a further reflection of that government's confidence in the competitiveness of Queensland's coal deposits. Recent Queensland coal lease agreements are reported to include an excess freight element of $6–7 a tonne. In addition, coal companies pay a capital and operating cost charge which, respectively, pays off the railway over a ten-year period and covers all its operating costs. After the ten-year period has elapsed, the capital charge will be continued and added to the State's profit.[8] The Queensland government apparently attempts to tailor the freight rate charged to the average rent it believes can be extracted over the life of the project. Unlike a resource rent tax, however, negotiated freight rates cannot easily be changed to reflect annual fluctuations in profitability caused by movements in world prices. Furthermore, coalmines established in Queensland in the 1960s and 1970s pay much lower freight rates, whereas a resource rent tax would apply equally to all producers.

In New South Wales, the State rail authority does not appear to set freight rates to reflect the profitability of individual mines, but merely sets them reasonably high for all coal transport. If rail charges exceed rail costs, this may penalise the less profitable mines, though rebates are given at certain times to older mines in financial difficulty, like those in the Burragorang Valley. The State rail authority claims, however, that it is merely covering costs with its coal freight levy and is not extracting a rent. This claim tends to be supported by the

Commonwealth Grants Commission's report on State rail charges.[9] The New South Wales super royalties and super super royalties of $1.05 and $1.96 a tonne, on top of the basic royalty of $4.20 a tonne, do, however, represent a rather unsophisticated method of collecting perceived resource rents from new mines.

For States like New South Wales, Victoria and Tasmania, which have continued to at least partially subsidise infrastructure provision, the fiscal implications have been worsening budgetary situations and the deprivation of other areas of government capital expenditure such as schools, hospitals and public housing.[10] To bypass Loan Council and general revenue constraints imposed by the system of fiscal transfers, the States have exploited the range of innovative financing mechanisms discussed earlier, including leverage leasing, up-front capital loans by users (sometimes repaid by discounts on user charges), and supplier credit. When these devices are used to subsidise the provision of infrastructure, they frequently result in loss of efficiency and transfers from Commonwealth and State taxpayers to private companies and their (often foreign) shareholders and customers.

Public authorities

The pricing policies of public authorities such as the State electricity commissions have been subject to considerable criticism in recent years. It has been claimed that they are engaging in the sub-economic pricing of services to major bulk users like aluminium smelters and other rural and industrial groups with political muscle. On average (across different categories of customers), tariffs have frequently been set so that the authorities earn a very low if not negative real rate of return on funds employed, thereby 'short-changing' taxpayers of the return they should expect on their public investments.

Electricity authorities have stated in the past that their overall objective in calculating tariffs is to achieve a particular ratio of internal financing, to break even or to obtain a low (7 per cent in Victoria) nominal rate of return on assets valued at historical (rather than replacement) cost.[11] The structure of prices for individual customers is then determined on the basis of average historical costs, although major industrial and rural users have often been subsidised by retail and urban users.[12] As discussed previously, however, for customers who require augmentation of capacity the appropriate tariff is the long-run marginal cost (LRMC) of electricity supply. For large base load users like aluminium smelters, this is the total cost of generation at a new base load station plus an appropriate share of transmission and headquarters' administration costs. Charging a tariff well below the LRMC of electricity supply for users like aluminium smelters, which, before establishing in any location, have an extremely high elasticity of demand, will result in an overexpansion of generation and transmission capacity and a failure to achieve objectives of profitability. Expansion in system capacity may well be in line with the corporate objectives of the electricity authorities; a substantial body of literature indicates that the utility of public sector managers is closely correlated with the rate of growth of the organisation and the associated opportunities for prestige and promotion.[13] However, such policies are likely to result in an excessive allocation of capital, labour, fuel and other resources to electricity supply activities, which may put pressure on domestic interest rates and wages and also cause a loss of potential foreign exchange earnings from coal exports. The latter may cause a depreciation in the exchange rate and an increase in the price of imports. As a result of rising wages, interest rates and import prices, the viability of other productive activities in the economy may be jeopardised. Furthermore, if public authorities sustain losses as a result of these policies and taxes must be collected to cover deficits, additional allocative inefficiencies will be incurred.

All these trends were evident in the early 1980s when New South Wales planned a doubling of its generating capacity and Victoria a $10 billion expansion in its system. Studies at that time by Swan estimated that the annual subsidy to Alcoa's Portland smelter would be of the order of $34–150 million in constant 1982 prices, at a real discount rate of 5–10 per cent a year.[14] Treasury estimated that the subsidy to the Alcoa smelter from the waiver of most of the normal installation charges for the Portland transmission line alone would be of the order of $15–20 million a year, in 1981 prices.[15] Dick calculated that both the Tomago and Lochinvar smelters in the Hunter region would receive an annual subsidy of approximately $30 million in 1981 prices from underpriced electricity, at a real discount rate of 8 per cent a year.[16] Saddler and Donnelly calculated that the annual subsidy to Tasmanian bulk contract customers from taxpayers and retail customers in that State was between $65 million and $79 million in 1981/82 prices.[17] (The bulk users' cost to the system was calculated both at an average real rate of return on capital of 5 per cent a year and at the marginal cost of supply with a 5 per cent real interest rate.) Swan found that the overall subsidy to Tasmanian electricity consumers was between $30 million and $269 million a year in 1981/82 prices, using a real discount rate of 3–10 per cent a year.[18]

There have recently been some encouraging reforms in the State electricity commissions. In Victoria, the Cain Labor government has accepted a recommendation from the Department of Management and Budget that the State Electricity Commission be required to set tariffs so as to achieve a 4 per cent real rate of return on assets valued at replacement cost, after depreciation. Interest payments are included in the calculation of returns, as assets include outstanding debt. Since the Victorian State Electricity Commission, like the State Energy Commission of Western Australia, pays the government a 5 per cent turnover levy, the real rate of return achieved on this basis has been between 2.2 per cent and 2.8 per cent annually in recent years. The State Electricity Commission of Victoria will be expected to achieve the target rate of return only after a phasing-in period. The government has also announced that cross-subsidisation of different categories of consumers will be abolished and that each category will pay costs attributable to its level of consumption.

There is some debate about whether average rate of return targets of this nature are appropriate for electricity authorities.[19] It is argued that tariffs should ideally be set so that they equal the (short-run or long-run) marginal cost of supply, rather than to ensure the achievement of a target average rate of return on assets. The Victorian State Electricity Commission's approach anticipates that assets will be valued at their replacement cost, where this is defined as the cost of putting new power stations or transmission lines on new sites.[20] Furthermore, the target real rate of return specified is believed to be equal to the average rate of return in the economy (that is, normal profits), which would be incorporated into any calculation of marginal costs. Hence, there should be no conflict between these two tariff-setting criteria so long as there are constant returns to scale in the electricity supply system. However, if long-run marginal costs are declining or increasing, adherence to marginal cost pricing (and hence the objective of allocative efficiency) will result in losses or profits, respectively. In order to achieve the specified objective of profitability embodied in the financial rate of return target, electricity authorities will have to make consistent adjustments to marginal cost prices so that total average costs are recouped.

Another criticism of the target rate of return approach is that private firms will not necessarily earn the normal rate of profit every year. In times of economic downturn, therefore, electricity authorities, like private firms, should be allowed to keep tariffs somewhat below the trend level to offset the anticipated decline in demand caused by the recession. The shortfall could then be made good in times of more buoyant demand. Tariff flexibility of this kind is necessary to maximise long-run returns in a system with high fixed costs.

In 1982, the New South Wales Electricity Commission introduced an element of time-of-day and time-of-year tariff setting, at the same time as dramatically increasing tariffs. However, the Commission still does not pay any turnover levy to the State government, and certainly is not required to achieve a reasonable real rate of return on assets. In 1981/82, the Commission sustained a $51 million loss on its activities, though it holds depreciated physical and financial assets of $2.5 billion, valued at historical cost. Including interest payments, the Commission's return on capital (loan and equity) was $52.3 million in 1981/82. Swan calculated that in 1981/82 an implicit subsidy of $189 million was paid to electricity consumers, at a target return of 4 per cent real on assets valued at replacement cost. If a real return of 8 per cent is considered more appropriate, the subsidy was $619.6 million.[21] Cross-subsidisation of bulk industrial users by retail and domestic electricity consumers frequently meant that the bulk customers captured the lion's share of this subsidy.

Local councils

Local councils may, to a limited extent, also attempt to benefit their voters by their policies on infrastructure provision and pricing. In areas where unemployment is high, councils may try to subsidise the infrastructure requirements of major potential employers. However, pursuit of this policy can eventually result in an excessive burden on ratepayers, who may perceive the costs to be out of proportion to the benefits obtained in terms of increased direct and multiplier employment. In this situation councils may then attempt to secure greater contributions from developers towards providing infrastructure. Their capacity to do so may, however, be limited by their modest taxation powers—basically land taxes, or a small coal production levy in New South Wales.

In the Hunter region, both the Singleton and Muswellbrook shires faced severe budgetary constraints during the late 1970s and early 1980s. These shires had access to a small levy on coal produced, but this was an alternative to normal rates, rather than in addition to them. Furthermore, constraints on differential rating arising from rigid State regulations and the method of levying the coal tax actually caused revenue from this source to decline during the 1970s, at a time when the councils' need to install urban infrastructure for project workforces was at its greatest.[22] The borrowing capacity of local councils has also been severely constrained by State governments, which are themselves under tight Loan Council control. Local government is not represented on the Loan Council in its own right, despite attempts by the Whitlam government to initiate this. Hence councils have frequently fared badly in the allocation of the States' public authority borrowing programs, compared with larger public authorities like the electricity commissions and the rail authorities. Such borrowing constraints are particularly inappropriate, and inequitable to existing ratepayers, when higher income residents arriving to take up jobs on projects could and should be expected to contribute to the repayment of loans for infrastructure that they will use in future years. Even where councils did borrow substantial amounts, high interest rates were paid by existing ratepayers rather than capitalised in the loan until infrastructure was operational.

One of the most successful methods developed by the Singleton Shire Council to reduce its revenue shortfall was its venture into land development. It became the largest land developer in the shire, releasing serviced home blocks as well as industrial, commercial and home unit sites. With the profits from these sales, it not only financed further serviced block development but extended urban roads, sewage treatment, water supply, recreational and cultural facilities. The Council also persuaded the large mine developers in the shire to advance the funds to establish home sites that would be required by their future employees. This program both reduced the Council's need for expensive, and scarce, loan capital and provided serviced land at fixed prices to the mining companies.[23]

The Singleton Shire Council also secured per capita payments from mine owners for the provision of urban and social infrastructure, on the basis of the size of their construction and operational workforces. These negotiations were conducted under the guidelines of the State government's September 1982 infrastructure policy. However, despite all these innovations, inadequate local borrowing and taxation powers forced the Shire Council to increase local rates above those paid in comparable New South Wales country areas. Hence there was a substantial involuntary subsidy from local ratepayers to mining projects and the new residents employed on them. Parker has estimated that this subsidy was of the order of $350 per capita in Singleton shire over the period from 1978 to 1981.[24] The failure to grant councils in resource development regions differential rating powers or a means of raising the coal levy may have been motivated by the State government's desire to subsidise developers. By failing to offset the consequent revenue shortfalls with adequate grants, the State government shifted part of the burden of paying for these subsidies on to local residents and away from State taxpayers and voters. As such, this may have represented another method of subsidising infrastructure without drawing directly on State revenue and borrowing resources.

The federal system, with its imbalance between fiscal capacity and functional responsibility and the rather rigid mechanisms developed to overcome this, has a substantial impact on the efficiency and economic rationality of Australian policies on the provision and pricing of infrastructure. In the determination of policy, the financial capacity of governments within the federal system to provide subsidised infrastructure and services is equalled in importance by the relevant authority's perception of how these policies can be used to benefit its electorate, or powerful groups within it. If unemployment is high and potential developments are, rightly or wrongly, believed to be of marginal viability, the provision and pricing of infrastructure are likely to embody subsidies. If it is considered that new projects will be highly profitable and carry low risks, the same instruments may be used to extract resource rents. However, the capacities of different levels of government to provide subsidies to marginal projects, their eagerness to extract rents, and the methods used to achieve these objectives will be heavily influenced by their access to tax revenue and borrowings, as determined by legal interpretations of the Constitution and the operation of the Loan Council.

Various methods are employed to subsidise infrastructure provision and services, including leverage leasing, use of supplier credit, low or negative returns on capital employed, and sub-economic pricing of State-owned resources. Similarly, rents may be collected by methods such as excess rail freights and the private provision of State-owned infrastructure. These techniques are frequently designed specifically to maximise the responsible authority's command over resources within the federal system, but may cause an inefficient and inequitable reallocation of resources elsewhere in the economy. In the absence of fiscal imbalance and other constraints imposed by the federal system, authorities would be free, if they wished, to offer subsidies from taxes levied on the constituency that is expected to benefit from a project or on those benefiting from distortions in the economy, such as protected industries and some wage and salary earners. This would have the same effect as the beneficiaries taking a lower wage or a lower price for goods supplied, in order to make the marginal project viable. Instead, the subsidies are often paid for by taxpayers, infrastructure service consumers and producers who are outside the group expected to benefit from the project or from distortions in the economy. Moreover, there is rarely any attempt to determine whether the expected benefits to Australian residents of such subsidies will outweigh the costs. Similarly, if it were not for the constraints of the federal system, authorities would be able to levy a properly specified resource rent tax without fear that the funds raised would be offset against revenue transfers within the system. Ad hoc rent collections will probably not only fail to capture all rents available but will also be imposed on some activities which are not generating rents. This may force such enterprises out of business and result in a less than ideal use of human, capital and natural resources.

10 A Japanese perspective on resource trade with Australia

MAKOTO SAKURAI

Since the end of the 1960s the economic relationship between Australia and Japan has flourished, chiefly as a result of the development of resource trade between the two countries. In the 1970s, however, along with the evolution of a close economic relationship, there were some problems to be solved; for example, a price and quantity maladjustment in long-term contractual arrangements. For the Japanese investor these difficulties represented a very useful process of learning by experience.

The present economic recession is worldwide, and the stagnation of industrial production is likely to continue in both developed and developing countries. Nevertheless, the structure of industry in the Asian–Pacific region is changing rapidly. Japan is moving from an economy based on capital-intensive industries to one founded on higher technology. The Asian newly industrialising countries (the Republic of Korea, Taiwan, Hong Kong and Singapore) are shifting from labour-intensive economies to the pursuit of more capital—and technology-intensive economic structures. The members of ASEAN (except for Singapore) are catching up with the newly industrialising countries, and four of the ASEAN countries—Indonesia, Malaysia, the Philippines and Thailand—have performed well by comparison with other developing countries. These factors are bound to affect the economies of both Japan and Australia, and resources trade and investment between the two countries must be discussed within the broader perspective of these regional developments.

This chapter sets out to survey and analyse the principal issues in Japanese resource investment and trade with Australia. Three aspects will be covered: resources trade; major issues for Japanese investment in Australian resources; and the direction of future investment.

Japanese Resource Trade with Australia

Most of Japan's natural resources are imported, which is a typical pattern for countries poor in natural resources. Japan's postwar economic growth has produced some major changes in import and foreign investment patterns. In the early postwar period most Japanese resource imports depended on the spot market, but Japanese trade with Australia has expanded since the second half of the 1960s and rapid economic growth based on manufacturing industry has increased Japan's demand for Australian resources, necessitating the development of more permanent arrangements. Yamazawa identifies four trading categories in the importation of resources to Japan: importing on the spot market; importing through simple long-term contracts; the 'develop-and-import by loan-cum-purchase' technique; and the 'develop-and-import by captive development' technique.[1]

Most of Japan's resource trade relies on the develop-and-import by loan-cum-purchase technique, which has so far been the most important form of resource trade between Japan and Australia. By contrast, the develop-and-import by captive development technique has been popular in the United States and in European industrialised countries. This chapter compares the two techniques, and goes on to discuss the advantages of long-term contractual arrangements based on the first of them, and to examine the problems associated with long-term contracts.

A comparison of two resource trade techniques

A comparison of the two techniques and an examination of Japan's postwar economic history will reveal a number of reasons why Japanese firms adopted the develop-and-import by loan-cum-purchase technique. The comparison is undertaken from several perspectives: the industrial organisation of the market in terms of both supply and demand, the financial background, and uncertainty in the political climate and other non-economic factors.

There are significant differences between the two techniques for the organisation of industry. Captive development implies vertical integration from raw material to final product, a pattern that creates a market monopoly in both supply and demand. Historically, this has been the typical pattern for multinational companies procuring resources for North America and Europe. The loan-cum-purchase method does not involve integration, and its chief purpose is usually to establish long-term and stable import trade; in general, therefore, the loan-cum-purchase approach does not create a hold over the market. In the iron ore trade between Australia and Japan there is certainly a bilateral monopoly, with Japan as the dominant buyer and Australia as the dominant supplier, but a bilateral monopoly is quite different from a pure monopoly. A necessary condition for the develop-and-import by loan-cum-purchase technique is the existence of a high level of demand for the resources concerned. The development of resources is a lengthy process requiring a great deal of capital and a long gestation period for capital investment. A high level of market demand satisfies these requirements, and ultimately produces economies of scale in the development of resources.

The existence of differences in financial capacity provides another perspective on the development of Japan's trade in resources. In a perfect international financial market there would be no difference between participants in terms of financial capacity. In an imperfect financial market, however, investment in a captive development structure is not possible for resource consumers with limited financial capacity. By comparison with western multinational companies, Japanese firms at the time of Japan's emergence as an industrial nation did not have sufficient financial capacity for foreign investment; furthermore, Japan's technological background at that time was poor.[2]

Political uncertainties and other non-economic factors have become critical factors in the development of resource trade and investment. By comparison with the situation in the 1960s there have been increasing global uncertainties in the 1970s and 1980s, for example, fluctuations in oil prices and a worldwide economic recession. Developing resource-rich countries in particular have adopted an increasingly nationalistic attitude to resource development, an attitude that precludes the captive development approach to resource development. Uncertainty about the likely level of future demand immediately poses a serious adjustment problem for long-term contractual arrangements.

Advantages of long-term contracts

Since the second half of the 1960s most resource trade between Japan and Australia has been based on long-term contracts, and a number of studies of long-term contract trading have been published.[3] The theoretical basis for long-term contractual arrangements is found in the labour contract theory developed by Baily and Azariadis.[4] The simplest explanation of the effects of long-term contracts on price formation is illustrated in Figure 10.1.

The model parallels the labour contract theory in which the advantages of nominal wage stability are analysed. Figure 10.1a shows the relationship between the utility of the exporter and resource prices; Figure 10.1b shows the relationship between the disutility of the importer and the import prices paid. Price fluctuation in the spot market is indicated by the distance from F to G. Exporter utility decreases with decreasing resource prices and importer disutility increases with increasing prices. These conditions may be expressed as follows:

$$U = U(P),$$
$$U'(P) > 0, \; U''(P) < 0$$
$$T = T(P)$$
$$T'(P) > 0, \; T''(P) > 0.$$

Under these conditions, degrees of utility for both spot market trading and long-term contract arrangements can be measured. Exporter utility and importer disutility in the spot market depend on the average price (E); the exporter utility at E corresponds to $HE = U^{\star\star}O$; and the disutility at E corresponds to $H'E = T^{\star}O$. For long-term contract trading with fixed prices and quantities, the utility at the fixed price E corresponds to $H'E = T'O$. Therefore, by comparison with spot market trading, exporter utility is greater under long-term contractual arrangements and importer disutility is smaller. Clearly there are

Figure 10.1a   A resource trade model

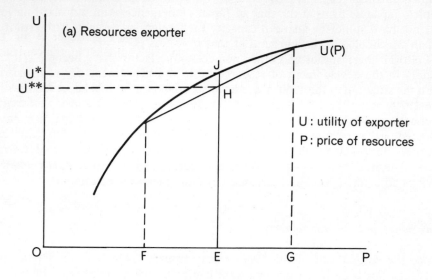

Figure 10.1b

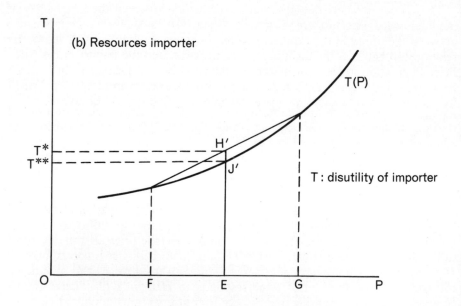

advantages for both exporter and importer in long-term contractual arrangements.

It is true that in the 1970s there were some maladjustment problems in long-term contractual arrangements. A misjudgment in supply and demand forecasts will cause the price level (E) to move towards either F or G; furthermore, it will be difficult to trade the quantity stipulated by the contract. But forecasts are made on the basis of a global economic outlook, which may itself be incorrect; and the advantages of long-term contractual arrangements are in any case not clearcut under strongly uncertain economic conditions.

There is ample support for the view that both Australia and Japan have benefited from long-term contractual arrangements in their mutual resources trade.[5] One factor that must be taken into account, of course, is the intervention of the Australian government in the setting of prices; this issue is discussed below.

Problems associated with long-term contracts

During the 1970s serious problems were experienced in the adjustment of traded quantities under long-term contractual arrangements, notably for iron ore in 1971 and for sugar from 1975 to 1977. (The beef trade also encountered problems in 1974 and 1977, but trade in beef between Australia and Japan was not conducted under long-term contractual arrangements.) Many studies have been carried out on the poor performance of long-term contracts under conditions of economic uncertainty, with the source of the uncertainty ranging from fluctuations in demand and supply to such factors as exchange rate movements. In response to conditions of increasing economic uncertainty, long-term contracts underwent such modifications as the introduction of clauses to allow for flexibility in quantities traded.

In a White Paper on resources published in 1971, the Japanese Ministry of International Trade and Industry proposed several policy strategies for stabilising resource imports: diversification of sources of supply; diversification of trading arrangements; stock-piling; and the use of inventory stocks.[6] In adopting these policy recommendations, Japanese manufacturers came to realise that they would have to extend their arrangements for importing resources from the traditional long-term contracts to joint ventures in captive development. Australia, for its part, as a resource supplier, has attempted to diversify its trading arrangements outwards to such partners as the Republic of Korea, a comparative newcomer in the resources market.[7]

Resource trade is dependent on resource development, which normally requires enormous capital investment, so it is not surprising that short-term adjustment of quantities and prices in response to economic uncertainty is not easy. However, the problems of long-term contractual arrangements can be largely solved by a sharing of the risks between the importer and the exporter. If the costs and benefits of risk sharing in long-term contractual arrangements are weighed in the balance, the net result will be positive. Future resource trade between Australia and Japan will continue to depend on long-term contracts, though some modifications will be necessary.

Major Issues for Japanese Resource Investment in Australia

Resource trade between Australia and Japan bears a natural relationship to Japanese investment in Australian resources, which, in turn, is fuelled by the

Figure 10.2   Japanese resource-related foreign investment in Oceania (annual flow and percentage share)

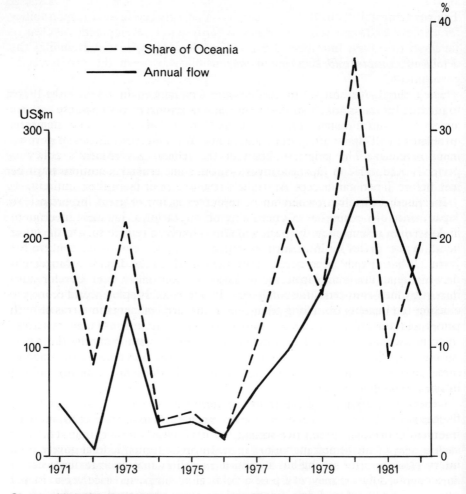

Source: Ministry of Finance *Monthly Monetary and Financial Statistics* December 1983 (special issue)

thriving Japanese economy. In a sense, Australian resources may be classified as a public good for the Japanese economy, a public good being defined as a widely used resource that is not easily substitutable. In this respect Australia, as a host country for Japanese investment, represents a reliable source of supply whose relationship with Japan is not clouded by political uncertainties. For the Japanese investor, however, the situation is complicated by the federal–State division of powers. This section goes on to examine the influence of Australian government intervention on resource price setting and on Japanese investment policy.

Government intervention and price setting

The fundamental distinction in Australia—that between federal responsibility for resource trade and State responsibility for resource development—is clear to Japanese investors, but there are problems for Japan in understanding the details of the complex division of responsibility between the two levels of government.

The federal government's mineral resources policy has altered since the 1970s to provide for increased Australian ownership of resources as a response to three areas of concern: export prices; the proportions of foreign and domestic ownership; and the contribution of the mineral resource industries to government revenues. The primary thrust of the federal government's policy is perfectly acceptable to Japanese investors, but some crucial conditions must be met before Japan can accept Australia's resource policies in their entirety.

Increased Australian ownership of resources is not of great importance to Japan, since ownership has not been a significant factor in Japanese investment in Australian resources in the past, and this is likely to remain so. On the other hand, export prices for Australian resources are a source of major concern for Japan. It has already been noted that the most widely used trade arrangement between Australia and Japan is the long-term contract under develop-and-import by loan-cum-purchase conditions. In a reasonably stable world economic climate, the benefits from long-term contractual arrangements in terms of both prices and quantities traded are positive; in fact, Australia–Japan resources trade is roughly equivalent to a bilateral monopoly, with Australia the major supplier and Japan the major consumer. (Of course, Australia–Japan trade in some resource commodities—for example, coal—does not conform to the bilateral monopoly model.)

Generally speaking, the Australian government should not attempt to influence prices but should allow the market mechanism to operate unhampered,[8] intervening only when the price-setting process is clearly unfair; intervention in such a case would be acceptable to Japan. In broad terms, federal government intervention in price setting has a political as well as an economic dimension— an economic solution may well pose a political problem, and vice versa. In any case, the ideal level of federal intervention in price setting is very difficult to define, even in a purely economic context.

Federal intervention and Japanese investment policy

Many studies have pointed out that the difficulty confronting a resource-based economy is to maintain equilibrium between the growth of the resources sector and the development of other sectors; in this respect, Australia is a typical resource-based economy. Moreover, most of Australia's resources are exported, and economic growth based on resource exports tends to create an expansion in the demand for both traded and non-traded goods. In principle, the exchange of traded goods operates according to the theory of comparative advantage, so that the non-traded goods sector will expand in parallel with the growth in the resource-based traded goods sector. Australia's manufacturing industries are facing some real problems, such as restructuring in order to raise productivity.[9]

Equilibrium among the various sectors of the economy (the resource, manufacturing and tertiary sectors) is a major macroeconomic objective for the Australian federal government, and to achieve the necessary balance in growth rates the federal government must intervene at the policy level in resource development and trading arrangements. Standard macroeconomic measures such as fiscal and monetary policies will have to be employed, as well as policies for industrial and regional development. Regional development policy has a major influence on investment in resource development. This is because a high proportion of the huge capital investment required for development must be devoted to providing such infrastructure as transportation facilities. Furthermore, depending on the way 'regional development' is defined, the provision of infrastructure may take place within a broader economic and environmental context: a resource development project may have the parallel social objective of creating a viable economic community. Thus infrastructure investment will expand to include community-related as well as project-related infrastructure. Regional development in this form will be welcomed by both levels of government in Australia.

Japanese investors and importers recognise the wisdom of this approach to regional development, but—obviously—they will be reluctant to expand their investment in infrastructure indefinitely. It would be better for the federal government to encourage resource-based regional development by adopting the principle of sharing the costs of the related infrastructure between the government and private investors.

The current trend in resource development towards emphasis on investment in infrastructure is broadly supported by the government of Japan, which has listed four objectives of Japanese investment in overseas resource development: to promote regional diversification of supply sources; to cooperate in requests for investment in related infrastructure; to engage in joint development ventures with overseas companies; and to support the processing of resources within supplying countries.[10] These guidelines will apply to Japanese resource investment in Australia.

The Outlook for the Future

The economic prospects for Japan must be taken into account in any consideration of Japanese investment and trade in Australian resources. In 1982 the Japanese government published a research study, *Japan in the Year 2000*, on the long-term economic outlook for Japan.[11] According to this study, Japan's annual rates of economic growth will range from 4.0 per cent to 4.4 per cent in the years from 1980 to 2000, and the index of energy consumption to gross national product will have fallen to 73 in the year 2000 (taking 1980 as the base year). The share of secondary industry in gross national product will also fall, but the share of the service sector will rise (Table 10.1).

On the basis of these forecasts, Japanese demand for Australian resources will expand more slowly than it has done in the past. Economic and political uncertainty has been growing since the 1970s, and a rapid decrease in the levels of uncertainty is unlikely. The probability of serious difficulties in the adjustment of resource supply and demand under long-term contractual arrangements means that governments in both Australia and Japan will have to intervene in policies for resource development and trade. In principle, however, trade and

Figure 10.3   Japan: the outlook for primary energy consumption per unit of gross national product (Base: 1980 = 100)

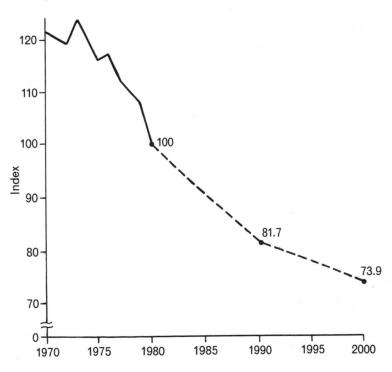

Source: Economic Planning Agency *Japan in the Year 2000* 1983

Table 10.1   Japan: the outlook for the industrial structure

	Nominal gross domestic product (¥tr)		
	1970	1980	2000
Primary industry	4.4	8.6	
—percentage of total	6.0	3.7	4.2
Secondary industry	31.6	89.6	
—percentage of total	43.1	38.2	31.5
Mining and manufacturing	26.2	68.8	
—percentage of total	35.7	29.3	21.6
Chemicals	5.8	12.7	
—percentage of total	7.9	5.4	1.5
Primary metals	2.9	8.4	
—percentage of total	3.9	3.6	0.8
Machinery	10.1	28.0	
—percentage of total	13.7	11.9	15.7
Others	7.4	19.6	
—percentage of total	10.1	8.4	3.6
Construction	5.5	20.9	
—percentage of total	7.4	8.9	10.0
Tertiary industry	37.3	136.5	
—percentage of total	50.9	58.1	64.2
Electricity, gas, water	1.6	7.1	
—percentage of total	2.2	3.0	1.5
Finance, insurance, real estate	9.3	36.5	
—percentage of total	12.6	15.5	8.5
Transport, communications	4.9	15.5	
—percentage of total	6.6	6.6	5.6
Services, etc.	21.6	77.4	
—percentage of total	29.4	33.0	48.6
Total	73.4	234.8	
—per cent	100.0	100.0	100.0
Statistical errors	−0.1	+0.2	
Gross domestic product	73.3	234.9	

Source: Economic Planning Agency Japan in the Year 2000 Japan Times, 1983

investment policies should be determined as far as possible by market conditions, and government intervention should be confined to complementary issues.

At the time of writing, Japanese importers are reluctant to enter into long-term resource contracts because of the risk of creating an oversupply of resources; the trend in Japanese resource trade has therefore reverted from long-term contractual arrangements to spot market trading. There has been no

Table 10A.1 Japanese foreign investment: total stock (accumulated approved investment from base year 1951, US$m)

	Japanese fiscal year							
	1960		1970		1980		1982	
	number	amount	number	amount	number	amount	number	amount
Manufacturing	104.0	127.5	1 294.0	926.0	7 213.0	12 573.0	8 763.0	16 952.0
—percentage of total	15.6	45.0	34.7	25.9	30.1	34.4	30.2	31.9
Primary (agriculture, fisheries, mining)	72.0	93.2	359.0	884.0	1 732	7 981	2 304	11 372.0
—percentage of total	10.8	32.9	9.6	24.7	7.2	21.9	7.9	21.4
Tertiary, others	489.0	62.4	2 079.0	1 766.0	15 003.0	15 943.0	17 996.0	24 807.0
—percentage of total	73.5	22.0	55.7	49.3	62.6	43.7	61.9	46.7
Total	665.0	283.0	3 732.0	3 579.0	23 948.0	36 497	29 063.0	53 131.0
—per cent	100.0	100.0	100.0	100.0	100.0	100.0	100.0	100.0

Source: Ministry of Finance *Monthly Monetary and Financial Statistics* December 1983 (special issue)

Table 10A.2 Japanese foreign investment by region and industry: Japanese fiscal year 1983 (percentage shares of stock)

	North America	Latin America	Asia	Middle East	Europe	Africa	Ocenia (Australia)	Total
Manufacturing	25.1	20.3	34.2	6.7	7.0	1.0	5.8	100.0
							(4.4)	
	27.9	*38.8*	*39.9*	*45.9*	*19.2*	*6.5*	*29.9*	*31.9*
							(25.9)	
Primary industry	9.6	14.5	50.1	0.4	7.5	5.4	12.3	100.0
							(11.1)	
	7.2	*18.6*	*39.2*	*16.9*	*14.0*	*24.7*	*41.7*	*21.5*
							(43.7)	
Tertiary industry, others	39.8	15.2	12.3	5.2	16.5	6.9	4.0	100.0
							(3.5)	
	67.7	*42.6*	*20.9*	*37.2*	*66.8*	*68.8*	*28.4*	*46.6*
							(30.4)	
Total	28.7	16.7	27.4	4.7	11.6	4.7	6.3	100.0
							(5.4)	
	100.0	*100.0*	*100.0*	*100.0*	*100.0*	*100.0*	*100.0*	*100.0*
							(100.0)	

Source: Ministry of Finance *Monthly Monetary and Financial Statistics* December 1983 (special issue)

188

clear policy direction from the Japanese government concerning this reversion, but it is likely that in the long run Japan's fundamental approach to resources trade will not differ substantially from the policy stance adopted in the light of the experience of the 1960s and early 1970s. Thus the basic elements of Japan's overseas resource development policies—diversification of supply sources, cooperation in the provision of related infrastructure, joint development ventures, and promotion of resource processing in supplying countries that are hosting Japanese resource investment—will probably also remain virtually unchanged.

The present situation is largely attributable to widespread fluctuations in business operations. On the supply side, for example, the main concern of Japanese manufacturing industries is not the price of resources but the use of excess production capacity; excess capacity is at present the most important concern of financial management in the manufacturing industries.

Given this short-term situation, Australia–Japan resources trade and development will probably stagnate over the next few years. Nevertheless, the basic relationship between the two countries is likely to be maintained with some minor changes, such as a scaling down of the relative importance of long-term contractual arrangements in total resources trade.

Some of the important concerns for Japan–Australia resource trade and investment were identified earlier in this chapter, but the crucial factor for Japanese investment in Australian resources is the political stability of Australia. Political stability in the host country is a fundamental requirement for direct foreign investment; and, though many of the world's resource-endowed countries are politically unstable, Australia, while rich in natural resources, may be classified among the most stable countries in terms of 'political risk'. Problems will arise in Japan–Australia resource investment and trade, but in the long run the established relationship between the two countries will continue and strengthen. To promote the development of this economic relationship, a sound mutual understanding must be built up in both the public and the private sectors through such avenues as the exchange of information.

11   Federal–State issues in external economic relations

JOHN WARHURST AND
GILLIAN O'LOGHLIN

This chapter is concerned with establishing the framework within which interaction between State and federal governments in the conduct of Australia's external economic relations takes place. The 'issues', when they appear in the discussion, are used to exemplify particular points rather than discussed in their own right; or, to put it another way, the most important 'issues' between governments in contemporary Australia are ones of constitutional principle and of appropriate intergovernmental structures. The key arguments are about which level of government ought to be carrying out which function, rather than about essentially transient, day-to-day disputes between governments. Recently there have been a number of such disputes between Australian governments about the extent to which State governments have a place in the daily working out of Australian external relations—political, economic and cultural. State government demands for representation at international conferences and for involvement in domestic preparations for international negotiations will be fully catered for only after the wider matters of principle have been settled.

Aspects of the Australian Federation

Within this context, discussion of the role played by the pattern of federal–State relations in influencing Australia's external economic relations must be based upon an understanding of contemporary Australian federalism, and external economic relations provide one window on the whole system at work. Aspects of the federal system requiring introduction include the functional pattern of intergovernmental relations within the cooperative style of Australian federalism; the particular problem of information distribution which, as governments now realise, this pattern creates; the interaction between the general political climate within the federal system and the approaches of federal and State governments to specific issues such as international trade; the expansion over the past ten to fifteen years in State government administrations, especially in departments concerned with central coordination and economic development; the relative unimportance of ideological and party differences in determining the substantial rather than the superficial behaviour of governments; the strengths as well as the weaknesses inherent in the federal system for equipping nations for dealings with other governments and with private firms; and the options for State governments wishing to intervene in the shaping of Australia's external economic policies.

Intergovernmental relations within the Australian federal system take place essentially between federal and State government departments with functional responsibilities, rather than (in any real sense) between governments as a whole.[1] In this way cooperative arrangements, which take into account the constitutional division of responsibilities, are negotiated by officials and ministers responsible for narrowly defined policy fields such as agriculture, secondary industry, resource development, and so on. The relevance of this pattern for Australia's relations with Japan was noted in the Myer report.[2] A myriad arrangements exist,[3] but central coordination within governments of intergovernmental relations has been limited. A coordinated approach by government to an objective which cuts across the traditional ways of managing policymaking, such as external economic relations with Japan, is not easily achieved.

A particular consequence of the segmented pattern of policy-making that is inherent in the traditional operation of cooperative federalism has been the very restricted distribution of information within and between governments. Where information, most of which is held by the federal government, is passed on from one government to another, distribution is often restricted to the functional equivalent at the other level of government.[4] State governments in the mid-1970s judged this problem to be so severe that they took the unique step of subscribing to a Canberra-based news service in an effort to increase their access to information originating from the federal government and other Canberra sources. The problem of lack of information for State governments is even more acute in functional areas such as foreign affairs and trade, where either there are no equivalent departments at the State level or the equivalents are new and relatively small. And it is these departments that are largely responsible for managing external economic relations.

Any specific issue that needs to be resolved within the federal system, such as the terms and conditions attached to trade in iron ore and coal between Japan and Australia, cannot escape entanglement both in other issues that divide Australian governments and in the general climate of intergovernmental relations. For example, shortly after the election of the Labor federal government in March 1983 the Premier of Queensland, Joh Bjelke-Petersen, warned the Prime Minister to keep out of the international coal negotiations that were then in train (*Australian* 25 March 1983), and, a little later, attacked the federal Treasurer in highly colourful language about the federal government's decision to refuse permission to a South Korean company to invest in Queensland's Jackson oil pipeline (*Australian* 5 April 1983). These clashes must be seen not only as reflecting the general climate of relations between the National–Liberal Queensland government and the Labor federal government but also partly as a spin-off from the intergovernmental tensions that surrounded the Tasmanian government's Franklin Dam plans.

Australian State governments in the recent past have greatly increased the size and quality of their bureaucracies in an attempt to exert what control they can over their regional economic environments. This expansion has occurred particularly in the Premiers' departments and the treasuries, and in variously named departments responsible for economic development.[5] It is these refurbished institutions that house the officers responsible for State government intervention in international trade matters, but they are only one facet of a new development, which now includes a whole range of defensive and aggressive schemes to assist industry located, or willing to be located, in one State rather than others.[6] The competition is fierce. In addition to narrowly economic concerns, State governments are very sensitive to their status within the federation, with the emphasis on 'State building' rather than 'nation building', so that participation in external economic relations is as much a response to internal as to external needs.

Despite some evidence of Labor/non-Labor conflict, federal–State relations are not dogged by party-generated differences in government policies, although leaders representing different parties do feel free to dress each other down publicly in a way that is not the case with members of the same party, who tend to be gentle with each other in public. This is best exemplified by the close public bond between the four Labor Premiers and the Labor Prime Minister at the moment. However, party labels are not the best predictors of how State and federal governments will act. All Australian governments share a commitment to economic growth, and their attitudes to international trade are similar. Of the areas in which party attitudes do matter, perhaps the most relevant in the context of external economic relations is industrial relations. Trade union intervention is criticised by non-Labor Premiers but not by Labor leaders.

A federal system of government is generally regarded as a handicap in dealings with either another country or with a private firm, and this has been the tenor of the comments of those who have considered the implications of federalism for Australia's external relations. This applies both to the Myer report and to a recent paper by the Commonwealth government's Japan Secretariat.[7] Neither is unaware of the benefits that may stem from federalism, but each does stress the problems. As the Myer report argues,

Australia's Federal system impinges on relations with Japan in two interrelated ways. First, it reinforces Japan's impression of Australia as a country lacking cohesion and broad consensus on national direction, particularly in basic policy areas such as foreign investment, mineral and energy resource development and industrial growth. Secondly, the Japanese are placed in a position of being able to derive advantage from playing one state off against another or the states against the Commonwealth. (p. 110)

This is fair comment, but more stress should be given to the concomitant advantages to Australian governments in their relations with business. For example, it can be argued that some firms pay more rather than less tax because of the existence of both federal and State taxes. Rather than enabling businesses to slip through the cracks between the two levels of government, the combination of governments may mean that government as a whole extracts more than it otherwise would (*Canberra Times* 4 April 1983).

The final aspect of federal–State relations that must be considered is the question of the political options available to State governments, given the constitutional division of responsibility. They have basically three options, which are not mutually exclusive. The first is to work solely through the federal government, relying on its representation of Australian interests but working to ensure that that representation takes into account the particular interests of one or all State governments; a State government must either convince the central government of the logic of its position or use threats and promises to achieve its goals. The second option is to go it alone, developing the expertise to promote the State, to promote industry and so on, without necessarily heeding what the federal government is doing, and cutting across it where State government goals appear to conflict with those of the central government. The third option is to blend in with the efforts of the federal government in a coordinated fashion, working together at times, separately at others, but always within agreed guidelines. In the industry promotion field in Australia, State governments have taken up all three approaches at one time or another, and sometimes simultaneously.

Differences Between the States

For some what is striking about the Australian States is their relative uniformity; for others it is their distinctiveness.[8] Differences between the States may be exaggerated, but they are not trumped up; the States have much in common, but also a lot that divides them. The real differences may be divided into permanent differences and variable or transient differences, a distinction that is illustrated by the arguments advanced in March 1982 by Mr K. Narusawa, economic adviser to the president of the Bank of Tokyo, at a seminar on Australian–Japanese relations in Adelaide (*Advertiser* 30 March 1982). Narusawa maintained that the reasons why South Australia lagged behind the eastern States in terms of Japanese investment included the absence of an international airport in Adelaide and the State's geographic position, which meant 'a long journey from Port Adelaide to Japanese ports'. The South Australian government could not do much about the State's geographic position, but later that year Adelaide airport was upgraded to international status.

Permanent differences

The main permanent differences between the states are size and population; location vis-à-vis both Japan and Canberra; the known presence of natural resources and balance between primary, secondary and tertiary industry in the local economy—though those factors may change slowly over time; and stage of development—some States have a far longer history than others of exploitation of their natural resources.

A State's size and population determine to a large extent the influence of its government within the federation. In Australia, New South Wales and Victoria contribute the majority of the representatives in both the federal Parliament and the federal Cabinet; the two larger States are also in the financial position to employ a larger bureaucracy. But they are less vulnerable than the smaller States to financial dependence upon the federal government. Tasmania, in particular, has a small public service, which limits the extent to which the State government can do the things it would otherwise choose to do. For similar reasons New South Wales and Victoria are influential in the private sector; most of the head offices of large private firms are located in either Melbourne or Sydney.

New South Wales and Victoria are also geographically closest to the centre of government, the national capital. Their leaders, in both government and the private sector, have had in the past—and to some extent still have—easier physical access to Canberra. The physical distance continues to contribute to the greater distrust of Canberra felt by the so-called 'peripheral' States—Queensland, South Australia, Western Australia and Tasmania. In terms of proximity to Japan the two States at most obvious disadvantage are South Australia and Tasmania, adding to the other disadvantages they suffer.

The distribution of natural resources among the Australian States means that Queensland and Western Australia are the main suppliers of Australian resource exports to Japan.[9] Western Australia relies heavily on only two commodities—iron ore and alumina—while Queensland (along with New South Wales) exports a very diversified range of products. All States, however, make some contribution. The Japan Secretariat has stressed that

[t]he implication of the States' commodity share of trade [with Japan] ... is that *all* States, however narrow or diverse their export pattern, have a vital interest in the development and well-being of the Australian trade relationship with Japan.[10]

The significance of the differences engendered by the stage which a State's development has reached has been argued most strongly by Garth Stevenson in attempting to explain different state attitudes to foreign investment.[11] Intergovernmental conflict may be the result, and States whose development has occurred comparatively late may have quite distinct interests. Stevenson shows how

... calls for economic nationalism emanating from Ottawa or Canberra, Toronto or Melbourne, can be interpreted as the dog-in-the-manger attitudes of those who grew rich on the first wave of foreign investment and who now want to slam the door on the second wave before the newer frontier areas can catch up. (p. 31)

Passing differences

Superimposed at any time on the permanent differences between the States are the transient differences related to governments, parties or personalities. But here too the differences are perhaps less important in the long run than the similarities.

The balance between the parties in government varies from year to year. At the time of writing there are five Labor governments in Australia (those of the Commonwealth, New South Wales, Victoria, South Australia and Western Australia) and three non-Labor governments (those of Queensland, Tasmania and the Northern Territory). Thus the present balance is heavily in Labor's favour, both because of the numbers and because of the significance of the governments that are Labor—the non-Labor governments include the two smallest.

Flowing on from party differences will be some differences in policies and in general attitudes to issues. Industrial relations, for example, is an issue favoured by non-Labor governments; it has been non-Labor Premiers such as David Tonkin of South Australia and Joh Bjelke-Petersen of Queensland who have been most forward in promoting to the Japanese the industrial relations climate of their States, and in criticising other States for their industrial relations and wages policies (Tonkin *National Times* 25 April–1 May 1982; Bjelke-Petersen *Australian* 25 March 1983).

Pressuring the Central Government

Where the Commonwealth government unarguably has the constitutional powers, the State governments may choose to exert what pressure they can against the central government to produce a decision favourable to their interests. One field of Commonwealth responsibility, and of demonstrated interest to Japan, in which this has happened in recent years has been import protection policy. State government pressure against the Commonwealth government has been exerted strongly in the direction of ensuring the maintenance of an increase in protection for domestic companies against imported products.[12]

This was so in a very recent case: protection of the Australian steel industry. The Japanese government attempted to convince the Australian government not to give further protection to the ailing domestic steel producer, Broken Hill Proprietary Co. Ltd (*Sydney Morning Herald* 31 July 1982). However, further protection was eventually given to that company and, while the impact of various pressures on the federal government cannot be isolated, State government voices were among the loudest in support of the local producer; Neville Wran, the New South Wales Premier, was a bitter critic of any suggestion that assistance should not be given to the company (*Australian Financial Review* 22 March 1983). Likewise, the South Australian branch of the Labor Party has recently called for a bar on the import into Australia of light commercial motor vehicles (*Canberra Times* 12 June 1983).

Independent State Government Action

Each State government devotes some resources within its capital-city-based administration to the management of external economic relations. Generally these activities are located in variously named departments of economic development, and to a lesser extent in Premiers' departments. The Victorian Department of the Premier and Cabinet contains an international relations branch, and the New South Wales government has attached an overseas trade authority to its Premier's Department. It is the Premiers' departments that are responsible for State government representatives outside Australia, including those in Tokyo. (There is some liaison with other departments; in Victoria, for instance, there is consultation with the Minister for Economic Development and with the Victorian Economic Development Corporation.) State government representation in Tokyo is the focus of the following section.

Information about these offices is presented in Table 11.1.[13] Four State governments, those of New South Wales, Victoria, Queensland and Western Australia, maintain their own public service representation in Tokyo, while the South Australian government pays a retainer and expenses to the Elders manager in Tokyo. The Tasmanian government has no office in Tokyo (the only Tasmanian office anywhere outside Australia consists of a tourist representative in New Zealand). In the cases of both New South Wales and Western Australia, representation in Tokyo dates back to the late 1960s.

The current pattern of representation has been in place since 1979, when the Queensland office opened. The senior representative of all governments is styled 'Commissioner'. Staff numbers are similar—about six; in the case of New South Wales this represents a drop from a peak of ten (*Sydney Morning Herald* 20 April 1982). Staff numbers are very small compared with those of the Australian Embassy in Tokyo, which maintains about 40 Australian-based diplomatic staff and over 100 staff in all. The two senior positions in each State office are filled by Australian citizens, and the staff are experienced: for example, the Queensland representative has worked in Tokyo for thirteen years and was previously the New South Wales representative; similarly, the head of the Victorian office has worked in Tokyo for many years, and at the time of his appointment in 1977 was deputy chairman of the Australian Chamber of Commerce in Tokyo.

What functions do the State government representatives perform? When the Queensland Premier opened the State's Tokyo office, he urged his Japanese audience to 'come to Queensland, not to Australia'.[14] That is a pointer to what the offices are about. Two general statements of purpose provided by State governments are appended to this chapter. The functions of State representatives, as summarised in 1981 by the Japan Secretariat, are to act

as contact points for Japanese and State business interests, to disseminate

Table 11.1 State government offices in Tokyo

State	Date established	Area of responsibility	Staff	Cost 1982/83 ($)
New South Wales	1968	Japan	6	820 000
Victoria	1977; Hume Bros (Aust.) Pty Ltd has acted as agent for the state from 1974	Japan, People's Republic of China, Republic of Korea, Philippines, Hong Kong	6; 2 Australian, 4 Japanese	552 800
Queensland	1979	Not formally defined; Commissioner travels to Korea, Taiwan, Northern Pacific Rim	6; 2 Australian, 4 Japanese	438 865
Western Australia	1968	—	6; 2 Australian, 4 Japanese	267 990
South Australia	mid-1970s—represented by Elders manager in Tokyo on a part-time basis			—
Tasmania	No state government representative—any trade dealings are handled by the Commonwealth Department of Trade			—

Source: Information provided by State governments

information about the State to the Japanese, to look after State visitors, and to promote State business interests including tourism.[15]

Some idea of the amounts of time devoted to different aspects of the work can be acquired from Table 11.2, which analyses the activities of the New South Wales government's Tokyo office during 1982.

Tourism-related activities stand out. One of the New South Wales office's staff is employed full-time as a tourist officer, and the Queensland office also employs a full-time tourist officer. Looking after visitors, including the State Premier, is also a time-consuming function. Reception facilities are maintained so that visitors, both government and private sector, can entertain their Japanese contacts. Another major function is the distribution of information; the Queensland office issues a bi-monthly business newsletter in Japanese and English to 600 companies in Japan and to others in Australia. Some of this marketing does lead to serious trade and investment inquiries, as shown in Table 11.2. However, it seems that major Japanese companies deal with State governments directly, either through the Japanese Embassy in Canberra or through the Consulates-General in Sydney, Melbourne, Brisbane and Perth.[16]

Do these activities complement or conflict with Commonwealth government representation in Tokyo? They have been subject to fairly strong criticism in the past. In April 1982 the Deputy Prime Minister, Lionel Bowen, argued that 'The States which have offices in Tokyo ... do us a disservice, as they compete with one another' (*Canberra Times* 16 April 1982), and went on to suggest that State government, foreign affairs and trade offices should be combined.

On the other hand, the Japan Secretariat accepts that the State offices have a role to play:

> The Embassy cannot properly hope to represent the legitimate interests of each State. The politics of Australian federalism require both Commonwealth and State representatives to be in Tokyo; the extent of communication between them depends on Commonwealth acceptance of State offices' legitimate presence and function, State recognition of the legal and practical limits of their powers, and goodwill on both sides. If each level is to recognise the aims of the other and do what it can to assist them in ways consistent with their own policy, information exchange is essential.[17]

Table 11.2 Activities of New South Wales government office in Tokyo, 1982

Direct investment enquiries processes	302
Trade enquiries processes	64
Overseas affiliation prospect submitted	41
Assistance to government departments, etc.—occasions	130
Assistance to private sector organisations—occasions	68
Tourism enquiries	2233
State government visitors assisted	33
Private sector visitors assisted	67

Source: New South Wales Premier's Department *Annual Report 1982*

This appears to be what happens in practice. State governments do believe that they have interests which cannot be adequately represented by the Commonwealth government, and when pressed they can give concrete examples. The South Australian government, for instance, believes that its own promotion of the State's wine in Japan has achieved better results than the Commonwealth government ever has for them. State offices are not accorded full legitimacy by all Commonwealth representatives, but a good working relationship exists in most cases. A former ambassador to Japan, Sir James Plimsoll, used to host regular fortnightly lunches for all State trade representatives. At the conclusion of his term, Plimsoll spoke positively of complementary action by Commonwealth and State governments to further Australian interests in Tokyo:

A constant dialogue has been conducted between the Australian Embassy and Japanese agencies, and between Australian State Government offices and Japanese buyers in both Tokyo and Australia. (*Australian Financial Review* 21 September 1982)

Commonwealth–State Coordination

The third option available to State governments is to cooperate with the Commonwealth government in coordinating their separate interests in external economic relations. This assumes, of course, that the Commonwealth government will willingly co-operate. The Myer committee reported that

[a]s to Commonwealth/State relations, the Committee recognises the difficulties of making any fundamental changes to Australia's Federal system, but suggests that greater efforts should be made to involve the particular expertise and capabilities of the States in improving the management of the relationship with Japan. To this end it recommends a Premiers' conference on relations with Japan to explore ways of coordinating State and Commonwealth interests and clarifying areas of responsibility. Preparations for this conference should be made by an ad hoc Committee of Commonwealth/State officials.[18]

The steps recommended here were taken by the Commonwealth government, despite some opposition to yet another federal–State committee. The conference of Premiers was held late in 1978, and it was decided that there should be a meeting of senior Commonwealth and State officials at least once a year, and more often if requested by State governments. The first of these meetings was held in Adelaide early in the following year, and at least one has been held each year since then. They are high-level meetings between a number of Commonwealth government permanent heads, including the heads of the Departments of Foreign Affairs, Trade, and Prime Minister and Cabinet, and State government delegations.

The main topics for discussions at these meetings, which have no formal agenda, have been what one would expect from observing the public debate: tourism, the pattern of foreign investment and foreign investment guidelines, and industrial relations. Some of these matters, like industrial relations, are essentially State responsibilities, while others, such as international airfares and airline routes, are based on commercial considerations and are largely out of the control of either State or federal governments.

The greatest of the State governments' needs is for more detailed information. The Department of Trade is now committed to sending regular trade statistics for each State to its government, so that the situation has improved since the Myer report identified 'shortcomings in the exchange of information between the Commonwealth and the States'.[19] The problem is not easily overcome, for structural reasons. The State governments do not have the staff resources in Tokyo to take greater advantage of closer contacts with the Embassy, while within Australia the Commonwealth Department of Foreign Affairs, unlike its counterparts in other federal systems, is not well equipped for serious communications with State governments.[20]

At the heart of federal–State issues is the fact that the State governments represent different economic and political interests, both from each other and from the Commonwealth government. These differences are lasting, although changes do occur from time to time with economic developments and as parties, personalities and governments change. In general the differences are marginal, but they can nevertheless become the basis for political conflict. Especially in economic hard times, each government will understandably want to squeeze every possible benefit in terms of production or employment out of the federal system. There are very rational political reasons for doing this, even if such a self-interested approach is economically irrational in national terms. The development of a small but elaborate administrative apparatus, which includes domestic departments and overseas offices, is a response to these needs. Even if very little can be achieved to increase a State's share of economic growth, there is a critical domestic audience which expects the attempt to be made by State governments.

Many of the issues in dispute can never be resolved. In some situations State governments are competing with one another, and with the rest of the world, for foreign investment or for world markets. In these cases solutions cannot be found in constitutional alteration, or in new forms of administration, or in greater efforts to communicate and cooperate. In terms of coping with relations with Japan, organisational reform is moving in the right direction. However, there would seem to be merit in the strengthening of Commonwealth Department of Foreign Affairs mechanisms for dealing with State governments by upgrading the Department's State offices and creating a unit within the Department in Canberra to coordinate the distribution of information to State governments. And, as many of the issues in dispute between State and Commonwealth governments inevitably involve the private sector, it would seem sensible to amalgamate the consultative committee on relations with Japan (the public–private meeting at the Commonwealth level) with the meeting of federal and State officials, either occasionally or permanently.

In evaluating the contribution of the federal system to Australia's relations with Japan, it is important to recognise that what is happening in the Australian federal system is not unusual. Governments within other federal systems with whom Japanese firms deal, such as Canada and the United States, behave similarly. State governments in these systems too are intervening in international trading relations. The Myer report was correct to be sceptical that, within the large firms and government institutions where it matters, there is any confusion in Japan about what Australian federalism means. Competition between State governments does allow some advantages to foreign investors and exporters, but equal advantage is given to domestic Australian firms by the same federal–State competition. What may have been played down in the past is the positive contribution the federal system may make to Australian capacity. As well as too many cooks spoiling the broth, it may be that two heads are better than one.

Appendix
Functions of the New South Wales and Victorian State Government Offices in Tokyo

*New South Wales**

1   Providing information about the State's resources and industrial development potential to Japanese business interests with a view to augmenting the flow of industrial investment into New South Wales.

2   Locating suitable affiliates for both Japanese and New South Wales companies and providing information on the financial status and manufacturing ability of potential business partners.

3   Providing assistance to both Japanese and New South Wales companies on such matters as licensing or selling of inventions, technology exchange and joint venture arrangements.

4   Identifying potential markets for New South Wales products in Japan.

5   Assisting New South Wales exporters in locating markets and customer and distributor organisations in Japan.

6   Furnishing information concerning commerce and industry to commercial, industrial and government organisations in New South Wales.

7   Assisting New South Wales government representatives and businessmen travelling to Japan to make suitable contacts.

8   Promoting tourism to New South Wales.

9   Keeping the government informed of political, economic and commercial developments in Japan which are of interest to the state.

---

*   Information supplied by the Premier's Department of New South Wales

10   Making appropriate arrangements for visits by government officials and mission representatives.

Victoria*

1   The promotion of overseas capital investment in Victoria, joint venture participation, and the two-way transfer of technology and expertise.

2   The promotion of Victorian exports, including assistance to Victorian businessmen wishing to establish appropriate contacts.

3   The processing of inquiries by overseas and Victorian industry.

4   The promotion of tourist travel to Victoria.

5   The preparation, servicing and/or assistance with visits to and from these countries by government representatives and commercial and industrial delegations.

6   Assistance with the maintenance of an industrial and commercial data bank in Tokyo and Melbourne in respect of areas of responsibility, with particular emphasis on Japan.

7   Assistance with the development of Victoria's sister-state relationships with Jiangsu Province in China and Aichi Prefecture in Japan, and visits by ministers and officials.

---

*   Information supplied by the Department of Premier and Cabinet of Victoria.

12 Resource markets and resource trade issues

BEN SMITH

Although the States of Australia are the formal owners of most of the mineral or energy resources located within their territories, the Commonwealth has substantial powers to control the pattern of development of those resources. Among the more important of these (alongside the general taxation power) are the Commonwealth's powers to regulate international transactions, trade and foreign investment.

The mining industry is heavily dependent on export sales. Excluding oil and gas, more than two-thirds of Australia's value of mine product is exported in unprocessed or processed form. The large increases in the production of iron ore, coking coal, bauxite and nickel, which provided the bulk of the rapid growth in the value of mine output in the late 1960s and early 1970s, were almost exclusively dependent on export sales. The more recent (or prospective) growth in steaming coal and uranium production, together with the increased processing of bauxite to alumina and aluminium and the development of the large North-West Shelf gas field, has again been (or will be) almost wholly export-oriented.

The Commonwealth's power to regulate trade in mineral products may be exercised through either quantitative or fiscal measures. Examples of the former are the iron ore and manganese export embargoes that existed until 1960, while the coal export levy is the major example of fiscal regulation. In principle, fiscal measures have to be employed in a non-discriminatory way, in the sense that they have to apply equally to equal cases.[1] Quantitative controls can be used much more selectively. Thus there is a general embargo on the export of natural gas, but half of the output from the North-West Shelf has been exempted. In the 1950s and 1960s there was an embargo on uranium export, except to the United Kingdom, and recent rules have required the satisfaction of Commonwealth safeguards before customers can be approved. Indeed, for all mineral exports it is necessary to obtain Commonwealth approval, which will be granted, subject to satisfaction of a given set of requirements, except where a specific embargo exists. Although the Commonwealth has to exercise its export control powers in a 'non-discriminatory' way, the absence of any restriction on the setting of necessary requirements allows the Commonwealth in effect to control the volume of exports from each individual mineral project if it chooses to do so.[2]

There is a high level of foreign ownership in the Australian mining industry, reflecting the large volume of funds invested in the past twenty years, the technical, organisational and marketing advantages of large international mining companies, and their relatively favourable access to international capital markets. In some areas, and probably increasingly, foreign participation by customers has been important in securing overseas markets for the output of mining or mineral-processing projects. Consequently, the capacity for foreign firms to become involved in mining or processing activities, and the nature of the mix of foreign involvement within projects, are often critical factors in determining whether those projects can proceed.

Commonwealth control over foreign investment is operated through executive decision by the federal Treasurer on advice from the Foreign Investment Review Board, operating within the policy guidelines set. In general, these require a 50 per cent Australian equity share in new projects, but they have a degree of flexibility that allows that rule to be waived (temporarily or relatively permanently) or interpreted broadly,[3] or that allows other restrictions to be imposed—for example, on the amount or source of foreign borrowing that can be employed to finance a project. Thus the regulation of foreign investment can be tailored, to some extent, to meet Commonwealth views about the desirable rate of minerals industry development generally or about the desirable rate of development of particular mineral sectors.

The existence of Commonwealth powers that can be used to impose a considerable amount of control over resource developments, whether or not those powers are exercised for a purpose central to their nature, has the capacity to generate substantial federal–State conflict. The States generally perceive themselves as the owners of their mineral and energy resources, entitled to exploit them as they wish within broad limits. The Commonwealth, on the other hand, sees itself as having a responsibility to ensure that resources are exploited in the best interests of Australians and that the benefits from that exploitation are spread among Australians, which implies that the resources are Australian resources and not State resources. Notwithstanding the formal ownership of the resources by the States, the constitutional powers provided to the Commonwealth and the High Court's interpretations of those powers mean that, in the bulk of cases and for most purposes, the resources are Australian resources unless they remain in the ground. In practice, however, the political constraints on exercising a national resource property right are substantial; the Commonwealth can afford to exercise its full power only rarely and in major cases. Thus McColl has argued that the effective prohibition of sand mining on Fraser Island through the revoking of export licences created a political climate in which the Commonwealth was subsequently forced to back away from its interest in environmental protection.[4] One impact of the division of powers, and of political conflict about their exercise, is that a degree of instability and uncertainty is generated for the overall policy environment affecting mineral developments.

The issues discussed in the preceding paragraph are dealt with more fully in other chapters; the interest here lies in the impact that Australian policy uncertainty may have on Australia's trade in mineral products, given the nature of the market in which that trade is conducted, and this is discussed later.

Aside from the use of Commonwealth powers to achieve what some might regard as illegitimate objectives, those powers are also (and more generally) exercised for purposes more obviously central to their nature. In particular, export control powers are, in the vast majority of cases, exercised for purposes which have directly to do with the market for Australia's mineral exports or the impact of that market on Australian producers and consumers. While it is not clear what the purpose of foreign investment regulation is—in that area the policy itself seems, publicly at least, also to be the objective—it clearly falls under the heading of legitimate exercise of Commonwealth power.

Nevertheless, in these cases also there is scope for federal–State conflicts of interest, and for the possibility of counteractive policy stances resulting from the lack of possession by either level of government of the full power to ensure that its objectives are met (or from the lack of the political support that would enable those powers to be used).

The main concern of this chapter is with trade and trade policy issues; the regulation of foreign investment is discussed elsewhere in this volume. The following section deals with the structure of the international market for Australia's main mineral exports, the nature of the trade arrangements entered into, and the trade policy issues arising in that context. The remainder of the chapter considers possible problems created by federal–State divergences of interest in the formulation of mineral trade policy.

Australia's Minerals Trade and Trade Issues

The pattern and direction of minerals trade

Table 12.1 indicates the relative importance of Australia's major mineral export commodities and the changes that have taken place since the mid-1960s. Total export value is now heavily concentrated on three commodity groups, coal, iron and aluminium, which together provide 75 per cent of export revenue. In 1960 there were virtually no exports of any of these commodities. The bulk of export revenue for aluminium comes from sales of the intermediate product, alumina (about 79 per cent in 1981/82), with unprocessed bauxite accounting for most of the remainder (about 15 per cent). In the classification iron, less than 10 per cent of export revenue came from sales of iron and steel products in 1981/82, and exports were dominated by unprocessed iron ore. The older established lead, zinc, copper and tin exports included a relatively high proportion of refined metals, and the bulk of nickel exports were in the form of metal or high metal content smelter products.

More than three-quarters of the coal export tonnage is coking coal, around 75 per cent of which is purchased by the Japanese steel industry. A little over half

Table 12.1 Australia's principal mineral/metal exports, 1964/65 – 1981/82

	1964/65		1974/75		1981/82	
	$Am	%	$Am	%	$Am	%
Aluminium[a]	12	5.1	382	14.0	1318	20.1
Copper[a]	7	3.0	155	5.7	140	2.1
Iron[a]	14	6.0	928	34.1	1314	20.0
Lead[a]	80	34.2	145	5.3	308	4.6
Manganese	1	0.0	39	1.4	61	0.9
Mineral sands	26	11.1	128	4.7	124	1.9
Nickel[a]	—	—	107	3.9	377	5.7
Tin[a]	5	2.1	44	1.6	99	1.5
Tungsten	—	—	10	0.4	41	0.6
Zinc[a]	38	16.2	125	4.6	286	4.4
Uranium	—	—	—	—	203	3.1
Coal	51	21.8	661	24.3	2292	34.9
Total	243	100.0	2724	100.0	6563	100.0

Notes: a Includes exports of processed and unprocessed ores and concentrates
Sources: Smith (1977); Barnett and Hemphill (1983)

of steaming coal exports go to Japan but, overall, sales to Japan account for around 80 per cent of coal export revenue.[5] About 73 per cent of iron ore export tonnage is sold to Japan, and Japan's share as a source of iron ore export revenue is a little higher than that figure.

Between them, coal and iron ore represent 53 per cent of Australia's total mineral and metal export value and almost 75 per cent of receipts from unprocessed mineral exports. Sales of these commodities under long-term contracts to the Japanese steel industry alone account for over one-third of total mineral exports and almost half of unprocessed mineral exports.[6] In recent years Australia has supplied a little under half of Japan's import requirements of coking coal and iron ore and a somewhat higher, but declining, share of steaming coal imports. The absolute importance of the coal and iron ore trades to Australia, coupled with their large concentration on a single market, have made them a focus of attention in Australian discussion of mineral trade issues.

The aluminium trade is substantially more diversified. Long-term contract sales of bauxite and alumina to the Japanese aluminium industry were important to the initial development of Australia's major bauxite deposits, and Australia has met a large share of Japan's aluminium raw material requirements. However, the Japanese market has been small relative to Australia's potential production capacity. High transport costs for bauxite have generally inhibited access to alternative markets,[7] so the major development of the industry has taken place through the establishment of large-scale refining of bauxite to higher value, lower bulk alumina. Access to markets in Europe and North America has been provided by the involvement of international aluminium companies, either directly in mining and refining or in the refining activity only. In the latter case, bauxite has been supplied to refiners under the same types of long-term contracts as are used for international sales. With the substantial reduction in the size of the Japanese aluminium industry, sales of bauxite and alumina to Japan will diminish further in importance, but the newer development of increased aluminium smelting in Australia will be fairly heavily oriented towards Japan and other expanding Asian markets. Thus, trade in aluminium products is likely to become more regionally oriented in future, with long-term contracts and/or participation in aluminium projects by Asian customers providing a major part of the security for the investments involved.

The bulk of Australia's exports of refined nickel, lead, copper and tin are directed to European and North American markets. Exports of refined zinc are fairly strongly concentrated in the Western Pacific, but only very small shares of the exports of any of these commodities are sold to Japan. Exports of ores and concentrates and of unrefined smelter products, however, are relatively heavily dependent on the Japanese market. Thus, for these higher transport-cost commodities, the proximity of the Japanese market has, to some extent, permitted an extension of mining beyond that which Australia's competitiveness in the processing activity would otherwise have allowed.[8]

Exports of manganese ore were at first concentrated heavily on the Japanese market, but the degree of dependence on Japan has now declined to below 50 per cent as other Asian and European markets have been developed. The markets for both uranium and mineral sands exports are relatively diversified across Asian, European and North American markets.

Minerals trade arrangements, policy uncertainty and the demand for mineral exports

The nature of mining and processing is such that both producers and consumers of mineral products have a substantial concern to obtain guaranteed long-term access to markets or sources of supply. This is due to the large size and highly capital-intensive nature of mining or processing developments, to the relatively long lives of those investments and, sometimes importantly, to the need for different processing technologies for different mineral raw materials. The interest in securing markets or sources of supply before development is intensified by the high cost of shipping minerals internationally, which tends to limit the geographic area within which feasible (or acceptable) markets or sources of supply may be found. The heavy regional concentration of much of Australia's minerals trade has already been described. A new mining or processing development may not provide a significant addition to world production capacity, but it may involve a substantial increment within the regional market on which it mainly impinges. Given the long lead times in bringing new mines or new processing facilities on stream, there is a need for mechanisms to ensure a matching of capacity expansion if the market is not to be seriously over- or under-supplied.

For much of the world's minerals trade, the security sought for mining and processing investments and the necessary matching of minerals supply with consumption are provided by vertical integration between processing and mining activities. This has been most evident historically in the world market for aluminium, and the pattern has been repeated, with some important variations, in the development of Australia's aluminium industry. The alternative to vertical integration is the long-term sales contract between independent minerals producers and consumers. For a number of reasons, the bulk of Australia's resources trade (and, indeed, that of the Pacific region generally) has been conducted under these contractual arrangements rather than through transfers of minerals between the mining and processing divisions of vertically integrated firms.[9]

For any large, long-lived project, investors are concerned not only about the economic conditions and policy environment prevailing at the time the investment is made but also about likely changes in those variables over the life of the project. In particular, uncertainty about the future policy environment generates risks that make investments less attractive than they would otherwise be.

Where an export-oriented resource development is established within the vertically integrated framework of an international company, risks associated with policy uncertainty will be reflected in the costs to the company concerned of making the necessary investment. From the viewpoint of the overseas parent company and consumer of the output, the apparent risk may be lessened somewhat by the capacity of the Australian subsidiary to evaluate potential problems at first hand and to make representations to the relevant governments in Australia about the effects of particular policy changes.

Where, as is more general in Australia's trade, resource developments are established under arm's-length, long-term contracts, the impact of policy uncertainty may be somewhat greater. Although the extent of this varies across commodities, long-term contracts involve a degree of reciprocal transfer of investment risk between buyer and seller.[10] Thus, uncertainty about the future Australian policy environment may have a smaller impact on risks faced by investors in mineral developments but may increase risks faced by overseas purchasers of the output from those developments. The effects may then be seen both on the willingness to invest in resource developments in Australia and on the willingness to contract to purchase mineral exports from Australia.

While the actual degree of uncertainty surrounding Australian supply capacity and cost is independent of the form of long-term trade arrangement entered into, the risk perceptions associated with that uncertainty may not be. Arm's-length purchasers may be fairly heavily dependent on contractual partners or media reports to provide them with information, and neither source will necessarily have an incentive to provide sober, accurate assessments of policy issues and effects. Thus such purchasers may be rather more concerned about policy uncertainties (and about other factors such as labour relations) than might purchasers with direct investment interests and a capacity to make independent assessments of conditions. To the extent that conflicts of policy interest between federal and State governments, or between either level of government and the mining industry, become open subjects of debate involving exaggerated assessments of the consequences of particular policy actions, the nervousness of arm's-length contractual purchasers may be considerably increased.

The essence of the problem is that overseas purchasers of Australian minerals have a necessary concern about both State and federal policies towards resource developments and trade, through their contractual dependence on Australian supplies and the risk-distributing elements of those contracts, but do not deal with those governments at first hand in the way that vertically integrated firms are able to do. Thus they may be less able to understand the relationships between different arms and levels of government policy, to perceive the policy motivations and likely outcomes, and to represent their own interests and constraints in dealing with the consequences of particular policy changes.

The inferior efficiency of long-term contracts compared with vertical integration as a means of providing security and risk distribution within the minerals trade has been discussed previously in a purely commercial context.[11] The present discussion suggests that the same conclusion extends to their relative degrees of efficiency in dealing with risks arising from policy uncertainties. More positively, it suggests a need for channels of communication between governments in Australia and overseas purchasers to allow policy interests and intentions to be more readily discerned and to provide for the impacts of particular policies on purchasers to be seen to be taken into account. There are, in any case, difficulties in direct dealing between governments and private foreign concerns, so that communication must often be established indirectly through various fora and public speeches. The absence of any cohesive and visibly coordinated approach to policy formulation in Australia, coupled with the inevitable need for different levels of government to communicate publicly (and, therefore, simultaneously to a domestic electorate and to overseas purchasers) may make for substantial difficulties in promoting a reasonably stable policy environment.

Commodity Market Conditions

The preceding discussion has been concerned, somewhat narrowly, with the possible impacts of the policy formation process and uncertainties surrounding the outcome of that process on the demand for Australian mineral exports—that is, on the quantities that overseas consumers may wish to contract to purchase from Australia at any given (expected) price. Closely associated is the possibility that the price obtainable for (some) mineral exports may, within limits, depend on the level of Australian supply and/or the cohesiveness of Australian bargaining strength—the possibility that Australia as a whole may have some monopoly power in the market. Where that is the case, the nature of the overall Australian interest in obtaining 'appropriate' export prices may diverge from that of the State interests in enlarging their market shares. First, as in all cartels, the collective surplus-maximising interest is unlikely to be that which maximises the gains to all parties (unless complex redistributions of benefits are undertaken). Second, the nature of the federal system may result in different focuses of concern at Commonwealth and State levels, so that a State collective interest may not coincide with the Australian collective interest as perceived by the Commonwealth. These issues are taken up in the last section of this chapter.

The rest of this section focuses on the market conditions for Australian mineral exports and the nature of any Commonwealth policy interest in seeking to regulate trade flows and market prices. After a general review of the markets for other commodities, the main focus is on the coal and iron ore trades.

General minerals market and policy issues

Australia is a large, or significant, world producer of a number of mineral commodities. Most strikingly, Australia produces between 60 per cent and 90 per cent of the western world's output of major mineral sands products and almost one-third of world bauxite output. In the case of mineral sands, the possibility of influencing world market prices has received limited attention in two instances. First, in debate over the environmental effects of sand mining, it has been argued that restriction of Australian output in environmentally sensitive areas would increase world prices to an extent which would increase Australia's overall gain from mineral sands trade, or at least would not reduce that overall gain very significantly.[12] To put it the other way round, overproduction of mineral sands due to a failure to take account of environmental costs would have the added disadvantage of worsening export prices for the commodities concerned. This argument was, in fact, incorporated in the assessment of costs and benefits of sand mining on Fraser Island on which the Commonwealth government relied in deciding to terminate export licences.[13] Second, the Commonwealth was involved for a period in arrangements with producers to limit supplies of zircon, which, because of its co-production with other mineral sands, was in excess supply and obtaining depressed world prices. The stimulus in that case was the low rate of return being earned by producers with relatively high shares of zircon in their output mix—that is, the motivation was short-term industry assistance, rather than exploitation of Australia's international monopoly power in any purposeful way.

The international bauxite industry has been, to some extent, cartelised by the formation of the International Bauxite Association. Australia is a member of the Association, but participates in information exchange and market assessment only and does not follow Association policies with respect to taxation or output controls. Although Australia is by far the largest producer in the Association (both Queensland and Western Australia rank alongside the two next largest producing countries), there has been no interest in strengthening the market power of the cartel by active participation. Rather, Australia has benefited from the price-raising effects of the cartel and from uncertainties about dependence on non-Australian supplies, which have provided significant incentives for expansion of the Australian mining and processing industry despite distance from the major North American and European markets. In fact, it appears that

Australia has sought to play a moderating role in Association discussions, even though Australia's producer interest might be served by less moderate Association policies.

The main concern of the Commonwealth in relation to the bauxite/alumina trade has been over the prices at which these commodities have been transferred within vertically integrated companies, although the prices at which bauxite has been sold to contract purchasers have also been subject to review and the applications of export control procedures. The issues here reflect a concern about exploitation by overseas purchasers, rather than any desire to exploit Australian monopoly power, and are similar in character to those discussed later with respect to coal and iron ore.

In the market for aluminium, fairly high levels of effective protection for smelting in much of the world (through tariffs or subsidised power) limit potential markets for Australian output as, to a considerably lesser extent, do considerations of transport cost. A substantial share of the output from smelter developments will be directed to the regional market. Thus it is likely that the terms on which contract sales of aluminium can be made will not be independent of the quantity of Australian aluminium attempting to find a market, and the establishment of new aluminium smelting capacity in one State is likely to limit the possibilities of establishing new smelters in others. The possibility therefore exists of interstate competition to influence the location of smelters, in which any incentives provided will, to the extent that they encourage a larger overall capacity than otherwise, also need to compensate for any adverse effects on aluminium export prices. The Commonwealth has expressed some concern about these issues, but has focused on the inefficient use of Australian resources that may be involved without explicit reference to international market conditions.[14]

Australia is the world's fifth largest producer of tin, with about 6 per cent of world production. The Commonwealth has participated in all of the successive International Tin Agreements, and Australia has joined the producer organisation, the Association of Tin Producing Countries. Under the present Tin Agreement, exporters are subject to quota restrictions designed to put a floor on the world price of tin. Country quotas are allocated on the basis of historic production shares, and the allocation of Australia's quota among individual tin miners by the Department of Trade is on the same basis. The main division of opinion in Australia on the quota arrangements appears to be between the significant number of very minor producers, who are often forced to cease production by the effects of output quotas on the profitability of their operations, and the larger mines, which have a stronger interest in maintaining a higher world tin price. While all State governments are concerned to ensure equitable treatment for producers in their States, the main conflicts of interest probably arise between the States with larger operations (New South Wales and Tasmania) and those where tin mining is a smaller, more scattered, activity. Of possibly greater concern to the main producing States is the implication that, as a result of membership of the Association of Tin Producing Countries, the Commonwealth may be 'required' to move towards greater overall control of the conduct of tin mining. On the basis of recent decisions, the Commonwealth's external affairs power would allow it to override any State interests in that area.

Although Australia has a significant share of world lead and zinc production, its degree of monopoly power in the world market as a whole is small and there has been no Commonwealth interest in seeking to regulate the market. On the other hand, the Commonwealth has not discouraged participation by Australian producers in a degree of market control by major world producer companies.

Australia has a potentially large share of the world uranium market. As with sand mining, possible effects of Australian supply variations on the world price of uranium have been given some consideration in assessing the effects of environmental restrictions on mining and exporting uranium.[15] However, there is little evidence that that issue is of any consequence in the deliberations about the terms and conditions on which uranium exports will (or will not) be permitted. As with lead and zinc, the Commonwealth has not discouraged (and has refused to yield to United States pressure to act against) companies participating in private market regulation.

Australia's associate membership of the Intergovernmental Council of Copper Exporting Countries provides observer status and no voting rights. Australia's own share of world production is less than 1 per cent, and the Council itself has little prospect of exercising any effective monopoly power in the international market.

In summary, this brief review suggests that, although Australia may have a degree of monopoly power in some international minerals markets, Commonwealth policy has not been directed towards its exploitation. Where there has been Commonwealth regulation of trade, as in sand mining and uranium, the effects on Australia's terms of trade have generally been incidental to the exercise of policy. Indeed, successive Commonwealth governments have taken the view that Australia has a responsibility to make mineral products available to consumer countries at competitive market prices, and have sought to persuade other producers to that view in international fora. Australia's active membership of the International Tin Agreement is the only real exception, but Australia would be out of step not only with the major tin producers but also with the major consumers if it were not a party to the Agreement. Membership of the Association of Tin Producing Countries may be seen in a somewhat different light, but it may be diplomatically difficult to avoid, given the importance of the tin industry to Australia's ASEAN neighbours.

Coal and iron ore

The coal and iron ore trades are distinguished by their very heavy dependence on the Japanese market and by the substantial barriers to significant diversification of markets. The coordinated purchasing stance of the Japanese steel industry (and the possibility that this will extend to steaming coal purchases) has given rise to substantial concerns in Australia and elsewhere about the exercise of monopsonistic purchasing power in those markets. These concerns can be thought of as having two distinct components.

First, there is a concern that a lack of coordination in bargaining over export prices by Australian exporters may produce outcomes in which Japan's share of the gains from the bilateral coal and iron ore trades is increased at the expense of Australia's share.

Second, the heavy dependence of Australian and other regional suppliers on sales to Japan, and the importance of contracts to supply Japan in determining the rate and scale of mine developments, give rise to the concern that coordinated Japanese purchases may be able to stimulate development of a supply capacity greater than they are likely to require. With limited viable alternative markets the bargaining position of Australian sellers, whether coordinated or not, may then be substantially weakened by their own excess capacity and by competition from other supplier countries in a similar position.

The first concern can be thought of simply as follows. There is a joint gain from Australia–Japan trade in coal or iron ore, compared to each trading with alternative trade partners, largely because of the relatively low transport costs between the two countries. If the volume of bilateral trade is set, through contract arrangements, so as to maximise the (expected) joint gain, there will then be scope for bargaining over the distribution of that gain. If there were a single Australian seller and a single Japanese buyer, the bilateral monopoly bargain might be expected to result in a more or less equal distribution of the gain from trade.[16] Where, on the other hand, there is effectively a single Japanese purchaser but there are competing Australian sellers (which is substantially more the case for coal than for iron ore), it is likely that the bargaining outcome will result in a larger share of the joint gain from trade accruing to Japan and a smaller share accruing to Australia.

The important element of this story is that the level of Australian supply is assumed to be set to match the actual level of Japanese demand, so far as that can be accurately anticipated. Thus the problem from Australia's point of view is 'simply' to obtain a united bargaining stance from exporters in price negotiations, in order to obtain a 'fair and reasonable' share of the joint gain from the given volume of trade.

Commonwealth policy has, essentially, been directed towards that objective. Export control powers have been used to induce exporters to consult with the Department of Trade about market conditions and prices which should be aimed at in negotiations, allowing the Department to provide a collective view of the sorts of prices expected to be obtainable. Ultimately, the Department can withhold export licences if individual producers negotiate prices which appear unjustifiably lower than the reference prices earlier thought achievable. The present, relatively quiet, system of seeking coordination and of monitoring the bargaining process, in which the commercial judgments of companies collectively provide reference points that are revised in the light of negotiating experience, has evolved from the initially more open and assertive approach of the Commonwealth. Then, there was a tendency for the relevant department to make its own assessments of 'appropriate' prices, and for the minister to play a visible and central role in demanding that those prices be achieved.

A major problem, particularly in the coal trade, has been that, except in very tight supply conditions, Japanese purchasers are able to rearrange their tonnage uptake under contracts so as to place pressure on individual suppliers or to offer additional tonnage inducements to make weak price bargains. Since the operating margins for some producers are tighter than those of others, so that they can less readily afford to operate away from full capacity, it can prove very difficult to achieve any collective interest in negotiating strategies. Thus it is impossible to induce the same degree of cohesiveness in bargaining among exporters as is achieved by the Japanese steel industry.

On the other hand, a major reference price for Commonwealth assessments of bargain outcomes is the comparison of landed prices of Australian supplies in Japan with those from major alternative suppliers. That is, broadly, the Commonwealth has taken the view that Japanese purchasers should not obtain supplies more cheaply from Australia than from major competing sources. To the extent that there are transport cost savings in obtaining supplies from Australia, they should be fully reflected in higher f.o.b. prices for Australian exports. As a first offer in bargaining this seems a sensible position, but as an assessment of what is a 'fair and reasonable' ultimate outcome of the bilateral bargain it seems less realistic. It would seem plausible for Japanese purchasers to suggest that an equally reasonable outcome would be that Australian exporters should not obtain higher f.o.b. prices for sales to Japan than for sales to alternative European markets. Importantly, it appears that, overall, the Australian view of the appropriate division of the transport cost savings resulting from the relative proximity of the two countries is fairly closely approximated in prices achieved. Thus, within the feasible bargaining limits, Australian exporters could well be argued to have done better than they might have done.

However, all of the above discussion assumes that the contracts bringing forth the level of Australian (and other regional) supply capacity have been set to maximise the overall gains from trade to the parties involved, and that bargaining is concerned only with the distribution of those gains. The second and more recent concern, mentioned earlier, is that Japanese purchasers may contract to purchase greater supplies than are likely to be required, so that there is an average excess supply capacity in the regional market. Then, while it may be the case that all suppliers obtain (approximately and on average) the same landed price in Japan, that price will itself be depressed by the overall weak bargaining position of sellers across the market as a whole.

The fact that Japanese purchasers have negotiated contracts to obtain supplies from new, high-cost sources, opening up additional supply points and generating an overall capacity that appears both unwarranted and unnecessarily costly, has been cited as evidence of a strategy to promote excess supply and greater competition among suppliers.[17] Whether or not such a deliberate strategy has existed, the fact that contracts include no penalties for failure to uplift contracted tonnage provides little incentive for purchasers to be conservative in their contracting behaviour. That is, it may be sensible from their point of view (though inefficient overall) to contract to obtain the maximum quantities they *might* require, so that they do not run into problems of insufficient supply. On average, that will result in excess supply capacity and a weak market for sellers.

To the extent that the dominant Japanese purchaser position is employed as has been suggested, a more coordinated bargaining stance among Australian exporters in price negotiations will not, by itself, provide an effective counter. Since Australia is a major supplier to Japan and a relatively low-cost producer, some limitation of the rate of Australian capacity expansion probably does have the potential to influence the overall market in a way that would favour Australia as a nation. That would require the Commonwealth to use its export control powers not only to oversee price negotiations after mine production capacity had been brought on stream, but also to use them to control the rate at which new contracts and mine developments were brought into being. In the iron ore trade, where there are a few large projects and where only one State is involved, it is probable that the Commonwealth will, in fact, withhold export permission for the next feasible project until some judgment about overall market conditions is satisfied. In the coal trade, which involves a large number of projects with relatively small market shares and the interests of two State governments, the Commonwealth has not established any effective control over new capacity expansion.

Federal–State Issues in the Minerals Trade

The previous section has suggested that for a number of commodities the supply levels of Australian minerals are likely to influence the export prices obtainable for those products. This might have given rise to a monopoly interest in restricting supplies, to some extent, below the level that was efficient from the point of view of producer and consumer countries taken together, but there is no evidence of such a general monopoly interest on the part of the Commonwealth. On the other hand, extension of supplies beyond the efficient level will, to the extent that export prices are influenced, impose a double cost on Australia—both through the inefficient use of capital and labour resources (and, indeed, of mineral resources themselves) in the minerals industry and through the reduction in mineral export prices that this would cause.

The discussion of the coal and iron ore trades has suggested the possibility that extension of supplies beyond the efficient level *may* be induced by the contractual dependence on the Japanese market and a lack of incentive for purchasers to be conservative in their estimates of future demand. Beyond that, the incentive structures within the federal system may themselves be biased towards 'overdevelopment' of resources. In particular, the States may have incentives to seek to attract investment in mining or processing (and compete with one another in doing so), and to exploit their resources in a way that maximises job creation and direct and indirect (State) income generation, rather than the value of the resources being exploited.

To the extent that there is a tendency towards oversupply in Australia, any propensity on the part of purchasers to overcontract will be facilitated. Indeed, purchasers might argue that they are forced to contract to purchase the largest conceivable amounts by the pressures from producer countries to develop greater volumes of resources.

It does seem plausible to argue that the States have a 'development orientation' which may not (collectively, at least) be consistent with maximising the value of Australian resources. The allocation of mineral leases to the company that discovers deposits or, if they are already known, to the company that appears likely to develop them most rapidly, has an implicit bias towards excessive development. In general, State royalty receipts (or royalty-equivalent charges) are not huge, and are structured in a way that tends to make volume of output more important to revenue collection than aggregate profitability of mining activity. Moreover, the nature of federal–State fiscal arrangements may persuade States that the exploitation of their resources to yield the greatest (present) value of revenues from that exploitation would not, ultimately, benefit them; that is, they might anticipate that higher revenues would simply reduce their grants from the Commonwealth. Even if that were not so, to the extent that a forgoing of current development might result in a longer term gain in resource revenues but no short-term improvement, the relatively short political time horizon of incumbent governments may give little incentive to take a longer view.

Supposing the Commonwealth to be capable of taking a longer, more collective view, there may be a significant divergence between its interests and those of the States—even in a case, such as iron ore, where only one State is involved. The Western Australian government is likely to want new iron ore developments to proceed more rapidly than the Commonwealth considers desirable, and there have been many instances in which that State and the Commonwealth have been in dispute over appropriate price-bargaining strategies for iron ore. In part, these have reflected genuine differences in perceptions of market conditions and feasible bargain outcomes; and they have, to some extent, been generated by differences between the iron ore companies themselves. More fundamentally, however, they reflect the different trade-off that each government may (rationally within its own level of concern) be prepared to make between prices obtained for iron ore exports and the potential volume of those exports.

Where there are competing State interests in obtaining market shares, as in coal, the incentives for individual States to exercise control over the rate of development are still smaller. Each State has an interest in having a larger market share at the expense of other States. Alongside policies to encourage resource developments, there may be competition to attract contract purchasers to particular States and lobbying for Commonwealth policies to provide protection from competition from other States. Whether the Commonwealth has a collective Australian interest in efficient resource development or not, it may be constrained by State pressures to behave in an 'even-handed' way which allows more 'balanced', and possibly more rapid, development than it would otherwise have thought desirable.

All of this supposes that the Commonwealth itself has a collective national interest in efficient resource development, which may be constrained by counteractive policies or political pressures from more 'development-oriented' States. However, it is not clear that the Commonwealth has, over any length of time, shown less propensity towards 'development orientation' than the States. The methods of allocating, and the conditions of holding, mineral leases are the same on Commonwealth property as in the States, and the same incentives to early and rapid investment are present: the Commonwealth has at times maintained highly concessional tax treatment for mining and has subsidised exploration; the Commonwealth has maintained a domestic oil price above import parity to encourage domestic production; and Commonwealth ministers have lobbied purchasers to expand purchases of Australian minerals alongside similar State lobbying.

While it may be argued that a more efficient development of the Australian export coal industry would have involved a greater expansion of lower cost Queensland resources and a lesser expansion of higher cost New South Wales resources, pressures from the New South Wales government to achieve a more 'balanced' development may have been less important than the fact that the Commonwealth minister administering export controls represented a New South Wales coalmining electorate. In some respects, the subsequent need to seek coordination of the industry bargaining position in the export market has been a need to provide protection for the less efficient suppliers. It has been suggested that the major Queensland exporters have been weak bargainers because of their low costs (and that the Queensland government has facilitated this by charging low royalties).[18] But an equitable division of the joint gains from trade between Queensland exporters and the Japanese steel mills would probably result in lower prices than the Commonwealth has sought to achieve, and it may well be an efficient strategy (State and national) for Queensland coal to seek a greater volume of exports at possibly lower prices, rather than to limit sales and to demand prices matching those sought by New South Wales exporters.

While there are obvious tendencies towards inefficient and excessive development of Australian resources, given the nature of the markets into which they are sold, there is no clear division of responsibility between the Commonwealth and the States in this matter. Commonwealth concerns about export prices and bargaining issues have, to some degree, been attempts at shutting the stable door. Attribution of any blame for leaving it open in the first place is rather less obvious, both because the structure of the federal system itself provides incentives which may make State actions efficient from their own perspective if not from a national perspective, and because the Commonwealth cannot be said always to have pursued an efficient national interest. Indeed, the weight of State government influence, given the size of each State relative to the whole, may make it impossible for the Commonwealth to adopt a national perspective that is other than a balancing of State pressures.

13 Summary and comment

PETER DRYSDALE

This book sets out to provide a clearer understanding of the nature, workings and problems of Australia's federal system, especially as it impinges upon the resources sector, and to explore the source and nature of policy conflict within the federal system over resource development and trade issues. It remains to summarise the main themes that emerge from the preceding chapters and to introduce some commentary from other perspectives. The authors of the commentary were discussants of the papers presented at the workshop which led to the preparation of this volume.[1]

The Constitutional Division of Powers

A major factor in the operation of the Australian Constitution is the interpretation that the Australian High Court is prepared to place on particular constitutional provisions. According to Saunders' analysis, the powers of the Commonwealth are broadly written and, so long as the High Court is prepared to interpret them broadly, the Commonwealth can exert effective control over a more and more extensive range of matters. Saunders argues that there has been, as a result of successive High Court decisions, a steady trend towards greater and greater concentration of power in the hands of the Commonwealth government.

Collins suggests that, in a search for 'objective' legal criteria as distinct from the 'subjective' processes of history and political preference, the technical tends to be stressed to the exclusion of the political element in Saunders' argument. A clear delineation of distinctive spheres for the different levels of governments may well be precluded by domestic political obstacles, by external influences upon the requirements of national power, and by the interdependence between these two aspects, internal and external, of Australia's national life and circumstances.

Domestically, any division of powers within a federal system immediately encounters two almost insurmountable obstacles. First, to divide powers is like cutting a cake, but the principles by which the cake is to be cut are inherently political. Second, the cake to be cut is itself constantly changing; it has something of the character of Norman Lindsay's magic pudding.

To take the first point: how are objective criteria for national powers to be achieved when no neutral criteria exist? Australia's major political parties are divided not least over their conceptions of appropriate national purposes and powers. Moreover, what is considered a deservedly national concern will vary not only according to partisan or ideological attachment, but also according to the observer's vantage point. As well as the powers themselves, the means of adjusting them cannot be quarantined from politics.

As to the second point, the pattern of politics within the Australian federal system is extraordinarily varied. Political accountability and the clarification of responsibility are valid concerns, but some of the recent federal–State cooperative devices described by Saunders demonstrate that accommodation between actors may be achieved politically only by blurring responsibility, thereby making accountability more difficult.

The division of powers within a federal system tends to be drawn chiefly according to domestic priorities, yet a nation must find its place in the world. Any review of the division of powers must acknowledge that changing international circumstances can alter the desirable dimensions of internal capacities. The setting of Australia's external political and economic relations is being transformed by new international regimes in diverse policy arenas, and this international milieu places a premium upon national cohesion and coherence in policy. The changes in Australia's external environment can be expected to produce new patterns in our domestic politics, for the two spheres are interdependent.

A change in the notion of legitimate national concern can originate externally: as the scope of international treaties alters and expands, so does the likely scope of the external affairs power of a nation, and hence of national government. Moreover, political responses are likely to be transnational as well as intergovernmental. Thus, following the Noonkanbah incident in Western Australia, and failing in its appeal to Canberra, the National Aboriginal Conference appealed directly to Geneva. That is at once the shape of politics to come and a reflection of increasing international interdependence.[2]

In the process of balancing external challenges to national action alongside regional claims and redistributions, the Constitution is unlikely to provide a guide to the deepest dilemmas. The polity will probably continue to muddle through in ways which may offend the law but succeed in other respects. This is an argument from political expediency brought out well in the penultimate scene of Norman Lindsay's *The Magic Pudding*.[3]

'I'm afraid this is unconstitutional', said the Mayor to the Constable.

'It is unconstitutional', said the Constable; 'but it's better than getting a punch on the snout.'

As well as self-inflicted, internecine injuries, blows can come from outside. Australia's political arrangements, and its division of powers, have to deal with both.

Sharman challenges certain assumptions in Saunders' contribution: the content of State power, the role of judicial review, and the growth of Commonwealth power. Any impression that the Commonwealth government has the lion's share of legislative powers and that what meagre residue remains with the States is soon to be lost to them, must be corrected. For most Australians, the bulk of the law that regulates daily life is State law. Jurisdiction remains the greatest single resource that States have to deploy against the Commonwealth. This has been the situation since federation, and there is no prospect that it is about to change. Talk of the growth of Commonwealth powers confuses the growth of general government activity and constitutional power with other forms of political influence, and uses the term power in a way that gives a misleading impression of the nature of intergovernmental relations. The growth in governmental bureaucracy has no special implications for the division of powers within the federation, except, perhaps, that relations between the levels of government are likely to become more extensive and complicated— and this may imply a growth in vulnerability rather than in power.

It is quite possible for the Constitution to remain unchanged but for the Commonwealth government to increase its influence. The central government has used its superior tax-raising ability to buy involvement in many areas of State activity to the extent that the scope of its influence is far greater than the ambit of its law-making power.

Federalism involves a fluid interaction between federal and State governments, and the gains and losses of power are difficult to assess. Take, for example, the operation of conditional grants to the States under section 96 of the Constitution, a mechanism by which the Commonwealth is assumed to have increased its power to shape policy in areas of State jurisdiction. Quite apart from the fact that most of these arrangements were welcomed or even initiated by the States, the political benefits to the Commonwealth are usually tentative and indirect, while those accruing to the States are direct and highly visible. Conversely, the cost to the States in the form of information about constraints on policy is slight, while the financial cost to the Commonwealth is both large and direct. It is hard to see such arrangements as amounting to a net growth of Commonwealth power.

In resource trade and development both the Commonwealth and the States have jurisdictional vetos, the States over resource development and the Commonwealth over international trade. It would be hard to find a better subject to illustrate the importance of the division of powers (however defined), the subtlety of intergovernmental relations, and the vigour and resilience of Australian federalism.

These comments on the argument in chapter 2 do not so much qualify its conclusions as add to the explanation of the accretion of Commonwealth powers, defined in a particular sense. They underline some important issues, especially for the outside observer of Australian political behaviour. The Australian Constitution is not an inflexible legal document, and the balance of the division of powers shifts over time in response to changing circumstances (national and international) in a way determined by a combination of judicial review and interpretation and other pressures, economic and political. In the long run this is clearly healthy; in the short run changes in the balance of powers can be a source of substantial conflict that may result in non-cooperative action between levels of government, not only in respect of the problem issue itself but also in other areas.

Federal–State Fiscal Arrangements

Despite a federal system of government within which individual States are large components of the whole, Australia has a highly centralised revenue-raising system. Indeed, Mathews' analysis in chapter 3 shows that the share of total government receipts, at all levels, accruing to the central government in Australia is higher than it is for many countries with unitary governments, including Japan. However, since State governments are responsible for providing most services, a large proportion of the revenue raised by the Commonwealth has to be redistributed to the States. In addition to its important power in determining tax-sharing arrangements and, consequently, overall State budgeting positions, the Commonwealth also exercises considerable control over State and local authority borrowings (including those by State government enterprises) through the Loan Council. This has implications, which are discussed later, for the provision by State governments of the infrastructure necessary for resource developments.

Clements draws attention to the effects of fiscal equalisation arrangements on the incentives for efficient resource development. Mineral-rich States are liable to receive smaller grants to offset their higher-than-average capacities to raise revenues from royalties, for example. Arrangements of this type discourage efficient resource tax raising and promote inefficient expenditure patterns on the part of the States. Clements also emphasises, along with Mathews, the taxation burden in Australia and the general need for fiscal reform.

Yonehara observes that the Japanese fiscal system is beset by many of the same problems as the Australian fiscal system, and that proposals for reform of each system have much in common. While revenue-raising structures in the two countries are remarkably similar, the methods of distributing outlays among the three levels of government (central, state or prefectural, and local or municipal) differ markedly.

In the context of resource development and trade, two major issues emerge from Mathews' detailed review of federal–State fiscal arrangements. They bear repeating here. The already centralised fiscal arrangements, and the way in which national equity principles are embedded into their operation, impose significant barriers to the introduction of a uniform and efficient system of resource taxation. While the States are content for the Commonwealth government to bear the odium of general taxation, they guard carefully the right to impose royalties and other levies on resource developments, since these taxes are not electorally unpopular. The fiscal equalisation arrangements, at the same time, encourage inefficient and hidden taxation and, perhaps, overexploitation of resource wealth.

State and Federal Objectives and Policies

Much of the discussion of federal–State differences of interest presupposes a fundamental divergence, in which the Commonwealth has a national interest in efficient, revenue-maximising strategies for resource development (including tough export price bargaining), while the States have a more parochial interest in rapid development for its own sake. Harris points out, in chapter 4, that in the historical context this is an inaccurate caricature. Until the 1970s all levels of government in Australia pursued a more or less unfettered development objective, and it is only recently that the Commonwealth has moved away from that stance. In the past few years there have also been signs that State governments have shifted their attitudes towards more consciously revenue-efficient resource development strategies, although it remains true that the federal system provides them with a less powerful incentive than national objectives might dictate.

McColl takes up the question of how to measure the benefits from resource development projects at the regional, State and national levels. Harris quotes a survey paper in support of the view that the effects of development on local economies are relatively minor because of low population densities.[4] Other studies, however, suggest quite high employment and multiplier effects. These estimates of the benefits from resource project development are based on input–output analysis, and the results (the limitations of which are familiar to economists) exaggerate the benefits if they incorporate effects beyond the project at the State or national level. Resources such as labour put into particular projects have an opportunity cost, even in times of high unemployment. A realistic assessment of the impact of resource development projects has to take into account both positive and negative effects beyond the project area, since other regions lose resources as well as gain from positive income or multiplier effects. No work of this kind has been done in Australia on the contribution of resource developments to State economies, although a framework exists for such an analysis.[5] There have, however, been studies of the impact of project developments at the national level that take this factor into account.[6] While the benefits from the sale of output and the costs of constructing and operating projects are unlikely to vary between national and State economies, the benefits and costs associated with financing the project may differ markedly, particularly when high levels of investment by other States are involved and when the flow of revenue to the federal government is taken into account.

McColl notes that most of the taxation revenues from resource developments initially flow to the federal government in the form of income tax collections. The States have sought other sources of revenue from resource developments, frequently with adverse effects on resource allocation, and a better way is needed of providing them with a larger share of the direct taxation returns from projects within their borders.

Shoyama introduces a Canadian perspective to the subject of conflict in policy interests and objectives between the federal and the State and provincial levels of government. The most obvious objective of public policy in pursuing resource development is to take account of the direct effects on incomes and jobs. Both developers and governments at both levels need to focus these direct impacts. Harris suggests in chapter 4 that the spin-offs from resource developments are frequently illusory and that this has led to a harder nosed appraisal of the benefits of resource development and the fiscal impact of projects. In Canada, the current tendency is to stress the spin-offs and economic linkage effects associated with resource developments rather more than has been the case in the past.

A feature common to both Australian and Canadian attitudes is the 'development ideology', which was important in both countries until the 1970s. In that decade the boom peaked, encouraging the belief that the exploration of publicly owned natural resources required compensation to the owner, a belief that rapidly reversed the hitherto favourable taxation status of mining operations, and there was a public policy effort to capture resource rents. Moreover, this reversion of resource rents to the public sector promoted a concern for social costs such as environmental impact, loss of sovereignty through foreign ownership, and damage to Aboriginal cultures.

One explicit objective of public policy that has been much more evident in Canada than in Australia is that of regional economic development. Perhaps this stems from the greater emphasis in Canada on regional disparity, which leads to an explicit and significant commitment in national economic policy to regional development.

It is clear that the constitutional framework and the division of powers between State and central governments set certain ground rules for resource development. The parallels between the formal structures in Canada and Australia are very close, hinged as they are on proprietory rights over resources on the one hand, and the trade and commerce and external powers on the other. In both countries powers tend to overlap, and there is frequent conflict of economic and political interest between constituent States as well as between the two levels of government. The federal system institutionalises this overlap and conflict, and political clout may be as important as legal power. Bargaining has to be accepted as a means of resolving conflict, so that public policy has to be adaptable rather than consistent and coherent. It is difficult to be sure whether economic efficiency is best achieved under a highly centralised or a more decentralised system of decisionmaking, but the federal system clearly demands as much skill in political as in economic and financial management.

Canada is probably more decentralised than Australia in its decisionmaking, especially in fiscal structure. An important consequence is that political bargaining has to be frequently deployed, rather than the blunt assertion of constitutional power. Oil and gas development in Canada provide a striking illustration of the complexities of resource development in a federal state. Here the producing provinces, the federal government, consumers in general and consuming provinces in particular, and an industry dominated by multinationals and the United States 'national interest', are all involved in the same struggle—against an international background with forces at play under no particular control. It is not surprising that really good policies are hard to find.

A second parallel policy area is control of foreign investment in resource development. The approach in Canada is essentially similar to that in Australia, being confined to the control of takeovers by foreign firms and the establishment of our own foreign business. But there is no formal attempt to set a target level of domestic equity, except in the petroleum sector. Export control policy is also mainly applied in the petroleum sector, with the significant addition of uranium.

A perspective that does not receive much emphasis in chapter 4 is the effect of continuing international economic stagnation on attitudes to and policies for resource development. Because of structural change in the world economy, competition among resource suppliers in a stagnant world market, and increasing costs of supply in many of Canada's resource industries, there is a gathering mood in Canada of cooperation between the provincial and the federal governments in resource development matters. The emphasis in Canada will probably continue to shift away from resource rents towards industrial benefits and job creation.

Indeed, this recent development in Canadian policy thinking underlines the fact that the presence of conflict in policy objectives among different levels of government, and the pervasiveness of flux in the bargaining between them, do not weaken the potential for, nor the facts of, policy cooperation in overlapping jurisdictions and the derogation of powers by political agreement as the need dictates.

The Minerals Exploration and Production System

Following the introductory chapters, which provide general background and perspectives on the working of the Australian federal system, chapter 5 focuses explicitly on the federal environment for resource exploration and mining development. Here Crommelin provides a detailed analysis of the legal aspects of exploration and mining tenement leasing and the degrees of control that State and federal governments are able to exercise.

On State territory the powers to authorise exploration and issue mining leases are exclusively those of the State concerned. (Offshore they reside with the Commonwealth.) The capacity of the Commonwealth to control resource developments in the States lies in its power to control exports, foreign investment and, to some extent, State government borrowings for providing infrastructure. There is a suggestion in chapter 12 that these powers have been used to influence the rates of development of the coal industry (slowing down development in Queensland, and thereby increasing the demand for New South Wales coal), but the major example was the Commonwealth's use of its export control powers to prohibit sand mining on the environmentally sensitive Fraser Island, in direct opposition to the Queensland government. Although there has been no similar episode (partly because of the political pressures induced), export-oriented resource developments do face the uncertainties of trying to meet both State and federal requirements concerning whether and how mining may proceed in environmentally sensitive areas, despite the Commonwealth's lack of direct powers in this area.

Ottley sees the development of the Australian mining lease system as a successful adaptation to changing conditions, revealing on area of Australian public policy where there has been widespread agreement between the parties— explorers, miners, and State and federal governments. The adaptation of exploration and mining lease procedures over the years has reflected the greatly increased cost of exploration; current outlays for exploration, especially offshore, are huge. The linking of the right to explore to the right to exploit in the petroleum-leasing procedures reflects the perceived need for guaranteed access after costly exploration. The costs of exploration in other areas are also high, and the Australian industry sees the linking of exploration rights with mining rights in these areas as a progressive step. The current leasing procedures are intended to prevent resources from being locked away by companies who can buy exploration rights and leave them unused, but the equity of the system is brought into question when valuable resources cannot be developed within the time scale implicit in the procedures.

Another interest in this area is whether the conditions attaching to the leasing and licensing procedures encourage more rapid development of resources than might be desirable, from the viewpoint of both private developers and the national economy. Some provisions may encourage premature development, and others have the opposite effect. This issue is taken up again in chapter 6 and throughout the subsequent discussion.

The question of the land rights of the Aboriginal people and the power of Aboriginal land councils in the development of mining tenements is perceived by some as a special problem. Crommelin points out that Aboriginal land rights is not a separate issue; any private landowner has similar rights and is qualified for similar concessions.

Resource Taxation in the Federal System

While heavily critical of existing forms of taxation (royalties and excess rail freight charges, for example) and pointing to the advantages of a resource rent tax along the lines advocated by the present federal government, Willett sees no reason in principle why such a tax would have to be administered by the Commonwealth government. An appropriate resources tax could be administered at the State level, and federal involvement might lie in assistance with the specification of the tax and, possibly, the provision of guarantees against revenue shortfalls in periods of depressed market conditions. A less conflictual approach to the resource taxation problem might have more chance of success than proposals that States forgo their charges to make way for a Commonwealth resource rent tax, which would then be distributed back to them.

However, another view is that the prospect of the States (or at least of some States) adopting any approach suggested by the Commonwealth—no matter how beneficial to their interests—is remote unless they are forced to do so. The resource taxation issue is unlikely to be resolved rapidly. The industry is concerned about the disruptive effects on mineral developments if taxation competition in the resources area is not alleviated.

A major focus of Willett's chapter is on the methods of allocating exploration and mining leases. He argues that the competitive environment for acquiring leases, whose retention is partly conditional upon levels of investment spending and rate of development, leads to overinvestment in exploration and mining— both in the sense that investments have been undertaken and in the sense that the scale of investment has been larger than optimal. The general thrust of this argument finds support in Crommelin's chapter. However, while it may be valid to argue that exploration and early development work have been unduly accelerated, it is less clear that actual mining development has occurred earlier than justified. The main problem may be that the capacity capable of being developed into new mines, which has absorbed considerable investment funds in the process of identification and proving-up, may well have been excessive.

Although the incentive towards excessive development provided by the lease allocation mechanisms is consistent with the development orientation believed to characterise State governments, the allocation of leases on Commonwealth territory seems to proceed in identical fashion. Only very recently has the Commonwealth suggested the auctioning of oil leases without any conditions relating to the rate of investment in exploration or mining. Thus there is in general no present source of conflict between levels of government on this issue.

Trengove notes that Willett's approach in chapter 6, with its tentative support for the use of a resource rent tax, relies heavily on the efficient taxation approach. An efficiency theory of government supposes that government activity enhances the overall efficiency of resource allocation and that revenue to purchase public goods is raised in the least distorting manner. This leads directly to a consideration of so-called optimal taxation—the levying of taxes more on inelastic activities, the limiting case of which is the taxation of pure economic rent. Even if the efficiency theory of government is discarded, the optimal taxation problem remains relevant in the consideration of changes at the margin. The impact of replacing one tax instrument with another, regardless of the purposes to which the government intends to put the marginal gain in revenue, if any, needs to be considered. If the switch from, say, ad valorem royalties to a resource rent tax does represent a move in the direction of increased efficiency in taxation, the lot of both taxer and taxed can be improved: either the mining company's profits may be left unaltered, with tax receipts enlarged, or receipts may be held constant, with profits enlarged. In general, a combination of the two is possible. However, the new form of tax might carry with it an additional lump-sum element. It might succeed in lowering returns to the firm or project, but without adversely affecting the efficiency of resource allocation—that is, without adversely affecting the firm's incentives to explore, develop and mine.

It may certainly be the case that, for many existing projects, there is ample potential for the 'negotiation' of new forms of taxation that would raise tax receipts and lower company profits but would not threaten the projects' survival. If the impact of the new regime on future projects is taken into account, however, it is difficult to see how reductions in the profitability of existing projects—even if efficiency of resource use is not harmed in those projects—can do anything but lower the incentive to invest in future exploration and mining activities.

In Trengove's view Willett's argument is more concerned with long-term than short-term issues, and results in a tendency to pass off some of the severe informational problems inherent in the more theoretically 'ideal' taxes as being merely 'administratively difficult' to implement. It seems inevitable that taxes must in the end be based on things that are easily and objectively measurable. It is perhaps a little ironic that the mounting pressure to move away from royalties towards taxation of super profits should come at a time when there is substantial pressure (admittedly from a different part of the political spectrum) to change the overall tax base from a concept of income towards the more easily measured consumption concept. Chapter 6, with its emphasis on efficient taxation, relies on the risk-sharing motivation for government participation—government equity—in resource development. This approach is consistent with the 'principal–agent' context in which much of the academic literature is framed. The suggestion is that the government, as the principal, should share the risk of project development with the presumably risk-averse managing agent, the mining firm. But these assumptions about the propensity to bear risk could well be inappropriate, and in any case various market institutions already achieve considerable diversification of risk. If governments genuinely wanted to maximise their tax receipts, then a free-for-all auction, with no strings attached, could well do the job—the winner of such an auction being the most optimistic and risk-taking bidder.

Fraser accepts Willett's broad conclusions, but suggests that the implementation of the preferred approach—a combination of lump-sum bidding and a profit-related resources rent tax—has a number of political and practical implications that need to be pursued beyond the broad conceptual level reached in the chapter; for example, revenues from profit-related taxes would be subject to greater fluctuation than those derived from production-based taxes.

In the area of Commonwealth–State revenue sharing, economists are unlikely to win arguments by appeals to economic efficiency alone. Cooperation between the Commonwealth and the States, rather than competition, is a prerequisite for progress in this area, and it is probably better strategy to move away from generalities and focus on particular minerals, as the Commonwealth is presently doing in its application of a resource rent tax to the petroleum sector. Ownership of resources provides a natural and logical guide to the question of who should control the rents, but problems could arise where ownership differs between, say, onshore and offshore fields. For the Commonwealth's resource rent tax on petroleum to work, the Commonwealth will have to compensate the States for the loss of royalty revenue from onshore production.

The Mining Industry in a Federal System

Chapter 7 provides a broad industry perspective on operating in a federal system. The importance of Macleod's contribution is the indication it gives of the wide range of areas of intervention or satisfaction of regulations (at all levels of government) necessary to get mining development off the ground. The key message is that the involvement of federal and State governments, at different levels and stages of project development, does complicate matters—probably more than is really necessary.

Emerson takes issue with the assertion in Macleod's chapter that current views on mining taxation 'start with the assumption that governments can spend these resources more wisely and effectively than shareholders'. The relationship between the State and the mining company is modelled on the principal–agent relationship, in which each party contributes potentially productive assets. In a mining venture, the State's contribution is the grant of mineral-bearing land on behalf of the community, so that the benefits of contributing the mineral asset should accrue to the community at large. Emerson concludes that the most appropriate taxation revenue base for a government is resource rent, because it is less distorting than other taxes and is therefore consistent with a wider tax base and higher levels of expected government revenues.

Further, the high-risk nature of minerals exploration is not an argument for no special taxation of mining industries; rather, it can be an argument for risk sharing between the State and mining firms. Risk sharing can be accommodated through the relative reliance for revenue from a mine on the lump-sum bid made at an auction of mineral rights and the tax based on the revealed rent value of the mine. The process of lease allocation for onshore minerals by State governments in Australia is effectively one of bidding for work program expenditures. Competition between mining firms on this basis leads to a dissipation of rent, which, as Willett explains, is detrimental from a national perspective.

Also, from a national perspective, State government policies to encourage local processing of minerals are economically inefficient. Policy instruments that have been used for this purpose include differential royalty rates and requirements that a specified proportion of mine output be processed locally. Higher royalties are applied to mine output exported from the State in unprocessed form, which amounts to an export tax (with exports defined in terms of State rather than national boundaries). Imposing minimum levels of local processing on mining firms that otherwise would not process locally absorbs, through inefficiency, profits earned at the mining stage, and can lead to a loss of national taxation revenue.

Reform of minerals policy arrangements would be extremely difficult without Commonwealth–State cooperation. Australia is fortunate to be in a situation where mining taxation reform can benefit both Commonwealth and State governments: no party need be worse off as a result of mining taxation reform.

McDonald injects another industry perspective in stressing the huge change of circumstances in which the minerals industry in Australia now operates. Shoyama's account of the shifting attitudes in Canada towards support for resource developments echoes this concern, and such changes of focus are becoming important in Australia. The characteristics of the prospects for Australia's resource trade have altered radically since the 1960s and 1970s, and governments may be coming to understand this.

The likelihood of only modest world economic growth; intense competition among resource suppliers, especially from developing countries, in the resource and processed goods trades; high dependence on markets in Japan, an economy whose growth rate has peaked and whose resource-based industries are static because of resource saving and lack of competitiveness: these changed prospects demand that the main priority for Australia must be the development of fiscal and other policies which support the international competitiveness of nationally beneficial resource developments.

State and Federal Foreign Investment Regulation

Chapter 8 sets out the nature of foreign investment regulation in Australia, and makes the point that there is substantial bipartisan support for the foreign investment guidelines now in force at the federal level. The rationale for Australia's foreign investment policy requires further exploration, but one point of interest is the possibility that Japanese purchaser equity in projects (coming late) might be impeded by Australian equity requirements.

In examining the rationale for foreign investment regulation, Findlay suggests that an underlying theme of the operation of the policy is conflict between federal and State governments, whether regulation is motivated by public interest or political expediency. Federal–State conflict over the exercise of policy is not addressed in the chapter.

If rigidly applied, the fixed local equity guidelines operate to reduce incentives for transfer pricing, to retain some of the rent value of mineral projects, and to avoid the resource allocation costs of inefficient taxation and leasing procedures. All these outcomes are sought in the public interest, but it must be emphasised that the use of equity guidelines for these purposes is a second-best policy. Moreover, the fixed-rule equity guidelines have inherent disadvantages: risk sharing becomes inefficient because, although the domestic economy retains more of the rent value of the project to compensate for the extra risk, the rents are dissipated to offset the cost of risk bearing; and forms of ownership are inefficient becasue the more costly joint ventures and long-term contracts take the place of vertically integrated operations, which are ruled out by the equity guidelines.

In fact, however, the local equity rules are not rigidly applied, and this suggests that foreign investment regulation may be motivated by political expediency; it may be employed by the Commonwealth to achieve 'balanced' development between States and regions, and used in a discriminatory way as part of the broad strategy of building up a coalition of political support, trading off gains in some States against losses in others. Either way, the theme is one of conflict between State and federal governments.

Financing and Charging for Infrastructure

The issue of how infrastructure is financed and charged for returns attention to some of the questions raised in chapter 3 on federal–State fiscal arrangements. In Perkins' view, the nature of these arrangements provides States with little incentive to provide and charge for infrastructure services in an efficient manner—while Loan Council obstacles to funding might prevent infrastructure from being delivered as and when it is needed.

Swan underlines the clear message in chapter 9: some semblance of economic rationality is required in the provision and pricing of public infrastructure to supplement, if not supplant, the allocation of scarce resources through subsidy. The problem posed by the allocation of subsidies on non-economic criteria is exacerbated by the federal system, with its imbalance between functional responsibility and fiscal capacity.

Loan Council allocations bear little relation to the economic returns to society from project investments. Two recent Loan Council developments relate to a Commonwealth veto on new projects (instead of the far more desirable course of evaluating proposals on the grounds of economic viability) and the freeing of electricity project borrowings from Loan Council control for a trial period (overseas borrowings still require approval). It is hard to understand why the State-owned electricity industry, in which there is substantial overcapacity in certain States and considerable inefficiency in public utility, should receive favoured treatment.

The taxpayer should not be required to subsidise an inefficient public sector; efficiently run private companies should be encouraged to provide their own power, and sell any surplus to the grid in competition with State instrumentalities.

In a few cases in Queensland, Western Australia, and South Australia, States have implemented the 'user pays' principle by requiring developers to provide townships, railways and port facilities. Perkins justifies less than full provision of infrastructure by State or local governments in single-enterprise mining towns on the grounds that the project might fail, leaving the government authority high and dry. But Swan suggests that the enterprise would have a more accurate perception of the long-term viability of the project and would pay for infrastructure only if it were viable.

The Commonwealth Treasury's policy of rational charges and high real rates of return on public investments has never really been implemented. The required rate of return approach would inject some rationality into public sector investments, but there are other possible avenues for reform also, such as competition between the public and private sectors in the provision of services presently provided by statutory authorities, privatisation of power stations and railways, and much greater provision of infrastructure generally.

Bloomfield observes that there is a wide divergence between what actually happens, and what economists might suggest (in an ideal world) the basis ought to be for funding infrastructure and charging for its services. In focusing on the sources of that divergence, reference must also be made to the agenda of political considerations whose reality must be recognised if our understanding of why Australian governments manage the resource sector the way they do is to be advanced.

It becomes clear from Perkins' analysis that the provision of infrastructure has become the vehicle for an interventionist role by governments, whether in the form of subsidy, through public financing, or as a method of collecting economic rent. The practice by governments of providing infrastructure as a measure supportive of industrial development is a common one in the Australian economic developmental tradition under governments of whatever political persuasion. The structure of intergovernmental relationships in the Australian federal context provides a valuable key to understanding why this practice has become so important.

A large part of the answer is to be found in the tensions between governments as a result of existing federal fiscal arrangements, and particularly the effects of the present fiscal imbalance and revenue-sharing arrangements on the attitudes of State governments towards independent revenue sources.

Political perceptions are also important, and they do differ markedly—and not necessarily on party lines—from government to government within the federation. To illustrate, it is useful to make reference to three broad approaches to the appropriate role of government in the management of resource development. The first is the market or *laissez faire* approach, which envisages a minimal role for government in a predominantly private enterprise environment. The second is a developmentalist approach, which regards government as having an entrepreneurial role in a 'mixed economy', in terms of providing incentives to encourage private development. Third, there is a nationalist or interventionist approach, which sees it as desirable for government to take the initiative by controlling resource development and ensuring that the community receives an appropriate return on the exploitation of its resources. All these perspectives are familiar from 40 years of Australian experience, and each has been adopted at different times by national and State governments. Given the ways in which powers are allocated within the Australian federal system, the tensions between these three approaches are unlikely, in the short term at least, to be resolved.

It is also clear that the provision of infrastructure, and the nature of government intervention in its provision, cannot be separated from the wider array of other government interventions in resource development and their cumulative effect. For example, the industry obviously regards government involvement in providing infrastructure as inseparable from the whole range of government interventions in respect of the industry. Requirements on companies to finance infrastructure are perceived as a variant form of taxation, as are measures to extract economic rent through user charges on services. Efforts to increase direct revenue from mining companies through resource rent tax or 'super' royalties have a clear effect on the companies' willingness to contribute to social infrastructure costs, as local governments have discovered. The cumulative effects of Commonwealth export levies, State royalty payments, Commonwealth company tax, State infrastructure user charges, and local front-end payments for social infrastructure suggest a far more complex arithmetic, in which infrastructure provision is a contributing factor. In this context, Perkins' analysis offers an opportunity to scrutinise the redistributive effects of *one* set of interventions.

The level of indirect subsidy inherent in the way infrastructure needs are met is influenced not only by whether a project is of marginal profitability but by the relative bargaining positions of government and enterprise. The scale and capital intensity of new mineral projects, the size of proponents, the level of overseas investment, and the existence of international investment alternatives have combined to erode the bargaining position of government. Major projects have the potential to be so important to a State economy that they are dealt with in an ad hoc way, in a bargaining situation in which, in order to secure the benefits of development to their own regions, State governments may be prepared to trade away other obligations, on matters such as the cost recovery from the provision of infrastructure. More recent trends away from subsidy towards revenue raising through user charges, up-front payments and the like testify to the dynamic character of the relationship. This flexibility over time in response to fluctuations in world markets, differing demands for particular resource commodities and differing regional needs contributes significantly to the diversity in infrastructure arrangements around Australia.

Perkins' concern about the effect of Loan Council constraints may be somewhat misplaced in view of the diminishing role of that body. Current estimates suggest that less than a quarter of Australian public sector borrowings now remain within its control.

It is clear from Perkins' argument, and from other comments, that the existing practices of governments in the provision of infrastructure and charging for services are far from perfect. The reality must be recognised that governments, and in particular State governments, will be concerned primarily with those courses of action that maximise their own influence and secure for them the widest scope for autonomous action. If, in the process, governments find themselves obliged to select inefficient instruments, that will be regarded as one of the costs. The question remains of whether it is possible, given the rigidities of the existing federal allocation of powers and the divergent interests and obligations of different governments within the Australian federal system, to do any better.

McDonald argues that while the policy advocated by Perkins might be appropriate in a perfect world, it is inappropriate in the real but imperfect world. Given the market imperfections and distortions of the real world, a clear distinction must be made between the valuing and the pricing of resources if resource allocation is to maximise economic welfare. To allow for the imperfections and distortions, resource allocation and pricing decisions need to be guided by cost–benefit analysis. In such an analysis of a resource project the full economic value of the resources required by the project is charged against it, and the economic value of the project's benefits is credited to it.

However, the resources are priced at the highest level, consistent with maximising economic welfare, that allows the preferred project to use them. It may therefore be necessary to price the resources to the preferred project at less than their full economic cost in order to allow that project to proceed and the community's economic welfare to be maximised.

It is also important to make a distinction between private and public sector entities and their respective operating criteria. Governments and government organisations should not operate according to the narrow financial efficiency criteria of the private sector. Rather, they should employ broadly based economic criteria, assessing the implications of distortions and imperfections in the real world and making policy and pricing decisions in the light of these to maximise the community's economic welfare.

Japanese–Australian Resource Trade

In chapter 10 Sakurai reviews the long history of resource trade relationships between Australia and Japan, describing methods of trade, the Japanese preference for long-term contract trade with Australia and the policy trend in the Ministry of International Trade and Industry towards stable resource imports, and making pointed reference to the changed forecast for Japan's resource needs to the year 2000. His argument suggests that Japan would prefer to continue its trade relations with Australia without becoming deeply involved in resource project development.

Charlton and Reynolds note that there are few Australian resource investments in which Japanese companies have taken a significant equity position. Japanese lenders do provide finance and regard Australia as a relatively secure borrower, especially in respect of investment in the production of commodities required by Japan. Japanese lenders have also provided finance to North and South America for resource projects. Japan's strong trade performance has meant that current account surpluses are balanced by increasing external investment, a considerable proportion of which goes into productive enterprises in developing countries. The question is whether Japanese investment strategy in the resource development area changes significantly under these circumstances.

It is instructive to describe the perspective of a foreigner contemplating potential investment in a resource project in Australia in terms of a little parable—the Parable of the Japanese Investor.

An honourable (but anonymous) citizen of Japan called 'Mr Smith' decides personally to investigate developing a mineral deposit on behalf of his company.

After obtaining all the technical data it is considered that the project will give a reasonable rate of return on the equity invested and that it is a viable risk/reward for his company.

Mr Smith then decides he should visit Australia and speak to the government about his company's proposed development.

After talking to his good friend Mr Iwasearchy, he realises there are three levels of government, federal, State and local. Mr Iwasearchy tells him not to worry about the local government because they will 'do as they are told' by the State government. The State government is a good friend and does 'special deals'.

So Mr Smith, full of enthusiasm, embarks for Australia to see the friendly State government.

On arrival, Mr Smith is introduced to all the senior State government personnel, and he has many hours of fruitful discussions, all encouraging his investment in their State of opportunity. Mr Smith is just about ready to say he will recommend going ahead when the State government tells him about the foreign investment policy of the federal government and that he had better go and see them as well.

The State government tells Mr Smith about the two levels of government in Australia, federalism, etc., which leaves Mr Smith slightly confused. Nevertheless, undaunted, he sets out for Canberra.

Here Mr Smith is courteously received by senior federal personnel. He is carefully informed of the foreign investment requirements of 50 per cent Australian equity, the need for an environmental impact statement for both federal and State governments (because Mr Smith's deposit is on farming land which has been cleared but not yet cultivated), the rate of income tax and the possible effects of withholding tax, and the requirements of export licences.

So Mr Smith has to sell 50 per cent of his project to an Australian resident. Mr Smith knows what it is worth, so if he gets the right price he should still be able to proceed. But alas! an Australian citizen called Ned Kelly is the only one interested, and he will only pay half price.

Sadly, Mr Smith returns to his hotel room, gets out his personal computer and puts in some variables plus Mr Kelly's reduced price. Fortunately the result shows a sufficient rate of return, and although it is not nearly as attractive as it had been he can still proceed.

On the aeroplane from Canberra, Mr Smith sits beside a learned fellow traveller (lft) who starts to tell him all about the federal–State relationships, fiscal equalisation, concurrent powers grants, special grants, relativities, and claimant States, which has the effect of thoroughly confusing him. He also mentions that it is illegal to look for uranium in Victoria and that, in the semi-State of the Northern Territory, it is difficult for explorers because of federal Aboriginal laws. Mr Smith listens with stoic passivity to all this, together with a diatribe on the deficiencies of the federal–State industrial arbitration systems. Finally the lft mentions something called 'rrt' that will take all the 'cream' out of the resource projects. If this does not shake Mr Smith, then the next comment, that the State governments already have a resource tax, certainly does. (His friendly State government did not tell him that!)

By now in a highly excited and emotional state, Mr Smith quickly goes back to his friendly State government official and confronts him about his 'special deal'.

After a thorough examination, and after talking to other companies with 'special deals' (which are of course secret), Mr Smith finds out that he will have to pay for all the infrastructure, which will mean that he will

1 pay up-front capital for houses, shops, swimming pools, cultural halls, sewerage and water, also sporting grounds and recreational parks for his employees, the service population and the railway workers, not to mention an odd regional road here and there;

2 pay all up-front capital for the track and rolling stock for the railway and its workshops—and, in spite of this payment, the State government also wants an additional profit component about four times over the actual costs of rail haulage;

3 pay up-front capital for a portion of the port facility and agree to fund the balance over a period of years;

4 pay a mineral royalty on each tonne produced, stamp duty and payroll tax, and so on.

Horrified by all this, Mr Smith also learns that any hopes he had of using Japanese manufactured goods and fabricated steel products will not be realised because of tariffs and a preferential system favouring local producers. Mr Smith does not need to use his personal computer (made in Japan) to tell him that his rate of return is now close to negative.

But he thinks all this surely cannot be true in a great, resource-rich country like Australia, so, in desperation, he goes to the top of the State government with his tale of woe, and suggests that there now should be talk about his 'special deal'. He is told that this *is* the 'special deal'—we want you to invest here. (Imagine the special deal given to an Australian company!)

Finally, he is told the State government will sort it out—'leave it all to us'.

'That is exactly what they want,' says Mr Smith, 'all of it'. So he hurriedly packs his bags and goes home to Japan, buys the minerals he requires on the spot market and lives happily ever after.

Charlton and Reynolds present this little story in a spirit of good humour, but every parable has its moral. While it is well and good to pontificate over the intricacies of federalism and States' right, State and federal governments should not think of the mining industry as being like Norman Lindsay's magic pudding, which could be cut into innumerable slices and consumed without getting any smaller.

Shoyama notes the emphasis in chapter 10 on the background of recessionary conditions that has been slowing the growth of the Japanese economy markedly. The pronounced structural shift away from industries consuming heavier materials and energy has reinforced the slowdown in the growth of Japanese demand for resource commodities.

Japanese resource investment has had the securing of long-term supply at acceptable and stable prices as its motivating force, rather than earning potential alone. Where simple purchase on the basis of long-term contracts cannot be relied upon for these ends, two alternatives have been adopted: the financing of development by loan capital, with tied purchase commitments; and 'captive development' or direct equity investments, usually involving local partners. Perhaps it is not surprising that the loan-cum-purchase technique has been favoured, in that there has been some sensitivity to possible objection by the host country to aggressive direct investment.

There is a new but understated emphasis in the Sakurai chapter on 'increasing uncertainty' and the problems that arise with rigidly fixed terms as to quantities and prices in long-term contracts negotiated during earlier boom times. An important aspect of these contracts was simple provision for price escalation under inflationary conditions. But to include adjustment provisions anticipating reductions of prices and quantities would tend to undermine the viability of major resource projects. Adjustments in more directions may now be required, even though the stake in loan financing or equity investment builds in a countervailing force. A reluctance to join in the financing of infrastructure can be understood in this context.

Finally, Sakurai notes the overriding concern of the Japanese investor with 'political stability'. It can be inferred that the political complexion of the government, particularly at the national level, is an important aspect of stability. So too, explicitly, is the potential for federal–State conflict in policy formulation over all the areas covered in chapter 4 and explored in detail in other chapters. Nevertheless, security of supply, and therefore diversification of supply sources, within or among separate countries, is a prime objective of policy, whether enunciated in Japan at the company or the official level. Hence the readiness to pay premium prices, as is evident in the coal trade, which involves Canada as a supplier alongside Australia and other sources. The coal development in the north-east of British Columbia has to be regarded as a competing source in this light.

One channel for the flow of Japanese investment in Canada has been the opening up of the banking sector to foreign-owned banks effected five years ago. This remains on the agenda for Australia. In any case, the array of issues noted by Sakurai in the Australian situation is also encountered in Canada, even though both countries remain, for similar reasons, preferred outlets for Japanese investment.

Another question was raised in the context of comment on chapter 10: whether Japanese resource purchasers now have a greater desire for ownership links which, if difficult to obtain in Australia, might divert Japanese demand to alternative suppliers. From a federal–State perspective, it seems likely that the less populous, more resource-rich States are less supportive of Australian ownership requirements than the more populous States. Queensland, for example, may well regard American, Japanese or European firms as no more foreign than firms owned largely by residents of New South Wales or Victoria. On the contrary, they may find that dealing with non-Australian companies gives them a degree of independence from Canberra in the world at large. However, there has been little evidence so far of any serious conflict of interest that would impede resource developments. If States such as Queensland or Western Australia felt that they were losing resource development opportunities because of foreign investment controls, they would probably be able to persuade the Commonwealth to relax its stance (as indeed it has tended to do when investment has slackened in the past).

Federal–State Issues in External Economic Relations

Chapter 11, by Warhurst and O'Loghlin, looks at the structure of State government representation overseas, particularly in Japan, and considers the possibility of State competition to attract resource purchasers or resource investments. It appears that the overseas offices of State governments are mainly designed to provide information to prospective investors.

Galligan observes that, despite being pronounced 'obsolete' by Laski in 1939[7] and 'trivial' by Riker in 1970,[8] federalism is alive and well in Australia. In an obvious sense federalism matters, because of the sheer complexity it imposes upon any policy area (such as resources development) that involves both levels of federal government. The basic consequences of federalism are the fragmentation of political power and the disaggregation of public policymaking. Thus we find that in the particular area of resource development and trade, as Warhurst and O'Loghlin set it out, federalism entails a complex and uncoordinated functional pattern of intergovernmental relations that includes duplication of State offices in Japan, conflicts of interest between federal and State governments, competition among States and lack of information flows—in short, a morass of disparate institutions, activities and interrelationships. Warhurst and O'Loghlin ferret out the details of the various State government offices in Tokyo. It turns out that these offices are little more than symbolic indicators of direct activity by the States in trade areas that vitally affect them, which is the significant point.

If federalism so complicates things, why continue with it? This question has animated generations of rational centralists and produced a whole sub-literature of indictment of the inefficiencies of federalism. But, as one arch-protagonist of 'organic federalism', Sawer, has recently admitted: 'There is no longer a simple confidence in central planning, Keynesian or otherwise'.[9] It has not always been recognised that the question can only be hypothetical, because once a federal system has been put in place it crystallises political parties, government bureaucracies and interest groups into a dynamic federal pattern that reproduces itself and institutionalises regional differences, whether perceived or real. There is therefore little point in proposing alternatives, but there is a point in evaluating the system as it stands.

Much has changed in political economy since the invention of federalism in its American form: corporations have become giant national and multinational enterprises; governments have become increasingly interventionist in pursuing their various, and often conflicting, policies; and direct government–corporate dealings have replaced market competition in large areas of development and trade. All these changes are features of the political economy of resources. Yet federalism has persisted. The structural changes in political economy towards huge government involvement and direct negotiations combine badly with federalism. The recent resurgence of interest in federalism over its impact upon resource development and trade has been premised on a view opposite to Riker's: that federalism makes no difference to outcomes. The leading argument that federalism affects outcomes, advantaging corporate developers, producing regions and Japanese buyers, and disadvantaging the public interest and national unity, was made by the Canadian Stevenson in 1976[10] and has tended to become an orthodoxy among Australian commentators. This view informs the Myer report on Australian–Japanese relations quoted by Warhurst and O'Loghlin: 'The Japanese are placed in a position of being able to derive advantage from playing one state off against another or the States against the Commonwealth'.

As Warhurst and O'Loghlin note, however, this is only one possible outcome that federalism allows. It did tend to be the case earlier for resource development in both Canada and Australia, but cannot be extrapolated to federalism per se. Federalism is diverse and resilient and allows, or if the conditions are right even stimulates, a dialectic reaction. Vertical competition between the federal and State levels of government to protect, enhance or regain their spheres of influence or taxation bases can set off a series of initiatives and counter-initiatives that produce more overall government intervention and higher total taxation than either level of government intended or would prefer. This was borne out in practice in Canada in the early 1980s when the federal Liberal government imposed the National Energy Program to redress the excessive earlier gains of Alberta in seizing the bulk of economic rent from oil and gas after the OPEC increases. There was no comparable development in Australia because our regional States were less entrepreneurial, because Australia's major oil and gas field is offshore, and because the resources boom collapsed. The original Laski thesis that federalism facilitates corporate conquest by fragmenting political power therefore does not necessarily hold; even less so does its more exaggerated modern formulation by Wheelwright and Crough that Australia is a 'client state' of giant transnational corporations that take advantage of our federal system.[11]

Federalism matters for resource development and trade because it affects outcomes, but the way in which it does so depends on the character and dynamic interactions of the various players reacting to the international market situation. So to find out how federalism affects outcomes these other factors must be investigated: first, the character and structure of the various players; second, their dynamic interrelationships; and third, the international market. Warhurst and O'Loghlin make two general points on these issues.

The first is 'the relative unimportance of ideological and party differences in determining the substantial rather than the superficial behaviour of governments'. Party political differences are not so significant for federal–State relations in the resources area. But if politics in the narrow party–Parliament–pluralist sense is not so important, what is? Here there is a certain lack of analytic rigour and clarity in the argument of chapter 11. Warhurst and O'Loghlin seem to suggest some mixture of institutional structures, different State economic interests, more varied political climate, and the like. But how much is due to each, and in what ways? There is a need for a more systematic unpacking and examination of all the complex parts. But that is a large task. On the other hand, one should be cautious about dismissing party and ideological differences without thorough investigation. Surely Premier Court's Liberal regime in Western Australia and Premier Petersen's National Party in Queensland have had some influence on resource development in those two States?

Also, the claim that intergovernmental relations within Australian federalism take place 'essentially between federal and State government departments', not between governments, is difficult to sustain. Typically, because of giant projects with enormous capital, infrastructure and risk aspects, governments do tend to be directly involved in the resources area. They cannot afford not to be, nor can corporations risk not negotiating at the highest political level and locking governments into projects. In Bass Strait, the North-West Shelf, Utah's export coalmines, the Tasmanian Dam and the Argyle diamond mine, to name only some of the major developments or controversies, governments have been directly involved. Warhurst and O'Loghlin note that a major function of Queensland's Tokyo office is looking after its Premier, and that despite the multitude of State government offices in Japan, 'major companies deal with State governments directly'.

On the contrary, the direct dealings between governments and corporations and between State and federal governments, as well as those between corporations and government departments and between State and federal government departments, are vital in the field of federalism and resource development. That is because the political economy of resources entails megaprojects of such size and importance, both politically and economically, that the various federal, State and corporate actors need to be directly involved at both the government and government department levels. Unfortunately, this area of direct government–corporate dealings is difficult to research and hence to give proper weight to.

Resource Markets and Resource Trade Issues

In a market structure largely dominated by arms-length, long-term contract purchases—where such contracts provide some degree of redistribution of investment risk—purchasers need to be concerned about the nature of policy and likely policy change in Australia. In chapter 12, Smith makes the point that, since both State and federal government policies are important in resource developments, it is necessary that both levels of government communicate with major purchasers to provide them with an understanding of policy thinking and directions. The difficulty has been that the two levels of government have tended to communicate separately and sometimes in contradictory ways. Partly because governments can really only communicate with private overseas purchasers through public speeches, and because those speeches are also heard and read by domestic electorates, the nature of federal–State rivalry in Australia tends to make public statements more contradictory and uncertainty-generating than reflects the position accurately.

The other issue considered in chapter 12 is the nature of Australia's position in major resource markets. If, as some believe, there is an inherent tendency to overexploitation of resources in Australia, has this adversely affected Australia's terms of trade for mineral products as well as generating domestic production inefficiencies? The importance of the question is that if, say, Queensland chooses to overproduce coal (reducing the value of its coal resources and potential revenues from those resources but affecting no one else), there might be no case for Commonwealth intervention. If, on the other hand, the export price for New South Wales coal fell in consequence, the case for Commonwealth regulation might be more pressing. Smith suggests that Australia is so large a supplier in many relevant markets that a tendency to oversupply would result in a deterioration in terms of trade. There is a further suggestion that Commonwealth action to regulate price bargaining without any control on the development of export capacity might be ineffective. Yet conflict will follow attempts to exercise such control.

McDonald identifies two key points in chapter 12. The first is Smith's conclusion that the absence of any cohesive and visibly coordinated approach to policy formulation in Australia may make for substantial difficulties in promoting a reasonably stable policy environment. State and federal government objectives in relation to resources can and do differ, while the absence of an integrated fiscal system in Australia, and of a satisfactory mechanism for sharing the costs and benefits of resource developments, means that the potential exists for a marked divergence between State and federal perceptions of project or policy costs and benefits. Because of institutional distortions, assessments of the net social benefits of a resource project by State and federal governments may differ quite markedly.

When resource development was rapid this difference was of less importance. Now, with relatively low growth prospects, which are also generally recognised as 'inadequate', there is an urgent need to integrate and harmonise State and federal perceptions of the costs and benefits of resource projects. Unless this is achieved, valuable projects will be frustrated by policy difficulties reflecting divergent assessments of costs and benefits.

The second point relates to the question of uncertainty and contracts. Smith considers different types of trade arrangements and also the roles the Commonwealth might play in influencing Australia's resource trade. The important point is the need to recognise the inherent uncertainty of resource markets and to develop commercial relationships accordingly, rather than simply to rely on long-term inflexible contracts or equity positions. There is no point in having long-term contracts, or an equity relationship, designed to ensure market access and stability, if the supplier cannot also remain competitive. On the other hand, in return for having to maintain an internationally competitive price, the supplier should be given explicit commitments in relation to market share.

This suggests the use of more 'sophisticated' contracts embodying conditions that provide for the adjustment of volume, price and any other relevant conditions, in any reasonable set of foreseen circumstances. In the negotiations the parties explicitly allow for likely (especially cyclical) changes in the economic and market environment, and provision is made in the contract for any variation in such circumstances. In this way the balance of risk and advantage is linked with changes in conditions. If the parties find it impossible to agree on contract conditions under reasonably likely market conditions, there is no basis for a contractual relationship.

Main Themes

Throughout this discussion a recurring theme is the level of economic efficiency of the federal fiscal arrangements governing resource development and trade in Australia. The federal system is generally pressed for its equity; but the confusion generated by competing resource taxation arrangements and ambiguities over State and federal exercise of authority are likely to damage the efficiency of one of the Australian economy's strongest sectors, especially as international commodity markets become increasingly competitive. The need is for a rationalisation of the tax structure between the federal and State governments, and this book suggests an agenda for policy action.

It must be said that there has not been a great deal of research in Australia on the economic consequences of the operation of our federal system. The contributions to this volume highlight the importance of some of the issues in this area and indicate a wide field for further study.

Notes

Chapter 1

Professor Shibata is responsible for that part of the argument of this chapter that introduces a Japanese perspective, and more particularly for the material included in the second, third and fourth sections. Dr Drysdale is responsible for the argument of the rest of the chapter.

1 A recent publication that contributes to remedying this deficiency is B.W. Head *State and Economy in Australia* Melbourne: Oxford University Press, 1983. A forthcoming volume is *Australian Resource Development: Bargaining at Many Levels*, edited by B. Galligan.

Chapter 2

1 K.C. Wheare *Federal Government* 4th edn, Oxford University Press, 1963, p. 10.
2 Geoffrey Sawer *Modern Federalism* Pitman Australia, 1976, p. 106. Sawer deliberately avoids a definition of federalism but, after an examination of different federal models, suggests that 'its most important feature is the creation of an area of guaranteed autonomy for each unit of the system'. The degree of autonomy determines the place of the system on the federal spectrum.
3 A.V. Dicey *An Introduction to the Study of the Law of the Constitution* 10th edn, London: Macmillan, 1959, p. 143.
4 *James* v. *Commonwealth* (1936) 55 CLR 1.
5 *Hume* v. *Palmer* (1926) 38 CLR 441, 483.
6 *Ex Parte Mclean* (1930) 43 CLR 472.
7 J. Quick and R.R. Garran *Annotated Constitution of the Australian Commonwealth* 1901, facsimile edn, Legal Books, 1976, p. 123.
8 ibid. p. 133.
9 Sections 76(i), 74.
10 *Amalgamated Society of Engineers* v. *Adelaide Steamship Co. Ltd* (1920) 28 CLR 129.
11 (1920) 28 CLR 129, 161–62.
12 (1920) 28 CLR 129, 160.
13 *Fairfax* v. *Federal Commissioner of Taxation* (1965) 114 CLR 1.
14 *R.* v. *Coldham; Ex Parte Australian Social Welfare Union* (1983) 57 ALJR 575; *Commonwealth* v. *Tasmania* (1983) 57 ALJR 450.
15 (1983) 57 ALJR 450, 495.

16 For a rare, recent example see *Gazzo* v. *Comptroller of Stamps* (Vic.) (1981) 56 ALJR 143. Murphy J, in dissent, attributed the result to 'the once-discredited doctrine of reserved powers . . . having a triumphant, if unacknowledged, resurgence' (at 154).

17 Sections 75 and 76.

18 *Commonwealth* v. *Colonial Combing, Spinning and Weaving Co. Ltd* (*Wool Tops* case) (1922) 31 CLR 421, *per* Knox CJ, Higgins, Gavan Duffy and Starke JJ.

19 *New South Wales* v. *Bardolph* (1934) 52 CLR 455.

20 (1922) 31 CLR 421.

21 (1922) 31 CLR 421, 441, 443.

22 Enid Campbell 'Commonwealth Contracts' (1976) 44 *Australian Law Journal* 14. See also G. Winterton *Parliament, the Executives and the Governor-General* Melbourne University Press, 1983, p. 46.

23 But cf. D. Dawson 'Commonwealth Prerogatives' in Saunders et al. *Current Constitutional Problems in Australia* Centre for Research on Federal Financial Relations, distributed by ANUTECH, 1982, p. 62.

24 (1975) 134 CLR 338, 396.

25 *Commonwealth of Australia Gazette* 21 June 1973.

26 *South Australia* v. *Commonwealth* (1941–42) 65 CLR 373, 429.

27 (1983) 57 ALJR 649.

Chapter 3

1 Russell Mathews 'Resource Development and Fiscal Equalization' in Stuart Harris and Geoff Taylor (eds) *Resource Development and the Future of Australian Society* Monograph No. 7, Centre for Resource and Environmental Studies, Australian National University, 1982, pp. 121–45.

Chapter 4

The research assistance of Jenny Tebbut in preparing this chapter is gratefully acknowledged.

1 A. Hirshman 'A Generalized Linkage Approach to Development, with Special Reference to Staples' in *Essays on Economic Development and Cultural Change in Honor of Bert F. Hoselitz* Supplement to *Economic Development and Cultural Change* 25, 1977, pp. 67–98.

2 R.C. Jensen and G.R. West 'The Nature of Australian Regional Input–Output Multipliers' *Prometheus* 1, 1, June 1983, pp. 202–21.

3 S. Harris 'Australian Resource Policies: Bargaining at Many Levels' in B. Galligan (ed.) *Australian Resource Development* (forthcoming)

4 S. Harris 'The Economics of Uranium Mining' *Current Affairs Bulletin* 54, 11, April 1978.

5 G. Stevenson *Mineral Resources and Australian Federalism* Research Monograph No. 17, Centre for Research on Federal Financial Relations, Australian National University, 1977.

6 G. Tullock 'Federalism: Problems of Scale' *Public Choice* 6, Spring 1969, p. 29.

7 A. Scott *Central Government Claims to Mineral Resources* Occasional Paper No. 8, Centre for Research on Federal Financial Relations, Australian National University, 1978.

8 P. Loveday 'Liberals and the Idea of Development' *Australian Journal of Politics*

and History 23, 2, August 1977, pp. 149–63; E.J. Harman 'Ideology and Mineral Development in Western Australia, 1960–1980' in E.J. Harman and B.W. Head (eds) *State, Capital and Resources in the North and West of Australia* Perth: University of Western Australia Press, 1982, pp. 167–96.

9   D. Horne 'Resources and the Cult of National Development in Australia' in S. Harris and G. Taylor (eds) *Resource Development and the Future of Australian Society* CRES Monograph No. 7, Centre for Resource and Environmental Studies, Australian National University, 1982, pp. 273–83.

10 B. Galligan 'Federalism and Resource Development in Australia and Canada' *Australian Quarterly* Spring 1982, pp. 236–51.

11 L. Layman 'Changing Resource Development Policy in Western Australia, 1930s –1960s' in Harman and Head (eds) *State Capital and Resources* pp. 149–63.

12 R. Stuart 'Resources Development Policy: the Case of the Export Coal Industry' CRES Working Paper, Centre for Resource and Environmental Studies, Australian National University, 1983.

13 Committee of Economic Enquiry *Report* Commonwealth of Australia, vol. 1, May 1965, ch. 8.

14 ibid., pp. 61, 196.

15 B.W. Head 'Some Economic Bases of Inter-state and Federal–State Conflicts' *Journal of Australian Studies* 9, November 1981, pp. 49–60.

16 Stevenson *Mineral Resources and Australian Federalism* p. 15; P.D. Groenewegen 'Federalism' in A. Patience and B. Head (eds) *From Whitlam to Fraser: Reform and Reaction in Australian Politics* Melbourne: Oxford University Press, 1979, p. 68.

17 Galligan 'Federalism and Resource Development'.

18 J. Brown 'Infrastructure Policies in the Pilbara' in Harman and Head (eds) *State, Capital and Resources*, pp. 237–55.

19 C. Emerson and P.J. Lloyd 'Improving Mineral Taxation Policy in Australia' *Economic Record* 59, 166, September 1983, pp. 232–44.

20 R. Mathews 'Resource Development and Fiscal Equalization' in Harris and Taylor (eds) *Resource Development and Australian Society*, pp. 121–45.

21 G. Sturgess 'Queensland Puts the Squeeze on Coal Miners' *Bulletin* 25 November 1980, pp. 118–20.

22 Stuart 'Resources Development Policy'.

23 Sturgess 'Queensland Puts the Squeeze on'.

24 Emerson and Lloyd 'Improving Mineral Taxation Policy'.

25 J.H. Cassing and A.L. Hillman 'State–Federal Resource Tax Rivalry: the Queensland Railway and Optimal Mineral Rights Leases' *Economic Record* 58, 162, September 1982, pp. 235–41.

26 D. Anderson *Foreign Investment Control in the Mining Sector: Comparisons of Australian and Canadian Experience* CRES Monograph No. 10, Centre for Resource and Environmental Studies, Australian National University, 1983.

27 G. Stevenson 'The Control of Foreign Direct Investment in a Federation: Canadian and Australian Experience' in R.M. Burns et al. (eds) *Political and Administrative Federalism* Research Monograph No. 14, Centre for Research on Federal Financial Relations, Australian National University, 1976, p. 43.

28 Harris 'Australian Resources Policies'.

29 Stuart 'Resources Development Policy'.

30 Horne 'Resources and National Development'; Layman 'Changing Resource Development Policy'.

31 H.C. Coombs 'How to Balance the Aboriginal Interest in Resource Development' in Harris and Taylor (eds) *Resource Development and Australian Society*, pp. 239–51.

32 *Mineral Resources and Australian Federalism*, p. 83.

Chapter 5

1   *The Case of Mines* (1568) 1 Plow. 310.
2   ibid.
3   *Australian Courts Act* 1828, 9 Geo. IV, c. 83 (Imp.), s. 24.
4   A.G. Lang and Michael Crommelin *Australian Mining and Petroleum Laws—An Introduction* Sydney: Butterworths, 1979, ch. 2.
5   ibid.
6   ibid.
7   *Coal Acquisition Act* 1981.
8   *Mining Act* 1971, s. 16.
9   *Mines (Amendment) Act* 1983, s. 45.
10 *Northern Territory (Self-Government) Act* 1978, s. 69.
11 *Cudgen Rutile (No. 2) Pty Ltd* v. *Chalk* [1975] A.C. 520.
12 Though uncommon, such restrictions are not unknown; e.g. *Petroleum Act* 1923 –1983 (Qld), s. 12; *Mining Act* (NT), s. 16.
13 Exceptions are New South Wales, Victoria and Tasmania.
14 See for example *Cudgen Rutile (No. 2) Pty Ltd* v. *Chalk* [1975] A.C. 520.
15 *Mining Act* 1968–1982, s. 67.
16 *Mining Act* 1980.
17 *Mines (Amendment) Act* 1983.
18 Cases are too numerous to list; a recent example is the *Diamond (Ashton Joint Venture) Agreement Act* 1981.
19 Again, there are numerous examples; an early one is *The Commonwealth Aluminium Corporation Pty Ltd Agreement Act of 1957* (relating to the Weipa bauxite project).
20 e.g. *Cooper Basin (Ratification) Act* 1975.
21 e.g. *Clutha Development Pty Limited Agreement Act* 1970.
22 e.g. *Alcoa (Portland Aluminium Smelter) Act* 1980.
23 This issue is the subject of various papers collected in Michael Crommelin and Andrew R. Thompson (eds) *Mineral Leasing as an Instrument of Public Policy* Vancouver: University of British Columbia Press, 1977.
24 Most recently in *Hematite Petroleum Pty Ltd* v. *Victoria* (1982–83) 57 ALJR 591.
25 *Parton* v. *Milk Board (Vic.)* (1949) 80 CLR 229, 259 (Dixon J).
26 Michael Crommelin 'Jurisdiction over Onshore Oil and Gas in Canada' (1975) 10 *University of British Columbia Law Review* 86, pp. 120–22.
27 Instead, some Australian States have sought to tackle this problem by means of differential royalty rates, which vary according to whether mineral processing takes place within or beyond State borders: e.g. *Commonwealth Aluminium Corporation Pty Ltd Agreement Act* 1957 (Qld).
28 (1975–76) 136 CLR 1.
29 ibid. 9.
30 *The Commonwealth* v. *Tasmania* (1983) 46 ALR 625, 57 ALJR 450.
31 *Australian National Airways Pty Ltd* v. *The Commonwealth* (Airlines case) (1945) 71 CLR 29.
32 *Hematite Petroleum Pty Ltd* v. *Victoria* (1982–83) 57 ALJR 591.
33 ibid. 601 (Mason J, with whom Brennan J agreed); 605 (Murphy J); query 595 (Gibbs CJ).
34 'Offshore Oil Legislation' Press Release, Canberra, 17 April 1964.
35 (1975) 135 CLR 337.
36 *Raptis (A.) & Son* v. *South Australia* (1976–77) 138 CLR 346; *Robinson* v. *The Western Australia Museum* (1976–77) 138 CLR 283.
37 The main statutes were: *Coastal Waters (State Powers) Act* 1980; *Coastal Waters*

(State Title) Act 1980; *Seas and Submerged Lands Amendment Act* 1980; *Petroleum (Submerged Lands) Amendment Act* 1980.
38   e.g. *Petroleum (Submerged Lands) Act* 1982 (WA).
39   *Minerals (Submerged Lands) Act* 1981, plus several ancillary statutes.

Chapter 6

The views expressed here are those of the author and should not be construed as reflecting those of the Western Australian government.

1   E.C. Brown 'Business–Income Taxation and Investment Incentives' in *Income, Employment and Public Policy. Essays in Honour of Alvin H. Hansen* New York: Norton, 1948, pp. 300–16; V.L. Smith 'Tax Depreciation Policy and Investment Policy' *International Economic Review, Papers and Proceedings* 64, 2, May 1974, pp. 1–14.

2   M. White and A. White 'Tax Neutrality of Instantaneous versus Economic Depreciation' in R.M. Bird and J.B. Head (eds) *Modern Fiscal Issues: Essays in Honor of Carl S. Shoup* Toronto: University of Toronto Press, 1972, pp. 105–16.

3   P.L. Swan 'Income Taxes, Profit Taxes and Neutrality of Optimizing Decisions' *Economic Record* 52, 138, June 1976, pp. 166–81, and 'A Review of the Northern Territory Government's Green Paper on Mining Royalty Policy for the Northern Territory', Canberra: Department of Economics, Australian National University, 1981; W. Mayo 'Rent Royalties' *Economic Record* 55, 150, September 1979, pp. 202–13.

4   R. Garnaut and A. Clunies Ross 'Uncertainty, Risk Aversion and the Taxing of Natural Resource Projects' *Economic Journal* 85, 338, June 1975, pp. 272–87, and 'The Neutrality of the Resource Rent Tax' *Economic Record* 55, 150, September 1979, pp. 193–201.

5   J.E. Stiglitz 'Taxation, Corporate Financial Policy, and the Cost of Capital' *Journal of Public Economics* 2, 1973, pp. 1–34; A.J. Auerbach 'Taxation, Corporate Financial Policy and the Cost of Capital' *Journal of Economic Literature* 21, September 1983, pp. 905–40.

6   Garnaut and Clunies Ross 'The Neutrality of the Resource Rent Tax'.

7   M. Gaffney (ed.) *Extractive Resources and Taxation* Madison: University of Wisconsin press, 1967; Northern Territory of Australia *Green Paper on Mining Royalty Policy for the Northern Territory* Darwin: Department of Mines and Energy, February 1981; D. Nellor 'Neutrality and Resource Rent Taxation' Supplement to D. Nellor, R. Clarke, C.T. Fletcher and M.G. Porter *An Evaluation of the Northern Territory Draft Mineral Royalty Bill* Melbourne: Centre of Policy Studies, Monash University, October 1981.

8   R. Dowell 'Profits Based Royalties and Productive Efficiency' *Resources and Energy* February 1980; Nellor et al. *The Northern Territory Draft Mineral Royalty Bill*; M.G. Porter 'Mining, Taxation and Economic Welfare' *Growth* July 1982, pp. 45–52.

9   C. Emerson and P. Lloyd 'Improving Mineral Taxation Policy in Australia' *Economic Record* 59, 166, September 1983, pp. 232–44; R. Garnaut and C. Emerson Mineral Leasing Policy: Competitive Bidding and the Resource Rent Tax Given Various Responses to Risk *Economic Record* 60, 169, June 1984, 133–42.

10 Commonwealth of Australia *Cash Bidding as a System for Awarding Offshore Petroleum Exploration Permits* Canberra: Department of Resources and Energy, January 1984; and 'Resource Rent Tax on "Greenfields" Offshore Petroleum Projects' Statement by the Treasurer and the Minister for Resources and Energy, 27 June 1984.

11   Swan *A Review of the Green Paper on Mining Royalty Policy.*
12   Northern Territory of Australia *Green Paper* Appendix B.
13   W.J. Mead 'Cash Bonus Bidding for Mineral Resources' in M. Crommelin and A.R.
     Thompson (eds) *Mineral Leasing as an Instrument of Public Policy* Vancouver:
     University of British Columbia Press, 1977, p. 55; J.B. Ramsay *Bidding and Oil
     Leases* Greenwich, Connecticut: JAI Press, 1980, p. 177; W.J. Mead, A. Moseidjord
     and P.E. Sorensen 'The Rate of Return Earned by Lessees under Cash Bonus
     Bidding for OCS Oil and Gas Leases' *Energy Journal* 4, 4, October 1983, pp. 37–52
     (p. 50).
14   Emerson and Lloyd 'Improving Mineral Taxation Policy in Australia'
15   H. Leland 'Optimal Risk Sharing and the Leasing of Natural Resources, with
     Application to Oil and Gas Leasing on the OCS' *Quarterly Journal of Economics* 92,
     August 1978, pp. 413–38.

Chapter 7

1   B.W. Mackenzie and M.L. Bilodeau *Economics of Mineral Expansion in Australia—
    Guidelines for Corporate Planning and Government Policy* Adelaide: AMF, 1984.
2   Hamersley Iron Pty Ltd and W.D. Scott & Co Pty Ltd *Report on the Effect on
    Employment and Australian Industry of the Expansion of Capacity to 46 Million Tonnes
    per Annum* Melbourne: CRA Ltd, January 1978.
3   T.M. Fitzgerald *The Contribution of the Mineral Industry to Australian Welfare*
    Canberra: AGPS, 1974.
4   *Minerals Industry Survey 1983* Canberra: Australian Mining Industry Council, 1983.

Chapter 8

1   *The Australian Financial System* Treasury Economic Paper No. 9, Canberra: AGPS,
     1981, pp. 177–79; *Foreign Investment Review Board Report 1982* Canberra: AGPS,
     pp. 38–39.
2   See *The Australian Financial System* pp. 199–205 for a chronological presentation of
     significant events in the evolution of foreign investment policy.
3   Australia, House of Representatives *Debates* 1969, pp. 1382–87 (16 September
     1969).
4   Australia, House of Representatives *Debates* 1972, pp. 1916–20 (26 September
     1972).
5   'Foreign Investment Policy of the Australian Government', statement by the Prime
     Minister, the Hon. E.G. Whitlam, Press Release No. 564, 24 September 1975.
6   Australia, House of Representatives *Debates* 1976, pp. 1283–92 (1 April 1976).
7   For example, the address by the Prime Minister, the Hon. R.J. Hawke, to the
     Foreign Policy Association, New York, 16 June 1983.
8   For comprehensive information on foreign investment policy, see *Australia's Foreign
     Investment Policy—A Guide for Investors* Canberra: AGPS, 1982.
9   Australian Bureau of Statistics *Foreign Ownership and Control of the Mining Industry,
     1974–75* Ref. No. 10.42.
10   Australian Bureau of Statistics *Foreign Control in the Mining Industry, 1976–77* Cat.
     No. 5329.0.
11   Australian Bureau of Statistics *Foreign Ownership and Control of the Mining Industry
     and Selected Mineral Processing Industries, Australia, 1981–82* Cat. No. 5317.0.

12   See *Foreign Investment Review Board Report 1980* Canberra: AGPS, ch. 5 and Attachment A; *Foreign Investment Review Board Report 1981* Canberra: AGPS, ch. 5 and ch. 6.
13   See *Australia's Foreign Investment Policy—A Guide for Investors*.
14   New South Wales government policy towards foreign investment is detailed in *Handbook for Industrialists* Government of New South Wales, 1983, pp. 15–16.
15   'Foreign Investment Policy', Statement by the Treasurer, the Hon. John Howard, Press Release No. 10, 20 January 1982.

Chapter 9

1   W.R.C. Jay 'The Shift to Specific Purpose Grants: from Revenue Sharing to Cost Sharing?' in R.L. Mathews (ed.) *Responsibility Sharing in a Federal System* Research Monograph No. 8, Centre for Research on Federal Financial Relations, Australian National University, 1975.
2   Campbell Committee *Final Report of the Committee of Inquiry into the Australian Financial System* Canberra: AGPS, 1981, pp. 195–203, 452–77.
3   P.O. Steiner 'Peak Loads and Efficient Pricing' *Quarterly Journal of Economics* November 1957, pp. 585–610; and J. Hirschleifer 'Peak Loads and Efficient Pricing: Comment' *Quarterly Journal of Economics* Autumn 1958, pp. 451–62.
4   See K.J. Arrow and R.C. Lind 'Uncertainty and the Evaluation of Public Investment Decisions' *American Economic Review* 1970, pp. 364–78; and 'Uncertainty and the Evaluation of Public Investment Decisions—Reply' *American Economic Review* 1972, pp. 171–72; and M.J. Bailey and M.C. Jensen 'Risk and Discount Rate for Public Investment' in M.C. Jensen (ed.) *Studies in the Theory of Capital Markets* New York: Praeger, 1972.
5   Department of the Treasury *Resource Development Maximising Opportunities* Submission to the Senate Standing Committee on Natural Resources; the Development of the Bauxite, Alumina and Aluminium Industries, Treasury Economic Paper No. 8, Canberra: AGPS, 1981.
6   P.L. Swan 'The Marginal Cost of Baseload Power. An Application to Alcoa's Portland Smelter' AGSM Working Paper 83–003, Sydney, January 1983.
7   S. Salsbury 'Economic Development and Finance: An Historical Perspective', in J.P. McAuley (ed.) *Planning and Financing of Resource and Infrastructure Development in NSW* Monograph 10, Planning Research Centre, University of Sydney, 1981, pp. 54–67.
8   G. Sturgess 'Queensland Puts the Squeeze on Coal Mines' *Bulletin* 25 November 1980, pp. 118–20.
9   Commonwealth Grants Commission *Report on State Tax Sharing Entitlements 1981. Vol. 111—Reports of Consultants* Canberra: AGPS, 1981.
10 R. Birrell 'Australia's Mineral Boom: Social and Resource Perspectives' in R. Birrell, D. Hill and J. Stanley (eds) *Quarry Australia* Melbourne: Oxford University Press, 1982.
11 C. Richardson and P. Wilson 'Pricing and Financing Guidelines for Victorian Public Authorities including the SECV' Paper presented to Conference on the Economics of Electric Power Systems, University of New South Wales, July 1983.
12 Victorian Department of Minerals and Energy *Electricity Pricing 1982/83* Melbourne, August 1982.
13 O.E. Williamson 'Managerial Discretion and Business Behaviour' *American Economic Review* December 1983, pp. 1032–57; W. Niskanen 'The Peculiar Economics

of Bureaucracy' *American Economic Review* 58, May 1968, pp. 293–305; H. Averch and L.L. Johnson 'Behaviour of the Firm Under Regulatory Constraint' *American Economic Review* December 1962, pp. 1052–69; R.P. Albon and P. Kirby 'Cost-Padding in Profit-Regulated Firms' *Economic Review* March 1983, pp. 16–27; A.E. Kahn *The Economics of Regulation* vols 1 and 2, New York: John Wiley & Sons, 1970.

14 P.L. Swan 'The Marginal Cost of Baseload Power'

15 Department of the Treasury *Resource Development Maximising Opportunities.*

16 H.W. Dick *Power Subsidies to Aluminium Smelters in NSW* Discussion Paper No. 18, Institute of Industry Economics, University of Newcastle, 1981.

17 H.D.W. Saddler and W.A. Donnelly 'Investment, Prices and Demand in the Tasmanian Electricity Supply System' Paper presented to Conference on The Economics of Electric Power Systems, University of New South Wales, July 1983.

18 P.L. Swan 'Marginal Cost Based Tariffs and Time of Day Pricing—An Introduction and Application to Tasmania' Paper presented to Conference on The Economics of Electric Power Systems, University of New South Wales, July 1983.

19 G. Aitchison 'Rate of Return Targets' Paper presented to Conference on The Economics of Electric Power Systems, University of New South Wales, July 1983; P.L. Swan 'The Marginal Cost of Baseload Power'; C. Richardson and P. Wilson 'Pricing and Financing Guidelines for Victorian Public Authorities'.

20 In a hydro system, this definition of replacement cost, which requires civil works and power stations to be built on new rather than existing sites, will have a considerable impact on average system costs, but the impact is likely to be less substantial for thermal power stations.

21 P.L. Swan, 'Real Rates of Return in Electricity Supply: New South Wales, Tasmania and Victoria' Paper presented to Conference on the Economics of Electric Power Systems: Tariffs and Industry Response, University of New South Wales, May 1984, p. 23a.

22 P.K. Parker, Market Town to Mining Town: Resource Development, Infrastructure Costs and Local Government in Singleton, Australia, unpublished Masters thesis, Australian National University, 1982.

23 ibid.

24 ibid.

Chapter 10

1 I. Yamazawa 'Nihon no Yunyu Senryaku to Tekkoseki Bōeki' (Japanese Iron Ore Trade and Import Strategy) in I. Yamazawa and M. Ikema (eds) *Shigen Bōeki no Keizaigaku* (The Economics of Resources Trade) Bunshindo, 1981.

2 K. Kojima 'Nichi-Go Shigen Bōeki no Arikata' (Japan–Australia Resources Trade) in Yamazawa and Ikema (eds) *Economics of Resources Trade.*

3 See for example B. Smith 'Long-Term Contracts for the Supply of Raw Materials' in J. Crawford and S. Okita (eds) *Raw Materials and Pacific Economic Integration* Croom Helm, 1978; Kojima 'Japan–Australia Resources Trade'; Yamazawa 'Japanese Iron Ore Trade and Import Strategy'; I. Nakatani 'Chukanzai Torihiki ni Okeru chooki Keiyaku Riron to Kakaku Koosho Model' (A Long-Term Contract Theory and Price Negotiation Model in the Transaction of Intermediate Goods) in Yamazawa and Ikema (eds) *Economics of Resources Trade.*

4 M.M. Baily 'Wages and Employment under Uncertain Demand' *Review of Economic Studies* January 1974; C. Azariadis 'Implicit Contracts and Underdevelopment Equilibria' *Journal of Political Economy* December 1975.

5   See, for example, B. Smith and R. Garnaut 'Trade and Investment Problems for Mining Development in Australia' in Yamazawa and Ikema (eds) *Economics of Resources Trade.*
6   Ministry of International Trade and Industry *Shigenmondai no Tenbo* (Perspective on the Resources Problem) 1981.
7   T. Mori 'Goshukeizai to Nihon no Chokusetsutoshi' (The Australian Economy and Japanese Direct Investment) in S. Sekiguchi (ed.) *Kantaiheiyo Keizaiken to Nihon no Chokusetso Toshi* (The Pacific Economic Basin and Japanese Direct Investment) Nihonkeizai Shinbunsha, 1982.
8   Smith and Garnaut 'Trade and Investment Problems'.
9   W.M. Corden *Inflation, Exchange Rates and the Economy* Oxford: Clarendon Press, 1977; W.M. Corden and J.P. Neary 'Booming Sector and De-Industrialization in a Small Open Economy' *Economic Journal* December 1982.
10 Resources and Energy Agency *Shigen Energuie Nenkan* (Year Book of Resources and Energy) 1982.
11 Economic Planning Agency *Japan in the Year 2000* Japan Times, 1982.

Chapter 11

1   J. Warhurst *Central Agencies, Intergovernmental Managers, and Australian Federal–State Relations* Occasional Paper No. 29, Centre for Research on Federal Financial Relations, Australian National University, 1983.
2   S.B. Myer *Report of the Ad Hoc Working Committee on Australia–Japan Relations* (Chairman S.B. Myer) Canberra: Commonwealth Government Printer, 1978, pp. 162, 262, Annex M.
3   See Advisory Council for Inter-government Relations *Register of Commonwealth–State Cooperative Arrangements* Hobart, August 1982; Department of Prime Minister and Cabinet *Australian–State Government Cooperative Arrangements* Information and State Relations Division, Canberra, May 1975; K.W. Wiltshire 'Australian State Participation in Federal Decisions' in R.L. Mathews (ed.) *Federalism in Australia and the Federal Republic of Germany: A Comparative Study* Canberra: Australian National University Press and Centre for Research on Federal Financial Relations, 1980.
4   Warhurst *Central Agencies*, pp. 17–19.
5   P. Loveday *Promoting Industry* University of Queensland Press, 1982, pp. 173–96; J. Warhurst (ed.) 'Perspectives on Premiers' Departments' *Politics* 17, 1, 1982, pp. 7–58.
6   Department of Industry and Commerce *Handbook of Services and Assistance to Industry Provided by Commonwealth and State Governments and Agencies* Canberra: AGPS, 1979; Australian Industries Development Association 'Industry Policy and the States' *AIDA Bulletin* 350, April 1983, pp. 12–20.
7   Myer *Report* pp. 101, 161; Japan Secretariat *The Commonwealth–State Relationship: Its Relevance to Australia's Relations with Japan* Research Paper CCRJ/25/81, October 1981.
8   J. Holmes and C. Sharman *The Australian Federal System* Sydney: George Allen & Unwin, 1977.
9   Japan Secretariat *The Commonwealth–State Relationship*, p. 14.
10 ibid., p. 14.
11 G. Stevenson *The Control of Foreign Direct Investment in a Federation: Canadian and Australian Experience* Research Monograph No. 3, Transnational Corporations Research Project, University of Sydney, July 1976. See also K. West 'Federalism

and Resource Development: The Politics of State Inequality' in A. Patience and J. Scott (eds) *Australian Federalism: Future Tense* Melbourne: Oxford University Press, 1983, pp. 107–22.

12   J. Warhurst *State Governments and Australian Tariff Policy* Research Monograph No. 33, Centre for Research on Federal Financial Relations, Australian National University, 1980.

13   For earlier discussions, see Myer *Report*, pp. 159–60; Japan Secretariat *The Commonwealth–State Relationship*, pp. 20–21.

14   B. Hocking 'Pluralism and Foreign Policy, the States and the Management of Australia's External Relations' *Year Book of World Affairs* London: Stevens & Sons, 1984 (published under the auspices of the London Institute of World Affairs) p. 1.

15   Japan Secretariat *The Commonwealth–State Relationship*, p. 20.

16   ibid., pp. 20–22.

17   ibid., p. 21.

18   Myer *Report*, pp. 13–14.

19   ibid., p. 158.

20   Hocking 'Pluralism and Foreign Policy', pp. 11–12.

Chapter 12

1   The coal export levy, however, was deliberately tailored (by relating the size of the levy to coal type and quality) so that it would impinge on particular producers differently.

2   Thus the export of mineral sands from Fraser Island was prohibited because of the failure to satisfy environmental requirements, notwithstanding that the Commonwealth has no direct power over environmental matters within the States.

3   In one case, for example, the 50 per cent local equity requirement for a new project (Norwich Park coal) was deemed to be satisfied by an equivalent expansion in the minority Australian equity share in the overall operating company, providing no effective Australian control over the development.

4   G.D. McColl 'The Mining Industry and the Natural Environment' *Resources Policy* 6, 2 (Special Issue *Current Status and Future Potential of the Australian Minerals Industry* June 1980), pp. 153–65.

5   This is partly due to the higher export price for coking coal and partly to the fact that prices for coal exports to Japan (and other Asian countries) are higher than for exports to Europe.

6   In fact, coal and iron ore sales account for half of Australia's total exports (of all commodities) to Japan. In substantial measure, both the growth in Australia's minerals trade and the emergence of Japan as Australia's major export market principally reflect a growth in trade with the Japanese steel industry.

7   The main exception to this, resulting from the negotiation of a favourable long-term shipping contract, has been the export of significant quantities of Weipa bauxite to a refinery in Sardinia in which Comalco is a participant. Subsequently, the refinery has shifted from 100 per cent to 50 per cent dependence on Australian bauxite.

8   An alternative, increasingly more realistic, interpretation is that continuing Japanese metals production inhibits the full realisation of Australia's competitiveness in processing.

9   For a review of the development and performance of long-term contract arrangements, see B. Smith 'Long Term Contracts for the Supply of Raw Materials' in J.G. Crawford and S. Okita (eds) *Raw Materials and Pacific Economic Integration* London: Croom Helm, 1978, pp. 229–70; B. Smith *Long-term Contracts and*

Financing Arrangements for Minerals Developments Research Paper No. 72, Australia–Japan Research Centre, Australian National University, 1980; G. Jackson 'Long-Term Contracts' Paper presented to the Australia–Japan Businessmen's Cooperation Conference, Sydney, 1978; B. Smith and P.D. Drysdale *Stabilisation and the Reduction of Uncertainty in Bilateral Minerals Trade Arrangements* Research Paper No. 65, Australia–Japan Research Centre, Australian National University, 1979. For a discussion of vertical integration arrangements and a comparison of them with long-term contracts, see Smith *Long-term Contracts and Financing Arrangements for Minerals Developments*; J. Stuckey *The Role of Marketing Arrangements in the Evaluation and Financing of Mining Projects* Research Paper No. 71, Australia–Japan Research Centre, Australian National University, 1980.

10   The risk distribution role of long-term contracts and the efficiency with which this can be performed in different kinds of markets are discussed in Smith *Long-term Contracts and Minerals Developments*.

11   Smith *Long-term Contracts and Financing Arrangements for Minerals Developments*.

12   For a conflicting assessment of this possibility, see A. Fitzgibbons and H. Hendrikx 'An Economic Evaluation of the Proposed Cooloola Sand-Mining Project' *Economic Analysis and Policy* September 1970, pp. 58–73; S. Bambrick 'An Economic Evaluation of the Proposed Cooloola Sand-Mining Project—Comment' *Economic Analysis and Policy* March 1971, pp. 30–48.

13   Fraser Island Environmental Inquiry *First Report of the Commission of Inquiry* Canberra: AGPS, 1976.

14   See, for example, Department of the Treasury *Resource Development: Maximising Opportunities* Treasury Economic Paper No. 8; Canberra: AGPS, 1981.

15   Thus the Ranger Uranium Environmental Enquiry devoted some considerable attention to assessment of the uranium market and the impact on that market of different levels of Australian supply: see Ranger Uranium Environmental Enquiry *First Report 1976* and *Second Report 1977*, Canberra: AGPS.

16   For a more intensive analytical discussion of the bilateral bargaining framework, see B. Smith 'Bilateral Monopoly and Export price Bargaining in the Resources Trade' *Economic Record* 53, 1977, pp. 30–50.

17   It needs to be emphasised, however, that the same phenomena might as readily be explained by a strategy of diversification for supply security reasons; see B. Smith 'Bilateral Commercial Arrangements in the Energy Coal Trade' in S.E. Harris and T. Ikuta (eds) *Australia, Japan and the Energy Coal Trade* Australia–Japan Research Centre, Australian National University, 1982, pp. 169–90.

18   See R. Stuart 'Resources Development Policy: The Case of the Export Coal Industry' CRES Working Paper, Centre for Resource and Environmental Studies, Australian National University, 1983.

Chapter 13

1   The commentators on each chapter, in order of appearance, are: Hugh Collins; Campbell Sharman; Ken Clements; Junshichiro Yonehara; Grey McColl; Tom Shoyama; Dennis Ottley; Chris Trengove; Bernie Fraser; Craig Emerson; Christopher Findlay; Peter Swan; Peter Bloomfield; Peter Charlton; John Reynolds; Brian Galligan; and Kerry McDonald. Comments were edited by Janet Healey. The summary and digest of discussion was prepared by Ben Smith, Peter Drysdale and Peter Bloomfield.

2   See Hugh Collins 'Aborigines and Australian Foreign Policy: Some Underlying

Issues' *Ethnic Minorities and Australian Foreign Policy* Canberra Studies in World Affairs, No. 11, pp. 50–77.

3   Norman Lindsay *The Magic Pudding* rept. Penguin, 1975, p. 152.

4   R.C. Jensen and G.R. West 'The Nature of Australian Regional Input–Output Multipliers' *Prometheus* 1, 1, June 1983, pp. 202–21.

5   J.T. Romans and D.H. Garrick 'Evaluating National Efficiency and Regional Distribution Efforts of Public Investments' *The Regional Science Association Papers* 28, 66, 1972, pp. 169–80.

6   L.H. Cook, G.S. Hundley and V.J. Lees *Structural Effects on the Australian Economy of Bauxite Mining, Alumina Refining and Smelting* Centre for Policy Studies, Monash University, 1983; R.W. Fraser 'The Contribution of Extractive Industries to the Western Australian Economy: An Application of ORANI-ORES' Discussion Paper 83–122, Department of Economics, University of Western Australia, 1983; M. Copland, K. McDonald, D. Gallagher and G. McColl *The National Economic Benefits of the Gladstone Aluminium Smelter* Comalco Ltd, 1981.

7   H. Laski 'The Obsolescence of Federalism' *New Republic* 3, May 1939, pp. 367–69.

8   W. Riker 'The Triviality of Federalism' *Politics* 5, 1970, pp. 239–41.

9   G. Sawer 'The Constitutional Crisis of Australian Federalism' in A. Patience and J. Scott (eds) *Australian Federalism: Future Tense* Melbourne: Oxford University Press, 1983, pp. 94–106.

10 G. Stevenson *The Control of Foreign Direct Investment in a Federation: Canadian and Australian Experience* Research Monograph No. 3, Transnational Corporations Research Project, University of Sydney, July 1976.

11 G. Crough and T. Wheelwright *Australia: A Client State* Penguin, 1982.

Bibliography

Books

Brannon, G.M. (ed.) *Studies in Energy Tax Policy* Report to the Energy Policy Project of the Ford Foundation, Cambridge, Massachusetts: Ballinger, 1975.

Corden, W.M. *Inflation, Exchange Rates and the Economy* Oxford: Clarendon Press, 1977.

Crommelin, M. and Thompson, A.R. (eds) *Mineral Leasing as an Instrument of Public Policy* Vancouver: University of British Columbia Press, 1977.

Dicey, A.V. *An Introduction to the Study of the Law of the Constitution* 10th edn, London: Macmillan, 1959.

Fitzgibbons, A. *Ideology and the Economics of the Mining Industry* Published for the author by Academy Press, 1978.

Gaffney, M. (ed.) *Extractive Resources and Taxation* Madison: University of Wisconsin Press, 1967.

Galligan, B. (ed.) *Australian Resource Development: Bargaining at Many Levels* (forthcoming).

Harman, E.J. and Head, B.W. (eds) *State, Capital and Resources in the North and West of Australia* Perth: University of Western Australia Press, 1982.

Head, B.W. (ed.) *State and Economy in Australia* Melbourne: Oxford University Press, 1983.

Herfindahl, O.C. and Kneese, A.V. *Economic Theory of Natural Resources* Columbus, Ohio: Merrill, 1974.

Holmes, J. and Sharman, C. *The Australian Federal System* Sydney: George Allen and Unwin, 1977.

Jensen, M.C. (ed.) *Studies in the Theory of Capital Markets* New York: Praeger, 1972.

Kahn, A.E. *The Economics of Regulation* vols 1 and 2, New York: John Wiley and Sons, 1970.

Lang, A.G. and Crommelin, M. *Australian Mining and Petroleum Laws—An Introduction* Sydney: Butterworths, 1979.

Loveday, P. *Promoting Industry* Brisbane: University of Queensland Press, 1982.

McDonald, S.L. *The Leasing of Federal Lands for Fossil Fuels Production* Baltimore: Johns Hopkins University Press, 1979.

McLure, C.E. Jr (ed.) *Tax Assignment in Federal Countries* Canberra: Australian National University Press, 1983.

McLure, C.E. Jr and Mieszkowski, P. (eds) *Fiscal Federalism and the Taxation of Natural Resources* Lexington, Massachusetts: Lexington Books, 1983.

Mathews, R.L. (ed.) *Federalism in Australia and the Federal Republic of Germany: A*

254

Comparative Study Canberra: Australian National University Press and Centre for Research on Federal Financial Relations, 1980.

Mathews, R.L. et al. *Australian Federalism 1980* Canberra: Australian National University Press, 1982.

Mishan, E.J. *Coal Benefit Analysis* 3rd edn, London: George Allen and Unwin, 1982.

Musgrave, R.A. *The Theory of Public Finance* New York: McGraw-Hill, 1959.

Ozawa, R. *Multinationalism, Japanese Style* Princeton University Press, 1979.

Patience, A. and Head, B. (eds) *From Whitlam to Fraser: Reform and Reaction in Australian Politics* Melbourne: Oxford University Press, 1979.

Patience, A. and Scott, J. (eds) *Australian Federalism: Future Tense* Melbourne: Oxford University Press, 1983.

Quick, J. and Garran, R.R. *Annotated Constitution of the Australian Commonwealth* 1901, facsimile edn, Legal Books, 1976.

Ramsay, J.B. *Bidding and Oil Leases* Greenwich, Connecticut: JAI Press, 1980.

Saunders, C. et al. *Current Constitutional Problems in Australia* Canberra: Australian National University Press, 1982.

Sawer, G. *Modern Federalism* Pitman Australia, 1976.

Scott, A. (ed.) *Natural Resources Revenues—A Test of Federalism* Vancouver: University of British Columbia Press, 1976.

Sekiguchi, S. *Japanese Direct Foreign Investment* Macmillan, 1979.

Sekiguchi, S. (ed.) *Kantaiheiyo Keizaiken to Nihon no Chokusetsu Toshi* (The Pacific Economic Basin and Japanese Direct Investment) Nihonkeizai Shinbunsha, 1979.

Wheare, K.C. *Federal Government* 4th edn, Oxford University Press, 1963.

Winterton, G. *Parliament, the Executives and the Governor-General* Melbourne University Press, 1983.

Yamazawa, I. and Ikema, M. (eds) *Shigen Bōeki no Keizaigaku* (The Economics of Resources Trade) Bunshindo, 1981.

Research Papers and Monographs

Anderson, D. *Foreign Investment Control in the Mining Sector: Comparisons of Australian and Canadian Experience* CRES Monograph No. 10, Centre for Resource and Environmntal Studies, Australian National University, 1983.

Burns, R.M. et al. *Political and Administrative Federalism* Research Monograph No. 14, Centre for Research on Federal Financial Relations, Australian National University, 1976.

Cook, L.H., Hundley, G.S. and Lees, V.J. *Structural Effects on the Australian Economy of Bauxite Mining, Alumina Refining and Smelting* Centre for Policy Studies, Monash University, 1983.

Dick, H.W. *Power Subsidies to Aluminium Smelters in NSW* Discussion Paper No. 18, Institute of Industry Economics, University of Newcastle, 1981.

Fraser, R.W. *The Contribution of Extractive Industries to the Western Australian Economy: An Application of ORANI–ORES* Discussion Paper No. 83–122, Department of Economics, University of Western Australia, 1983.

Garnaut, R. and Emerson, C. *Mineral Leasing Policy: Competitive Bidding and the Resource Rent Tax Given Various Responses to Risk* Department of Economics, Australian National University, 1981.

Gramlich, E.M., 'A Fair Go': Fiscal Federalism in Australia Paper for Brookings Survey of the Australian Economy, Centre for Economic Policy Research, ANU and Brookings Institution, Washington, 1984.

Harris, S. and Ikuta, T. (eds) *Australia, Japan and the Energy Coal Trade* Australia–

Japan Research Centre, Australian National University, 1982.

Harris, S. and Taylor, G. (eds) *Resource Development and the Future of Australian Society* CRES Monograph No. 7, Centre for Resource and Environmental Studies, Australian National University, 1982.

McAuley, J.P. (ed.) *Planning and Financing of Resource and Infrastructure Development in NSW* Monograph No. 10, Planning Research Centre, University of Sydney, 1981.

Mathews, R.L. (ed.) *Responsibility Sharing in a Federal System* Research Monograph No. 8, Centre for Research on Federal Financial Relations, Australian National University, 1975.

Nellor, D. and Clarke, R. *The Allocation of Mineral Leases by Work Programme Bidding* Centre of Policy Studies, Monash University, 1982.

Nellor, D., Clarke, R., Fletcher, C.T. and Porter, M.G. *An Evaluation of the Northern Territory of Australia Draft Mineral Royalty Bill* Centre of Policy Studies, Monash University, October 1981.

Nellor, D., Trengove, C., Hocking, D. and Parish, R. *Taxation of the Australian Resources Sector* Centre of Policy Studies, Monash University, April 1982.

Scott, A. *Central Government Claims to Mineral Revenues* Occasional Paper No. 8, Centre for Research on Federal Financial Relations, Australian National University, 1978.

Smith, B. *Long-term Contracts and Financing Arrangements for Minerals Developments* Research Paper No. 72, Australia–Japan Research Centre, Australian National University, 1980.

Smith, B. and Drysdale, P.D. *Stabilisation and the Reduction of Uncertainty in Bilateral Minerals Trade Arrangements* Research Paper No. 65, Australia–Japan Research Centre, Australian National University, 1979.

Stevenson, G. *The Control of Foreign Direct Investment in a Federation: Canadian and Australian Experience* Monograph No. 3, Transnational Corporations Research Project, University of Sydney, July 1976.

—— *Mineral Resources and Australian Federalism* Research Monograph No. 17, Centre for Research on Federal Financial Relations, Australian National University, 1977.

Stuart, R. *Resources Development Policy: The Case of the Export Coal Industry* CRES Working Paper, Centre for Resource and Environmental Studies, Australian National University, 1983.

Stuckey, J. *The Role of Marketing Arrangements in the Evaluation and Financing of Mining Projects* Research Paper No. 71, Australia–Japan Research Centre, Australian National University, 1980.

Swan, P.L. *A Review of the Northern Territory Government's Green Paper on Mining Royalty Policy for the Northern Territory* Department of Economics, Australian National University, 1981.

—— *The Marginal Cost of Baseload Power. An Application to Alcoa's Portland Smelter* AGSM Working Paper No. 83–003, Sydney, January 1983.

Warhurst, J. *State Governments and Australian Tariff Policy* Research Monograph No. 33, Centre for Research on Federal Financial Relations, Australian National University, 1980.

—— *Central Agencies, Intergovernmental Managers, and Australian Federal–State Relations* Occasional Paper No. 29, Centre for Research on Federal Financial Relations, Australian National University, 1983.

Government and industry reports

Advisory Council for Inter-government Relations 'Intergovernmental Aspects of the Provision of Infrastructure for Major Resource Projects' Draft Discussion Paper, Hobart, 1982.

—— *Register of Commonwealth–State Cooperative Arrangements* Hobart, 1982.

Australian Bureau of Statistics *Catalogue of Publications* Canberra, 1984. Publications containing mining statistics are listed under sub-group 84 of the catalogue.

Australian Mining Industry Council *Minerals Industry Survey 1983* Canberra, 1983.

Australia's Foreign Investment Policy—A Guide for Investors Canberra: AGPS, 1982.

Committee of Economic Enquiry *Report* vol. 1, ch. 8, Canberra, May 1965.

Commonwealth Grants Commission *Report on State Tax Sharing Arrangements 1981* Canberra: AGPS, 1981.

—— *Report on State Tax Sharing and Health Grants 1982* Canberra: AGPS, 1982.

Copland, M., McDonald, K., Gallagher, D. and McColl, G. *The National Economic Benefits of the Gladstone Aluminium Smelter* Comalco Ltd, 1981.

Department of Industry and Commerce *Handbook of Services and Assistance to Industry Provided by Commonwealth and State Governments and Agencies* Canberra: AGPS, 1979.

Department of Minerals and Energy, Victoria *Electricity Pricing 1982/83* Melbourne, August 1982.

Department of the Prime Minister and Cabinet *Australian State Government Cooperative Arrangements* Canberra, May 1975.

Department of Resources and Energy *Discussion Paper on Resource Rent Tax in the Petroleum Sector* Canberra: AGPS, December 1983.

—— *Cash Bidding as a System for Awarding Offshore Petroleum Exploration Permits* Canberra, January 1984.

Department of the Treasury *Resource Development: Maximising Opportunities* Treasury Economic Paper No. 8, Canberra: AGPS, 1981.

—— *The Australian Financial System* Treasury Economic Paper No. 9, Canberra: AGPS, 1981.

Economic Planning Agency, Japan *Japan in the Year 2000* Tokyo: Japan Times, 1982.

Electricity Commission of New South Wales *Performance and Future Direction* Statutory Report to the Minister for Energy, Sydney, 1983.

Fitzgerald, T.M. *The Contribution of the Mineral Industry to Australian Welfare* Canberra: AGPS, 1974.

Foreign Investment Review Board Reports Canberra: AGPS, various years.

Fraser Island Environmental Inquiry *First Report of the Commission of Inquiry* Canberra: AGPS, 1976.

Hamersley Iron Pty Ltd and W.D. Scott and Co. Pty Ltd *Report on the Effect on Employment and Australian Industry of the Expansion of Capacity to 46 Million Tonnes per Annum* Melbourne: CRA Ltd, January 1978.

Industries Assistance Commission *Crude Oil Pricing* Canberra: AGPS, September 1976.

—— *Petroleum and Mining Industries* Canberra: AGPS, May 1976.

Japan Secretariat *The Commonwealth–State Relationship: Its Relevance to Australia's Relations with Japan* Research Paper CCRJ/25/81, October 1981.

Mackenzie, B.W. and Bilodeau, M.L. *Economics of Mineral Expansion in Australia— Guidelines for Corporate Planning and Government Policy* Adelaide: Australian Mining Federation, 1984.

Ministry of International Trade and Industry, Japan *Shigenmondai no Tenbo* (A Perspective on the Resources Problem) Tokyo, 1981.

Northern Territory of Australia *Green Paper on Mining Royalty Policy for the Northern Territory* Darwin: Department of Mines and Energy, February 1981.

Ranger Uranium Environmental Enquiry *First Report 1976* and *Second Report 1977* Canberra: AGPS, 1976, 1977.

Report of the Ad Hoc Working Committee on Australia–Japan Relations Chairman S.B. Myer, Canberra: Commonwealth Government Printer, 1978.

Resources and Energy Agency, Japan *Shigen Energuie Nenkan* (Year Book of Resources and Energy) Tokyo, 1982.

Index

Italicised page numbers are for tables/figures. References to footnotes are to the page in the text in which they occur. A reference such as 203&n1 means that the footnote continues the discussion of the text.